RM
NOT L
FLOOR

W9-AXC-261

UNDERSTANDING PUBLIC-KEY INFRASTRUCTURE:

Concepts, Standards, and Deployment Considerations

Carlisle Adams
Steve Lloyd

MTP

MACMILLAN
TECHNICAL
PUBLISHING
U·S·A

About the Authors

Carlisle Adams has been involved with the design, specification, and standardization of various aspects of public-key infrastructures for many years and is recognized internationally for his contributions in these areas. He has participated actively in the IETF Public-Key Infrastructure—X.509 (PKIX) and Common Authentication Technology (CAT) working groups, and he has authored or co-authored a number of standards-track and informational specifications, including RFCs 2025 (SPKM), 2144 (CAST-128), 2479 (IDUP-GSS-API), 2510 (CMP), 2511 (CRMF), 2560 (OCSP), and 2612 (CAST-256). He also contributes to several other PKI standardization efforts, including ISO/SC2, ISO/TC68, ANSI X9.F.1, and the U.S. FPKI TWG.

Dr. Adams holds B.Sc. and M.Sc. degrees in computer science and a Ph.D. in Electrical Engineering. He is currently Senior Cryptographer and Senior Manager—Standards Program at Entrust Technologies. His activities and research interests include the structured design and analysis of symmetric block ciphers (including the CAST family of algorithms) and the design, analysis, and standardization of security protocols for the Internet.

Steve Lloyd has more than 15 years experience in data communications and distributed systems security. His areas of expertise include distributed message handling systems and directory services, TCP/IP, security protocols, security architectures, and public-key infrastructure technology. Steve has extensive consulting experience on these topics, including presentation of numerous seminars to a wide range of international audiences. He also frequently has been an invited speaker at various trade conferences and symposiums.

Steve holds a bachelor's and master's degree in computer science, and he is currently a Senior Consultant with the Advanced Security Technology Group at Entrust Technologies. His primary areas of responsibility include standards participation, interoperability initiatives, customer requirements analysis, consulting, and market trend assessment.

Dedication

To
Marion, Raphael, Gabrielle, Nathanael
and to
Brenda, Brandon, and Alex
with all our love and appreciation

Acknowledgments

Of all the people who contribute to the creation of a book, the author is only the most obvious. In our case, it is a pleasure to explicitly thank those whose significant contributions to this work might otherwise have gone unnoticed. In alphabetical order, they are the following: Rob Adams, Sharon Boeyen, Dave Fillingham, Barbara Fraser, Merike Kaeo, Steve Kent, Hoyt Kesterson, Sandra M. Lambert, Tim Matthews, Tim Polk, Paul Van Oorschot, and Dave Solo. The list of those who gave words of encouragement or offered support in numerous other ways is long; thanks to all of you!

We also owe a big "thank you" to Entrust Technologies, and particularly to the EVP and CTO, Brian O'Higgins, for generously allowing us to work on this project (as long as we got all our other work done!) and for giving us complete freedom to write whatever we wanted on this topic. (Now is probably as good a time as any to state that all opinions expressed in this book belong solely to the authors; any similarity to the actual PKI products of any vendor is entirely coincidental.)

The people at Macmillan Technical Publishing (Linda Engelman, Jen Garrett, Lisa Thibault, Karen Wachs, and the rest of the team) have been terrific at getting us to do the best job we could while somehow managing to keep the whole project on schedule. Thank you for making this book such a pleasant experience.

Finally, I (Carlisle) would like to thank my co-author (Steve), without whom this would be only half the book it is today.

As the other co-author, I (Steve) would like to take this opportunity to thank Carlisle for allowing me to collaborate on this effort with him. It has been both a pleasure and an honor, and as much work as this was, I would do it all over again!

Carlisle Adams
Steve Lloyd
Ottawa, Canada
August 1999

About the Technical Reviewers

These reviewers contributed their considerable practical, hands-on expertise to the entire development process for *Understanding Public-Key Infrastructure: Concepts, Standards, and Deployment Considerations*. As the book was being written, these dedicated professionals reviewed all the material for technical content, organization, and flow. Their feedback was critical to ensuring that *Understanding Public-Key Infrastructure* fits our reader's need for the highest quality technical information.

Robert L. Adams has more than 12 years of computer and network security experience. He is currently the Technology Strategist for Cisco Systems Global Alliances group with an emphasis on security and directory technologies. As such, he works with a wide variety of high technology companies on creating partnering programs, molding technology into partnering programs, and evangelizing new technologies throughout the industry. In the past, he has participated in the standardization process for IPSec and has been the architect for a number of IPSec implementations. He is a graduate of Penn State University with a B.S. in Computer Science.

Merike Kaeo (CCIE #1287) has been in the networking industry for more than 10 years. Merike has been employed with Cisco Systems, Inc. since June 1993 where she has worked primarily on technical issues relating to router performance, network routing protocols, network design, and network security. From 1988 to 1993, Merike worked at the National Institutes of Health in Bethesda, Maryland, designing and implementing the original FDDI backbone for the NIH campus using Cisco routers. She received her BSEE degree from Rutgers University in 1987 and completed her MSEE degree from George Washington University in 1998. Merike is the author of *Designing Network Security* (Cisco Press, May 1999).

Dr. Stephen T. Kent is a Chief Scientist of Information Security at BBN Technologies. Dr. Kent is also the Director of the Security Practice Center at GTE Internetworking and the Chief Technical Officer at CyberTrust Solutions. In his role as Chief Scientist, Dr. Kent oversees information security activities within BBN Technology and works with government and commercial clients, consulting on system security architecture issues. In this capacity, he has acted as system architect in the design and development of several network security systems for the Department of Defense and served as principal investigator on a number of network security R&D projects for almost

20 years. As Director of the SPC, Dr. Kent monitors all security-related aspects of the service offerings of GTE Internetworking Services. He reports to the President of GTE Internetworking and coordinates with engineering, operations, and marketing to ensure the security quality of offerings. As CTO for CyberTrust Solutions, Dr. Kent provides strategic direction for this certification authority business, reporting to the General Manager of CyberTrust. Over the last 20 years, Dr. Kent's R&D activities have included the design and development of user authentication and access control systems, network layer encryption and access control systems, secure transport layer protocols secure e-mail technology, multi-level secure (X.500) directory systems, public-key certification authority systems, and key recovery (key escrow) systems. His most recent work focuses on public-key certification infrastructures for government and commercial applications, security for Internet routing, and security for mobile computing. Since 1977, he has lectured on the topic of network security on behalf of government agencies, universities, and private companies throughout the United States, Europe, Australia, and the Far East. Dr. Kent received the B.S. degree in mathematics from Loyola University of New Orleans and S.M., E.E., and Ph.D. degrees in computer science from the Massachusetts Institute of Technology. He is a Fellow of the ACM and a member of the Internet Society and Sigma Xi.

Macmillan Technical Publishing would also like to offer our sincere thanks to Barbara Fraser, Tim Polk, and Hoyt Kesterson for their invaluable input on several chapters of this book.

Feedback Information

At Macmillan Technical Publishing, our goal is to create in-depth technical books of the highest quality and value. Each book is crafted with care and precision, undergoing rigorous development that involves the unique expertise of members from the professional technical community.

Readers' feedback is a natural continuation of this process. If you have any comments regarding how we could improve the quality of this book, or otherwise alter it to better suit your needs, you can contact us at networktech@mcp.com. Please make sure to include the book title and ISBN in your message.

We greatly appreciate your assistance.

OVERVIEW

PART III DEPLOYMENT CONSIDERATIONS

CONTENTS

Foreword

Public-key infrastructures (PKIs) are becoming a central part of enterprise security architectures. A PKI provides a focal point for many aspects of security management, as well as serving as an enabler for a growing number of standard and custom security applications. Most standard protocols for secure e-mail, Web access, virtual private networks, and single sign-on user authentication systems make use of public-key certificates and, therefore, require some form of PKI. Given the rapid evolution of PKIs in many enterprises, *Understanding Public-Key Infrastructure* is a very valuable book for any corporate IT manager, CIO, system security administrator, or application or protocol developer.

I have taught one- and two-day seminars on network security for over a decade, for audiences around the world. At the end of each seminar, I am often asked what books I recommend for further study, additional topics, more details, and so on. It's an obvious question, but one for which I rarely have a good answer.

Most of the books on network security I have reviewed fail to provide the right set of information for most readers. Many books devote too many pages to information that will be of little use to most readers. They may go into great depth discussing cryptographic algorithms, but few readers need to understand why the DES has 16 rounds (versus 12 or 20) or how the Merkle-Hellman trapdoor knapsack public-key algorithm was broken in the early '80s.

Other books devote page after page to discussion of cryptographic authentication protocols that were published, analyzed, found to contain flaws, and never implemented in any product! Some network security books devote multiple chapters to the politics of export control, an interesting topic, but not one that will help a reader design a system, make a more informed product purchase decision, or aid in system architecture trade-offs. Finally, almost no books combine useful background information and motivation for security technology choices, along with a good exposition of technical details.

I am pleased to say that this is a book I will recommend to my students, without hesitation. Although PKIs are just a part of the overall security landscape, *Understanding Public-Key Infrastructure* does an outstanding job of covering all the bases, and it does so in a highly informative and very readable fashion. Having reviewed chapters of the book during its preparation, I can honestly say that it was a pleasure to see how Carlisle and Steve approached the topic. They don't waste the reader's time with topics that are of only narrow, academic interest. The book is well structured, with chapters that focus on well-bounded topics, and it presents material in context, providing both the motivation and the technical details essential to developing a solid understanding of this complex topic. Most chapters are brief, making it easy to read this book incrementally, which is an important feature for all of us who have too much to read and not enough uninterrupted time.

Carlisle Adams and Steve Lloyd are an ideal team to author this book. They have extensive experience in the PKI arena, including standards development and operational experiences with large-scale PKIs for the U.S. and Canadian governments. I have had the pleasure of working with Carlisle, in my capacity as co-chair of the IETF PKIX Working Group, on several IETF standards, including the Certificate Management Protocol [RFC2510], and Certificate Request Message Format [RFC2510]. I have also interacted with Steve during his involvement in the U.S. DoD Defense Message System and its related PKI in the first half of this decade. The result of this collaboration is an excellent guide to public-key infrastructure, one that will likely service as an oft-cited reference text.

Stephen Kent
Chief Scientist—Information Security
BBN Technologies
Chief Technical Officer
CyberTrust

INTRODUCTION

Introduction

Without a doubt, the promise of *public-key infrastructure (PKI)* technology has attracted a significant amount of attention in the last few years. Virtually every day some facet of PKI addressed in a newspaper, trade journal, or a conference paper. We hear and read about the promise of authentication and non-repudiation services provided through the use of digital signature techniques, and about confidentiality and key management services based on a combination of symmetric and asymmetric cryptography—all facilitated through the realization of a supporting technology referred to as *PKI*. In fact, many people consider the introduction of PKI technology to be the very enabler of secure global electronic commerce.

Although the foundation for PKI was established over two decades ago with the invention of public-key cryptography, PKI technology has been offered as a commercially viable solution only within the last few years. But what started as a handful of technology vendors a few years ago has seen the birth of dozens, perhaps hundreds, of vendors that offer one form or another of PKI-related service. Further, the commercial demand for PKI-based services continues to increase, and available evidence appears to suggest that the momentum behind PKI may very well continue to grow for the foreseeable future.

Still, as a technology, PKI is fairly new. And to many, PKI technology is shrouded in mystery to some extent. This situation appears to be exacerbated by the proliferation of conflicting documentation, standards, and vendor approaches. Furthermore, there appears to be no comprehensive book devoted to PKI that provides a good introduction to its critical concepts and technology fundamentals.

Thus, the authors share a common motivation in writing this book: To provide a vendor-neutral source of information that can be used to establish a baseline for understanding PKI. In this book, we provide answers to many of the fundamental PKI-related questions, including

- What, exactly, is a PKI?

- What constitutes a digital signature?

- What is a certificate?

- What is certificate revocation?

- What is a Certification Authority (CA)?

- What are the governing standards?

- What are the issues associated with large-scale PKI deployment within an enterprise?

These are just some of the questions we explore in this book.

Motivations for PKI

It is important to recognize that PKI is not simply a "neat" technology without tangible benefits. When deployed judiciously, PKI offers certain fundamental advantages to an organization, including the potential for substantial cost savings. PKI can be sued as the underlying technology to support authentication, integrity, confidentiality, and non-repudiation. This is accomplished through a combination of symmetric and asymmetric cryptographic techniques enabled through the use of a single, easily managed infrastructure rather than multiple security solutions. (See Chapter 2, "Public-Key Cryptography," Chapter 3, "The Concept of an Infrastructure," Chapter 4, "Core PKI Services: Authentication, Integrity, and Confidentiality," and Chapter 5, "PKI-Enabled Services.") PKI offers scalable key management in that the overhead associated with the distribution of keying material to communicating parties is reduced significantly when compared with solutions based solely on symmetric cryptography. (See Chapter 2 for a description of symmetric and asymmetric cryptographic techniques.) Judicious deployment of a single, unifying PKI technology can also help to

- Reduce administrative overhead (when compared with the deployment of multiple point solutions)

- Reduce the number of sign-on events required by end-users

- Reduce paperwork and improve workflow efficiencies through more automated (and more secure) business processes

- Optimize work force productivity (by ensuring that users spend less time contending with the security infrastructure and more time on the job at hand)

- Reduce requirements for end-user training related to the use of the security services (because there is one security solution rather than many)

Not only does PKI technology have the potential to realize cost savings, but in some cases it might even be a source of revenue for an organization (through support for new services that might otherwise not be offered). Benefits and related business considerations associated with PKI technology are discussed further in Part III, "Deployment Considerations."

Note

We would like to emphasize that we have made every attempt to ensure that this book is as vendor neutral as possible. In fact, some of the original text has been modified at the request of one or more reviewers when (unintentionally) it even remotely appeared that we were advocating one approach over another. As authors, we are describing in this book our "vision" of what constitutes a *comprehensive PKI*. Although this viewpoint occasionally aligns more closely with some environments and certain specific vendor products than others, we hasten to point out that we are not aware of any one vendor that offers all the services that are described within this book.

We also recognize that some environments are necessarily more closely aligned with a subset of the components and services described herein (because of their specific requirements and target users), and we fully understand that these environments may never need to fully align with what we refer to as a *comprehensive PKI*. This is as it should be. This book is not about the "Internet PKI," nor is it meant to be limited to the "enterprise PKI"—although, arguably, the enterprise environment is much closer today to our notion of the comprehensive PKI than many alternative deployment environments. This book attempts to describe all aspects of a PKI; specific environments will implement subsets as needed. We have provided a discussion of some of today's PKI variations at the end of Chapter 5 in order to clarify these concepts.

Audience

The main purpose of this book is to provide a fairly comprehensive overview that will help the reader better understand the technical and operational considerations behind PKI technology. You will benefit from this book if you are responsible for the planning, deployment, and/or operation of an enterprise public-key infrastructure. Those who are simply interested in the basic principles behind a PKI should also find this book useful.

We hope that this book will become an educational tool for many and a handy reference guide for others. This book is not intended to resolve extremely detailed implementation questions, although it can serve as a primer for someone who will eventually be more interested in the finer implementation details.

Organization

The book is organized into three parts. Part I provides essential background information necessary to better understand the concepts and principles behind the PKI. Part II addresses standards and related activities (for example, industry-sponsored interoperability initiatives) related to PKI. There are two primary purposes for including this section in the book. First, it provides an overview of the major standards bodies involved in the PKI arena and discusses the main focus of each group, giving a roadmap to some of these activities. Second, it deonstrates the relative maturity and stability of this area, highlighting the fact that a solid basis for implementation and interoperability has already been laid. Finally, Part III discusses PKI deployment considerations, providing guidance for some of the initial and fundamental decisions that must be made prior to any PKI deployment.

Part I: Concepts

Part I of this book deals with fundamental PKI concepts. This includes background information (for example, a primer on cryptography is included) as well as detailed information with respect to public-key certificates and certificate revocation schemes.

Chapter 1, "Introduction," introduces Part I and provides a list of the contents of Part I on a chapter-by-chapter basis.

Chapter 2, "Public-Key Cryptography," provides a brief, non-mathematical introduction to the concepts of public-key cryptography relevant to the material presented throughout the remainder of the book. It includes the distinction between symmetric and public-key ciphers, the concept of a key pair, the services of this technology, terminology, and sample algorithms.

Chapter 3, "The Concept of an Infrastructure," discusses an infrastructure, highlighting its usefulness as an application enabler, its role in secure single sign-on, and its capability to provide end-user transparency and comprehensive security. This chapter also provides a working definition of PKI.

Chapter 4, "Core PKI Services: Authentication, Integrity, and Confidentiality," and Chapter 5, "PKI-Enabled Services," examine services that a PKI can provide. Chapter 4 discusses the core services of authentication, integrity, and confidentiality; Chapter 5 looks at PKI-enabled services such as digital time stamping, notarization, non-repudiation, and privilege management.

Chapter 6, "Certificates and Certification," introduces the concept of a certificate and discusses the process of certification. Certificate contents and format are described, along with the role of a Certification Authority (CA) and a Registration Authority (RA).

Chapter 7, "Key and Certificate Management," looks at the whole area of key/certificate life cycle management, including generation, publication, update, termination, key history, key backup, and key recovery.

Chapter 8, "Certificate Revocation," discusses common techniques for certificate revocation, both periodic publication mechanisms and on-line query mechanisms. Scalability issues, timeliness, and implementation considerations are discussed with respect to these techniques.

Chapter 9, "Trust Models," examines the concept of a trust model. Strict hierarchies, distributed architectures, the Web model, user-centric trust, and cross-certification are presented and compared.

Chapter 10, "Multiple Certificates per Entity," includes an examination of key pair uses, support for non-repudiation, and independent certificate management.

Chapter 11, "PKI Information Dissemination: Repositories and Other Techniques," looks at the area of certificate dissemination and repositories. It discusses the pros and cons of certificate publication, along with issues of scalability, replication, timeliness, and trusted versus untrusted storage/access.

Chapter 12, "PKI Operational Considerations," discusses client-side software, on-line requirements, physical security, and disaster planning/recovery, along with trade-offs between system security and ease of use.

Chapter 13, "Legal Framework," provides a brief discussion of some of the legal issues associated with PKI, including topics such as the legal status of digital signatures, roles and responsibilities, liability, and mitigation of risk.

Chapter 14, "Conclusions and Further Reading," concludes Part I and suggests some sources to consult for further reading in this area.

Part II: Standards

Part II of this book addresses standards activities and interoperability initiatives.

Chapter 15, "Introduction," introduces Part II and provides a list of the contents of Part II on a chapter-by-chapter basis.

Chapter 16, "Major Standards Activities," discusses some of the most prominent activities taking place within formal standards bodies as well as related efforts being undertaken outside the standards bodies.

Chapter 17, "Standardization Status and Road Map," provides the current and projected near-term standardization status of some of the most significant specifications.

Chapter 18, "Standards: Necessary but Not Sufficient," considers the fact that the existence of a "standard," whether it is the product of a formal standards body or not, is necessary but not sufficient to guarantee that the products of different vendors will interoperate with each other. Some of the reasons for this are given, along with a discussion of the usefulness of profiling activities and interoperability pilots.

Finally, Chapter 19, "Conclusions and Further Reading," provides concluding remarks and some suggestions for further reading.

Part III: Deployment Considerations

Part III of this book addresses deployment considerations. While not intended to be a deployment handbook, the primary purpose of this part of the book is to identify many of the deployment questions that should be asked (and answered) when considering any large-scale enterprise PKI deployment.

Chapter 20, "Introduction," introduces Part III and provides a list of the contents of Part III on a chapter-by-chapter basis.

Chapter 21, "Benefits (and Costs) of a PKI," discusses the benefits realized through the deployment of a PKI. It also discusses cost considerations. This chapter helps to identify sound business reasons for deploying a PKI in the enterprise environment.

Chapter 22, "Deployment Issues and Decisions," discusses a number of issues that should be resolved before initial deployment occurs. Essentially, this chapter provides a basic foundation for product selection.

Chapter 23, "Barriers to Deployment," addresses some of the more common hurdles to deployment, issues that one must consider in terms of long-term strategy.

Chapter 24, "Typical Business Models," explains some of the more common business models one may want to implement. It also provides a brief discussion of some of the global trust initiatives.

Chapter 25, "Conclusions and Further Reading," concludes Part III and offers suggestions for further reading.

PART I

Concepts

Introduction

This book is about *understanding Public-Key Infrastructure (PKI)*. The first step in understanding involves the *head*: knowing the concepts; becoming familiar with the terminology; and getting a sense of the parameters, the scope, the limits of a topic. This enables us to become conversant with others about the issues, to be able to read and follow the literature with a perceptive, critical eye.

The second step in understanding involves the *hands*: We learn by doing. We see what technical work others have done (and are doing) to enable concrete implementation of the concepts, and we set to work implementing the concepts for ourselves in our own environments. This, too, allows us to converse with others and to evaluate the literature fairly.

"Doing" leads to greater "knowing," which in turn results in more successful "doing," and so on. The end result is a fairly deep understanding of the topic under consideration.

The primary goal of this book is to be one of the tools in this process of understanding the PKI. Given that some level of "knowing" must come first, Part I, "Concepts," addresses this aspect of PKI understanding by discussing the underlying concepts and terminology, by explaining technical options wherever they arise, and by presenting the inherent strengths and limitations of this technology.

Part II, "Standards," focuses on "doing" by describing the relevant work being undertaken within the standards bodies and related initiatives to enable PKI implementation and interoperability. Part III, "Deployment Considerations," focuses on "doing" as well by discussing many of the practical issues and decisions involved in deploying a PKI in the real world.

Part I consumes the majority of the book. Parts II and III are essentially guidelines to get the reader started in his or her own PKI deployment.

The material presented in Part I is organized as follows:

- Chapter 2, "Public-Key Cryptography," provides a brief, non-mathematical introduction to the concepts of public-key cryptography relevant to the material presented throughout the remainder of the book. Included is the distinction between symmetric and public-key ciphers, the concept of a key pair, the services of this technology, terminology, and sample algorithms.

- Chapter 3, "The Concept of an Infrastructure," discusses the idea of an infrastructure, highlighting its usefulness as an application enabler, its role in secure single sign-on, and its capability to provide end-user transparency and comprehensive security. This chapter also gives a working definition of PKI.

- Chapter 4, "Core PKI Services: Authentication, Integrity, and Confidentiality," and Chapter 5, "PKI-Enabled Services," examine services a PKI can provide. Chapter 4 discusses the core services of authentication, integrity, and confidentiality; Chapter 5 looks at PKI-enabled services such as digital time stamping, notarization, non-repudiation, and privilege management.

- Chapter 6, "Certificates and Certification," introduces the concept of a certificate and discusses the process of certification. This chapter describes certificate contents and format, along with the role of a *Certification Authority (CA)* and a *Registration Authority (RA)*.

- Chapter 7, "Key and Certificate Management," looks at the whole area of key and certificate life cycle management, including generation, publication, update, termination, key history, key backup, and key recovery.

- Chapter 8, "Certificate Revocation," discusses common techniques for certificate revocation, both periodic publication mechanisms and on-line query mechanisms. This chapter discusses scalability issues, timeliness, and implementation considerations with respect to these techniques.

- Chapter 9, "Trust Models," examines the concept of a trust model. It presents and compares strict hierarchies, distributed architectures, the Web model, user-centric trust, and cross-certification.

- Chapter 10, "Multiple Certificates per Entity," discusses the concept of multiple certificates per entity, and includes an examination of key pair uses, support for non-repudiation, and independent certificate management.

- Chapter 11, "PKI Information Dissemination: Repositories and Other Techniques," looks at the area of certificate dissemination and repositories. It discusses the pros and cons of certificate publication, along with issues of scalability, replication, timeliness, and trusted versus untrusted storage/access.

- Chapter 12, "PKI Operational Considerations," examines PKI operational considerations and discusses client-side software, on-line requirements, physical security, and disaster planning/recovery, along with tradeoffs between system security and ease-of-use.

- Chapter 13, "Legal Framework," provides a brief discussion of the legal framework for PKI and includes topics such as the legal status of digital signatures, the *Certification Practice Statement (CPS)*, liability, and mitigation of risk.

- Chapter 14, "Conclusions and Further Reading," concludes Part I and suggests some sources for further reading in this area.

We begin, then, with a brief introduction to public-key cryptography.

2

Public-Key Cryptography

This chapter introduces the main concepts of public-key cryptography. The treatment is intentionally high level and brief, touching on only aspects directly relevant to an understanding of the remainder of this book. For a broader and more thorough discussion, please read the *Handbook of Applied Cryptography* by A. Menezes, P. van Oorschot, and S. Vanstone [MvOV97], *Applied Cryptography: Protocols, Algorithms, and Source Code in C* by B. Schneier [Sch96], *Cryptography and Network Security: Principles and Practice* by W. Stallings [Sta99], or *Cryptography: Theory and Practice* by D. Stinson [Sti95].

Symmetric Versus Asymmetric Ciphers

For as long as humans have communicated, there has been a desire to keep some communications confidential (that is, "hidden") from unintended recipients. Over thousands of years, countless methods for hiding data have been devised. One class of methods attempts to transform the words, letters, or bits to be communicated into something that looks like gibberish rather than a meaningful message. The intended recipient must be able to transform the gibberish back to its original form (in order to read the sender's message), but any other recipient—such as an eavesdropper—should be able to recover nothing more meaningful than the transmitted gibberish.

Two categories of mechanisms exist for performing the transformation of text to gibberish and back. The following section defines and discusses symmetric (*secret key*) ciphers; asymmetric (*public key*) ciphers are the focus of the "New Directions: Public Key" section.

Secret Key

Until the mid-1970s, the only mechanism known in the open literature for this transformation to gibberish and back was for the sender and the intended recipient to share some secret information that specified how the transformation was to be performed.

As one simple, well-known example of this, the shared secret information might specify that each letter in the original message is to be replaced with the letter 13 places ahead in the English alphabet. For example, *A* is replaced with *N*, *B* is replaced with *O*, *Z* is replaced with *M* (13 places ahead after wrapping around to *A* again), and so on. In this case, the secret information to transform the transmitted gibberish back into a readable message is identical: The letter 13 places ahead of *N* is *A*; 13 places ahead of *O* is *B*; 13 places ahead of *M* is *Z*; and so on.

To use the terminology commonly adopted in the field, the shared secret information specifying exactly how the transformation to and from gibberish is to be accomplished (for example, the value 13 in the preceding example) is called a *key*. The transformation to gibberish is called *encryption*; the transformation back to the original text is called *decryption*. The original message, called *plaintext*, is encrypted to gibberish, called *ciphertext*, which can then be decrypted by the intended recipient back to the corresponding plaintext. The entire confidentiality mechanism (that is, the encryption and decryption algorithms) is called a *cipher*. More precisely, the confidentiality mechanism is called a *symmetric cipher* when one of the following is true:

- When the encryption key and the decryption key are identical (as earlier, where both have the value 13)

- When one key is very easily derived from the other (as in a slight variation of the earlier example, where encryption is accomplished by rotating *ahead* five letters, and decryption is accomplished by rotating *back* five letters)

As noted earlier, symmetric ciphers, ranging from the very simple to the highly sophisticated, have existed for thousands of years, and new ones continue to be invented all the time. The earlier example is commonly known as *ROT-13* (or, more generally, as a *simple substitution cipher*). More modern examples include DES [FIPS46], IDEA [Lai92], RC5 [Rivest95], CAST-128 [Adams97, RFC2144], and the candidates for the Advanced Encryption Standard sponsored by the U.S. National Institute of Standards and Technology (for example, see "Advanced Encryption Standard Development Effort" [AES]).

Note

The Advanced Encryption Standard effort is NIST's process to select a symmetric cipher to officially replace the Data Encryption Standard (DES), primarily for U.S. government use but likely for much broader application as well. Scheduled to be chosen in the summer of 2000 from an initial field of 15 candidates, the AES cipher is expected to provide high cryptographic security for the next 20–30 years. Because of this long-term view, NIST requirements dictate that the AES will have a variable-length key size up to 256 bits (whereas many current ciphers have a key size up to 128 bits).

Although symmetric ciphers can possess some very desirable characteristics (such as a small implementation size, and encryption/decryption speeds that can reach tens of megabytes per second or more), they also suffer from some significant drawbacks in some environments. These include

- The need for secret key exchange

- Difficulties of scale

- Difficulties in initiating secure communication between previously unknown parties

The following sections briefly discuss these drawbacks.

The Need for Secret Key Exchange

For their security, symmetric ciphers rely completely on the fact that the sender and the intended recipient alone share some secret information (a key) prior to the transmission of the message. Therefore, the conveyance of this key requires that a separate, out-of-band, secure communication must occur prior to the intended communication. This additional step, although feasible in some environments, can be extremely difficult or highly inconvenient in some circumstances.

Difficulties of Scale

The secret key shared between Alice and Bob must be different from the secret key shared between Alice and Catherine; otherwise, the confidentiality of messages intended for Bob is compromised. In a community of 1,000 users, then, Alice could potentially have to maintain 999 secret keys (actually, 1,000 if she also wants to encrypt data just for herself). Because the same is true for each of the other users, this community could collectively hold something close to half a million unique secret keys! As the community grows, the storage and maintenance of such a large number of keys can quickly become unmanageable (a community of n users may require up to $n^2/2$ unique secret keys, including the key each user holds for him/herself). Manageability problems become even more pronounced when you consider that keys do not last forever but typically are replaced periodically with new ones to limit the amount of data encrypted under a single key.

Communications Difficulties between Unknown Entities

The need for a separate, out-of-band secret key exchange step can lead to tremendous difficulties when entities are unknown to each other (that is, when the entities have had no previous contact or relationship). Alice knows that there is a lawyer named Bob with whom she needs to have a confidential conversation. However, if she has not had any prior communication with Bob, how does she know with whom to share a secret key so that the confidential conversation can take place? That is, how can she be certain that she is sharing a key with Bob and not with David, who is posing as Bob to obtain Alice's confidential information?

Note that this fundamental problem (the need for an "introducer" between entities that have no previous relationship) is not unique to symmetric technology; it also arises in asymmetric technology. As you will see, however, the solutions to this problem are quite different in the two technologies (compare the following section, "Symmetric Central Server Architectures," with the later section, "Security between Strangers").

Symmetric Central Server Architectures

Some of the problems referred to earlier can be mitigated through the use of a symmetric-cipher-based central server architecture in which each entity in the community shares a secret key with the central server (usually called a *Key Distribution Center*, or *KDC*). In such an architecture, the number of secret keys that need to be stored and maintained in a community is essentially equal to the size of the community, and the central server can act as an "introducer" for entities that do not previously know each other. However, the security-critical central server must constantly be available on-line (because when the server is down, communication between entities is not possible). This represents a significant single point of failure and single point of attack for the entire community and can also represent a severe communications bottleneck in a large organization.

New Directions: Public Key

In the mid-1970s, two researchers named Whitfield Diffie and Martin Hellman steered the public-domain field of cryptography into some interesting new directions. (Recently declassified documents show that as early as the late 1960s, individuals in the British agency GCHQ knew of some of the concepts Diffie and Hellman introduced; however, such information was unavailable publicly and was certainly unknown to Diffie and Hellman.) Pondering some of the difficulties with symmetric ciphers discussed earlier, Diffie and Hellman imagined a world in which ciphers were *asymmetric*, in which the key for encryption and the key for decryption were related but conspicuously different. These keys would be so different, in fact, that it would be possible to publicize one without danger of anyone being able to derive or compute the other.

Such a concept was indeed new and interesting, but was it possible? Diffie and Hellman did not have a definitive answer; their paper, "New Directions in Cryptography," [DH76] did not contain a concrete example that provably met the requirements. What it did contain, however, was evidence that such a cipher *might be constructed*. It used, as a toy example, a cipher based on vector-matrix multiplication in which the sender and legitimate receiver only need to multiply a vector with a matrix to encrypt and decrypt, but any other unintended recipient needs to perform the more difficult task of matrix inversion to recover the plaintext. Their suggestion, in general terms, was that "difficult" mathematical problems that had a simple solution if additional information was known might be an attractive underlying basis for asymmetric ciphers. Technically, such problems are known as *trapdoor functions with high computational complexity*. (See also Merkle's early and independent work in this field [M78, M79].)

It is impossible to overemphasize just how radical the concept presented in Diffie and Hellman's paper was when it appeared. The idea of having a key that can be revealed publicly without compromising communications security was unheard of in the open literature and stimulated intensive research for a number of years. The search for concrete examples of asymmetric ciphers gave rise to a number of proposals (many of which were subsequently shown to be insecure). More fundamentally and perhaps more importantly, however, mathematicians, computer scientists, and engineers have been forced to explore the boundary between theoretical and practical complexity and to try to understand the inherent difficulty of certain mathematical problems, such as factoring or finding discrete logarithms over finite fields. Much progress has been made since the 1976 publication of the now-classic Diffie-Hellman paper, but research into asymmetric ciphers and all related subjects continues at an ever-increasing pace.

Public/Private Key Pair

As discussed in the previous section, asymmetric ciphers make use of two related but different keys. In this *key pair*, the keys are sufficiently different that knowing one does not allow derivation or computation of the other (even for a determined adversary with a lot of computing power at his/her disposal). This means that one of the keys may be made publicly available (for example, stored in an open database, listed in a telephone book, or printed on a business card) without reducing security—provided that the other key remains private. The idea that one of the keys in this pair can be revealed publicly was so radical and appealing that this whole method of protecting data quickly became known as *public-key cryptography*.

Note

The key that is not publicly revealed is generally referred to in the industry and the academic literature as a *private key*, rather than a *secret key*. This avoids confusion with the secret key of a symmetric cipher and derives from the idea that two people may share a secret, but a single person keeps something private.

Relationship between Keys in a Pair

The keys in a key pair of a public-key cipher are different, but they are also related (this is necessarily true because, for example, one must decrypt what the other encrypts). The relationship is mathematical and may rely on information known only to the creator of the key pair (such as the factorization of a large integer). However, security in this technology is based on the fact that it is computationally infeasible for anyone other than the key pair creator to derive the private key from knowledge of the public key. Theoretically, of course, the private key can always be derived, but the amount of time, memory, or computing power necessary to do so in practice must be prohibitively high.

Services of Public-Key Cryptography

The discovery of public-key cryptography has made a number of services available, some of which were either unknown or unachievable with symmetric ciphers. This section highlights some of the more important and/or more interesting of these services.

Security between Strangers

One of the driving motivations behind public-key cryptography was the inherent difficulty of enabling secure communication between strangers in a symmetric cipher environment. In particular, given the difficulty of computing the private key even if all other details of the cipher are known, it is possible in such a system to take the public key and disseminate it widely. For example, this key can be stored in a public repository (at some level, the electronic equivalent of a telephone book). Thus, even if Alice has had no previous communication with Bob whatsoever, she can look up his public key (analogously to the way she might look up his telephone number in the phone book) and protect data for him.

There is, of course, one caveat: Alice must feel fairly confident that the public key she retrieves really does belong to Bob. There are two general mechanisms for achieving this (without violating the assumption that Alice and Bob are strangers):

- *Alice trusts the repository*—This public repository may be trusted to return correct information. This is effectively the phone book scenario: When Alice looks up Bob's telephone number in the book, she assumes it is correct and does not do any independent verification of that number before using it to call Bob.

- *Alice finds a way to trust the information*—The public repository may be untrusted, but the information it returns can be independently verified for correctness.

In the paper world, a trusted public repository is achievable, at least to some degree. Alice does not worry that someone will break into her house and alter her phone book so that

Bob's telephone number is replaced with another number. In the electronic world, however, such unauthorized data modification is a legitimate concern: Public repositories, in general, cannot be trusted to return correct information. Thus, the information itself must be independently verifiable. A common mechanism to achieve this is the *public-key certificate*; see Chapter 6, "Certificates and Certification," for further discussion of this technology.

As the section "Communications Difficulties between Unknown Entities" noted earlier, both symmetric and asymmetric technologies require an "introducer." It may be argued, however, that the asymmetric "introducer" solution is preferable for a number of environments because an attacker must possess a much greater level of sophistication and skill to succeed. With the symmetric central server architecture, confidentiality is critical; simply being able to read the KDC data suffices to compromise the entire system. With the public repository (either itself trusted or holding independently verifiable data), confidentiality is unimportant: The attacker must be able to explicitly manipulate the contained data in a totally undetectable way. Such an active attack is generally harder to accomplish than the purely passive attack of trying to read data.

Encryption

With some public-key algorithms, encrypting data with the public key is possible; then, the resulting ciphertext can be decrypted only with the corresponding private key. Generally, however, the computations involved in public-key cryptography are slow enough that this is impractical for many environments. Typically what is done instead involves a two-step process, as follows:

1. The data is encrypted using a randomly generated symmetric key.

2. Then, the symmetric key is encrypted using the public key of the intended recipient of the data.

When the recipient receives the encrypted data, a similar two-step process takes place:

1. The recipient decrypts the symmetric key using its private key.

2. The symmetric key is then used to decrypt the actual data.

Even when the total amount of data to be encrypted is very small, the two-step processes presented here are typically used rather than direct data encryption/decryption using the public/private key pair. This serves to keep processing clear and simple so that there is never any confusion as to whether the output of a private-key decryption operation is data or a symmetric key.

Digital Signature

A service enabled by public-key cryptography that is not easily achievable with symmetric ciphers is the *digital signature*. This is analogous to a hand-written signature because a single entity can sign some data, but any number of entities can read the signature and verify its accuracy. However, it is much more secure because it is computationally infeasible for any other entity to create Alice's signature on some data (that is, forging is virtually impossible).

A digital signature fundamentally relies on the concept of a key pair. There must be a private key known only to Alice so that when she signs some data, the data is uniquely and explicitly tied to her. Furthermore, there must be a public key available to a wider group of entities (potentially all entities) so that the signature can be verified and identified with Alice. With a symmetric cipher, Alice might encrypt or compute a Message Authentication Code (MAC) on some data, but the symmetric key used would have to be revealed to any entity wishing to verify this value; see, for example, Federal Information Processing Standards Publication 113, "Computer Data Authentication" [FIPS113]. However, after the key is revealed, the value can no longer be identified with Alice, because this verifier holds the secret information (that is, the key) necessary to have created this value as well. Thus, the computation Alice performed cannot be considered to be a signature in any strict sense.

Conceptually, one can think of the digital signature operation as a private-key operation on data (where the resulting value is the signature). If Alice is the only entity who knows this private key, she is clearly the only entity who could have signed this data. On the other hand, any entity (because it is able to retrieve a copy of Alice's corresponding public key) can verify the signature by doing a public-key operation on the signature and checking whether this result corresponds to the original data. (Note that this data must have known redundancy for the signature/verification process to be reliable. All digital signature mechanisms, therefore, specify particular padding conventions for the data, to be applied prior to the signature process itself and to be examined and then removed as part of the verification process.)

Data to be signed may be of any arbitrary size (for example, a five-word e-mail message or a 10-megabyte file), but a private-key operation takes a fixed-size input and computes a fixed-size output. To address this problem, a *cryptographic hash function* is used (see the "Analysis and Design of Cryptographic Hash Functions" by B. Preneel [P93], and "Information Authentication: Hash Functions and Digital Signatures" by B. Preneel, R. Govaerts, and J. Vandewalle [PGV93] for an extensive discussion of this topic). Such a function has the property that it maps an input of arbitrary size to a fixed-size output (suitable for the input of a private-key operation), and it is very difficult (that is, computationally infeasible) to find two different hash inputs that produce the same hash output.

Thus, the signing operation is a two-step process:

1. The signer hashes the data to a fixed-size value.

2. The signer then subjects this value to a private-key operation.

Verification is a similar two-step process:

1. The verifier hashes the data to a fixed-size value.

2. The verifier then examines this value, the transmitted signature, the signing entity's public key (if the signature matches the key and the hash value, the signature verifies; otherwise, verification fails).

Data Integrity

A digital signature provides not only data origin authentication (evidence as to who originated the data), but also data integrity (evidence that the data has not been altered in any way). Difficulty in finding two inputs that hash to the same output is a result of the hash function's property. Thus, any alteration to the data (with virtual certainty) will lead to a different hash value, which will lead to a failure in signature verification. If the signature verification is successful, the recipient can feel confident that data integrity has been preserved.

Key Establishment

Public-key cryptography can also be used to perform key establishment (sometimes called key exchange) between two entities; that is, a protocol can use public and private keys such that, at the conclusion of the protocol, the two entities share a secret symmetric key known by no other entity.

Key establishment can occur in two ways:

- In *key transfer*, one entity generates the symmetric key and sends it to the other entity. Public-key cryptography can be used to protect the confidentiality of this transfer (for example, Alice can encrypt the symmetric key using Bob's public key).

- In *key agreement*, both entities jointly contribute to the generation of the symmetric key. Public-key cryptography makes such a procedure relatively simple (see, for example, the Diffie-Hellman key establishment protocol [DH76]), whereas this would be very difficult to achieve using purely symmetric technology.

Other Services

The advent of public-key cryptography has enabled a number of other interesting services beyond those listed in the previous sections. These include the construction of provably secure pseudorandom number generators, protocols for playing games (such as poker) and flipping coins over networks in a provably fair way, mechanisms for conducting secure electronic elections, and techniques for Alice to prove to another entity that she knows a secret without ever having to reveal the secret to anyone (known as *zero-knowledge* or *minimum-knowledge* protocols).

If you're interested in these services, see the references listed in the first paragraph of this chapter, or see the annual proceedings of the major cryptography conferences (particularly Crypto and Eurocrypt; for example, pages 667–698 in the *Handbook of Applied Cryptography* by A. Menezes, P. van Oorschot, and S. Vanstone [MvOV97]) over the past several years.

Algorithms

A number of public-key algorithms exist, and each is suitable for one or more of the services discussed in the previous section. The most well known examples are mentioned briefly here; see the *Handbook of Applied Cryptography* [MvOV97] or *Applied Cryptography: Protocols, Algorithms, and Source Code in C* [Sch96] for a much more complete enumeration.

RSA

The algorithm proposed by Ron Rivest, Adi Shamir, and Len Adleman in 1978 [RSA78], known as *RSA*, is one of the earliest and most versatile of the public-key algorithms. It is suitable for encryption/decryption, for signing/verification (and, therefore, for data integrity), and for key establishment (specifically key transfer). It can be used as the basis for a secure pseudorandom number generator as well as for the security in some electronic games. Its security is based on the difficulty of factoring very large integers. The current state of factoring research suggests that RSA keys should be at least 1,024 bits long to provide adequate security for the medium-to-long term.

DSA

The *Digital Signature Algorithm (DSA)* is a *Federal Information Processing Standard (FIPS)* publication of the *National Institute of Standards and Technology (NIST)* of the U.S. Department of Commerce [FIPS186]. It is a variant of the ElGamal signature mechanism [ElG85]. The DSA was designed exclusively for signing/verification (and, therefore, also for data integrity), but other algorithms in the ElGamal family can be used for encryption/decryption (and, therefore, key transfer if what is being encrypted and decrypted is a symmetric key). The security of these algorithms is based on the difficulty of computing logarithms in a finite field. The current state of research with respect to discrete logarithms suggests that DSA keys should be at least 1,024 bits long to provide adequate security for the medium-to-long term.

DH

The algorithm that Whitfield Diffie and Martin Hellman proposed, known as *DH*, is a wonderful example of elegance and simplicity [DH76]. The earliest public-key algorithm, it is exclusively a key establishment (specifically key agreement) protocol; each of two entities uses its own private key and the other entity's public key to create a symmetric key that no third entity can compute. It derives its security from the difficulty of computing logarithms in a finite field. As with DSA, the current state of research with respect to discrete logarithms suggests that DH keys should be at least 1,024 bits long to provide adequate security for the medium-to-long term.

ECDSA and ECDH

The DSA and DH algorithms can also be computed over the group of points defined by the solution to an equation for an elliptic curve over a finite field defined [Kob87, Mil86]. The resulting elliptic curve DSA (ECDSA) and elliptic curve DH (ECDH) algorithms have identical uses to their finite field counterparts earlier, but the security now rests on the difficulty of computing logarithms over the group of EC points. This different foundation leads to more complicated implementation and processing, but has the benefit of significantly smaller key sizes for a similar level of security. The current state of research with respect to discrete logarithms over EC points suggests that ECDH and ECDSA keys should be at least 192 bits long to provide adequate security for the medium-to-long term.

Note that it is possible to do elliptic curve RSA as well; however, due to the different security basis (integer factorization as opposed to discrete logarithms), the key sizes are not significantly smaller than "ordinary" RSA. Thus, the added complication has no perceived benefit, and ECRSA appears not to be used anywhere.

SHA-1

The *Secure Hash Algorithm SHA-1* (a slight revision of the original Secure Hash Algorithm SHA) is described in a NIST FIPS publication [FIPS180-1]. This hash algorithm was designed specifically for use with the DSA but can be used with RSA or other public-key signature algorithms as well. Its design principles are similar to those used in the MD2 [RFC1319], MD4 [RFC1320], and (especially) MD5 [RFC1321] hash functions proposed by Ron Rivest. Current computational capability suggests that the size of the SHA-1 hash value (160 bits) provides adequate security for at least the medium term (note that "SHA-2," with a longer hash value, is currently being developed with a view to very long-term security). Hash functions are not public-key algorithms but are included here because digital signature algorithms are always used in conjunction with hash algorithms to provide the services of signing/verification and data integrity. Thus, they are an essential component of the digital signature and integrity security services.

Summary

Public-key cryptography is a critically important technology. It realizes the concept of a digital signature; provides a practical, elegant mechanism for symmetric key agreement; and enables secure communication. The idea of a key pair (one key kept private; the other made publicly available) also enables other services and protocols including confidentiality, data integrity, secure pseudorandom number generation, electronic games, and zero-knowledge proofs of knowledge.

The underlying concepts of public-key cryptography, along with a number of the fundamental algorithms, have reached a stage of relative maturity. This is due to the intense scrutiny and research that has occurred in this area over the past two decades.

To bring the power of public-key technology to entities in a practical way, two related areas need to be explored:

* There needs to be a way to make this technology available to a wide variety of applications and environments in a uniform manner; this need for an *infrastructure* is discussed in Chapter 3, "The Concept of an Infrastructure."

* There needs to be a way to ensure that a public key actually corresponds to the entity with whom Alice wishes to communicate; the concept of a *certificate* is discussed in Chapter 6.

References

[Adams97]   Adams, C. "Constructing Symmetric Ciphers Using the CAST Design Procedure." *Designs, Codes and Cryptography* 12, no. 3 (November 1997): 71–104.

[AES]   National Institute of Standards and Technology. "Advanced Encryption Standard Development Effort." See http://csrc.nist.gov/encryption/aes/aes_home.htm.

[DH76]   Diffie, W. and M. Hellman. "New Directions in Cryptography." *IEEE Transactions on Information Theory* 22 (1976): 644–654.

[ElG85]   ElGamal, T. "A Public Key Cryptosystem and a Signature Scheme Based on Discrete Logarithms." *IEEE Transactions on Information Theory* 31 (1985): 469–472.

[FIPS46]   Federal Information Processing Standards Publication 46. "Data Encryption Standard." U.S. Department of Commerce, National Bureau of Standards, National Technical Information Service. Springfield, Virginia, 1977.

[FIPS113]   Federal Information Processing Standards Publication 113. "Computer Data Authentication." U.S. Department of Commerce, National Bureau of Standards, National Technical Information Service. Springfield, Virginia, 1985.

[FIPS180-1] Federal Information Processing Standards Publication 180-1. "Secure Hash Standard." U.S. Department of Commerce, National Bureau of Standards, National Technical Information Service. Springfield, Virginia, 1995.

[FIPS186]   Federal Information Processing Standards Publication 186. "Digital Signature Standard." U.S. Department of Commerce, National Bureau of Standards, National Technical Information Service. Springfield, Virginia, 1994.

[Kob87]   Koblitz, N. "Elliptic Curve Cryptosystems." *Mathematics of Computation* 48 (1987): 203–209.

[Lai92]   Lai, X. "On the Design and Security of Block Ciphers." *ETH Series in Information Processing*. vol. 1. edited by J.L. Massey. Hartung-Gorre Verlag Konstanz, Technische Hochschule, Zurich, 1992.

[M78]   Merkle, R. "Secure Communications Over Insecure Channels." *Communications of the ACM*. 21 (1978): 294–299.

[M79]   ———. *Secrecy, Authentication, and Public Key Systems*. Ann Arbor, Michigan: UMI Research Press, 1979.

[Mil86]   Miller, V. "Use of Elliptic Curves in Cryptography." *Advances in Cryptology, Proceedings of Crypto '85* (LNCS 218) (1986): 417–426.

[MvOV97] Menezes, A., P. van Oorschot, and S. Vanstone. *Handbook of Applied Cryptography*. Boca Raton: CRC Press, 1997. (See also `http://cacr.math.uwaterloo. ca/hac`)

[P93]   Preneel, B. "Analysis and Design of Cryptographic Hash Functions." (Ph.D. diss., Katholieke Universiteit Leuven, Belgium, January 1993).

[PGV93]   Preneel, B., R. Govaerts, and J. Vandewalle. "Information Authentication: Hash Functions and Digital Signatures." *Computer Security and Industrial Cryptography: State of the Art and Evolution.* edited by B. Preneel, R. Govaerts, and J. Vandewalle. Springer-Verlag (LNCS 741) (1993): 87–131.

[RFC1319]   Kaliski, B. "The MD2 Message-Digest Algorithm." Internet Request for Comments 1319. (April 1992).

[RFC1320]   Rivest, R. "The MD4 Message-Digest Algorithm." Internet Request for Comments 1320. (April 1992).

[RFC1321]   Rivest, R. "The MD5 Message-Digest Algorithm." Internet Request for Comments 1321. (April 1992).

[RFC2144]   Adams, C. "The CAST-128 Encryption Algorithm." Internet Request for Comments 2144. (May 1997).

[Rivest95]   Rivest, R. "The RC5 Encryption Algorithm." Proceedings of the Second International Workshop on Fast Software Encryption, Springer-Verlag (LNCS 1008) (1995): 86–96.

[RSA78]   Rivest, R., A. Shamir, and L. Adleman. "A Method for Obtaining Digital Signatures and Public-Key Cryptosystems." *Communications of the ACM* 21 (1978): 120–126.

[Sch96]   Schneier, B. *Applied Cryptography: Protocols, Algorithms, and Source Code in C, Second Edition.* New York: John Wiley & Sons, 1996.

[Sta99]   Stallings, W. *Cryptography and Network Security: Principles and Practice, Second Edition.* Upper Saddle River, NJ: Prentice Hall, 1999.

[Sti95]   Stinson, D. *Cryptography: Theory and Practice.* Boca Raton: CRC Press, 1995.

The Concept of an Infrastructure

This chapter introduces and discusses the idea of an "infrastructure" for security by considering the features and benefits of pervasive infrastructures with which we are currently familiar. This leads to a working definition of a *public-key infrastructure (PKI)* that will form the basis of understanding for all remaining chapters.

Pervasive Substrate

A *pervasive substrate* is a foundation or underpinning for a large environment (such as a corporate organization); an infrastructure may be considered a pervasive substrate. Two familiar sample infrastructures are the electronic communications infrastructure (that is, the network) and the electric power infrastructure. In the former, the *Local Area Network (LAN)* enables various machines to transfer data among themselves for a variety of purposes; in the latter, the power grid enables a plethora of electronic equipment to get the voltage and current they need for operation. Ultimately, however, the principle is identical: The infrastructure exists so that disparate entities can simply "tap into it" and use it on an as-needed basis.

An infrastructure for security purposes must recognize the same principle and offer the same fundamental benefits. A security infrastructure provides a security underpinning for the entire organization (however this "organization" might be defined) and must be accessible by all applications and objects in the organization that need security. The "entry points" into the security infrastructure must be convenient and uniform (like the TCP/IP stack or the power socket in the wall). Therefore, objects that want to make use of the infrastructure are not unduly hindered from doing so.

The pervasive security infrastructure is fundamentally the sensible architecture for many environments. This architecture avoids piecemeal, point-to-point, ad hoc, non-interoperable solutions, thereby introducing the possibility of manageable, consistent security across multiple applications and computing platforms. It is not difficult to imagine the chaos that would result from every pair of communicants running their own communications lines, or from every person running his/her own power generator at his/her own arbitrarily chosen voltage and current. Many facets of both ancient and modern society demonstrate that the uniformity and convenience offered by a well-designed, well-defined, pervasive infrastructure is worth the effort involved in the design and definition stages.

Application Enabler

The primary goal of the security infrastructure is to function as an "application enabler." The electric power infrastructure is an application enabler in the sense that it enables "applications," such as toasters and lamps, to operate correctly. Furthermore, the generality and utility of the electrical infrastructure is such that it can support "applications" (such as hair dryers, for example) that were unknown at the time it was designed.

Note

The word *application* is used with respect to the security infrastructure in the sense of any module that uses the infrastructure for security purposes, such as a Web browser, an e-mail client, or an IPsec-enabled device.

The security infrastructure enables applications to add security to their own data or resources and to add security to their interactions with other data or resources. The addition of security must be straightforward and quickly accomplished to be most useful. In particular, accessing the infrastructure is analogous to plugging an electrical device into a wall socket:

- There must be a known, easy-to-use interface.

- The result (that is, the service delivered by the infrastructure) must be predictable and useful.

- The way the infrastructure achieves that result need not be known to the using device.

In particular, it should make no difference to a toaster how electrical energy travels from a generating station to a house, or to the various wall sockets within the house. However, when the toaster is plugged into any particular wall socket, the predictable "service" delivered (a given voltage and current) to this well-known interface should enable the toaster to draw the energy it needs to operate correctly.

The security infrastructure must similarly have well-known entry points that can deliver a security service to using devices. *How it does this* need not be known by those devices, but *that it does this*, consistently and correctly, is essential.

The following three subsections discuss important aspects of the service delivered by the pervasive security infrastructure.

Secure Sign-On

The concept of "signing-on" (often called "logging-in") to an application is very familiar. Typically, the process involves the user entering some kind of user identification (user ID or username) along with some kind of authenticating information (a password or other secret value). Under the assumption that no one other than the legitimate user knows that user's authenticating information, this process can be (and commonly is) used to securely "introduce" the user to a specific application.

This process is familiar; its associated problems are just as familiar. If the application requiring sign-on is remote from the user (that is, on a different piece of equipment, such as another computer), passwords traveling over unprotected networks are subject to interception and eavesdropping, and even encrypted passwords do not necessarily protect against replay attacks. Furthermore, users are notoriously bad at picking "good" passwords (ones with sufficient length and unpredictability), remembering them without writing them down, and changing them frequently when their local security policy encourages them to do so.

A security infrastructure can help address some of these problems. In particular, having security as a pervasive infrastructure implies that a sign-on event to the infrastructure happens locally (that is, at the device through which the user is physically interacting), and the successful result is securely extended to the remote application when required. Thus, strong authentication mechanisms can be used for these remote sign-on events, and passwords need never travel over the network (in fact, need never be known outside the user's device).

The deployment of a security infrastructure, therefore, may not eliminate the use of passwords altogether (because this may be the mechanism for user authentication to the infrastructure itself). However, it can eliminate one of the most serious problems commonly associated with the use of passwords: their conveyance over untrusted and insecure networks.

Secure "Single" Sign-On

The sign-on problems cited in the preceding section are greatly exacerbated when a user needs to access multiple applications, all of which require an authenticated sign-on event. Using the same password for all applications reduces the overall security (by providing multiple points of attack); using a different password for each application reduces overall ease of use. Users can be instructed in proper sign-on procedures, but if those procedures impede the user's work, the user will find ways around the procedures, and these ways will typically be less secure.

The use of a pervasive substrate for security can greatly improve this situation. As stated in the previous section, the security infrastructure can enable the result of a successful sign-on event to be securely communicated to another device normally requiring sign-on, thus removing the need for a remote sign-on event. This feature can be extended so that a successful sign-on event can be communicated to *many* remote devices (as required), thus removing the need for *multiple* sign-on events. This type of feature is an integral concept to a security infrastructure. Like any system or application requiring sign-on, the security infrastructure has some explicitly-encoded sense of a user's "identity" (so that it can compare an attempted sign-on with what it expects of the legitimate user). However, that "identity" is understood throughout the full extent of the infrastructure (which could conceivably be global), so it is available to every system and application that plugs into the infrastructure.

One sign-on would, therefore, be sufficient to gain access to multiple devices, domains, servers, systems, applications, and so on (note that these sign-on events may still be combined with other access control [authorization] mechanisms; see Chapter 5, "PKI-Enabled Services," for further discussion). Thus, secure single sign-on is very desirable from a usability standpoint because the user has fewer passwords to remember and needs to know only a single procedure to access multiple systems. It is also very desirable from a security standpoint because passwords travel less frequently over the network and because there is a higher possibility that the single password chosen by the user will be a "good" one.

Note

Note that for environments that include a number of legacy applications, an actual single sign-on may be very difficult, or impossible, to achieve. In such situations, the discussion presented in this chapter is sometimes referred to as *reduced sign-on*. This may still represent a significant improvement in security, however, because each user has fewer passwords to remember and to manage.

Secure single sign-on is a service that can be delivered by the security infrastructure to all using applications and devices. The infrastructure incorporates the mechanisms required to securely disseminate authentication information when and where it is needed; applications "tap into" the infrastructure to access this information when necessary. This infrastructural service frees the user from having to sign-on multiple times. An additional, important security benefit is that a well-designed infrastructure can ensure that the users sign-on only to the local machine at which they are working. Thus, at least in some cases, passwords do not travel over a vulnerable network, greatly reducing the risks associated with password-sniffing and password storage/replay attacks.

End-User Transparency

A vitally important, yet often overlooked, feature of a pervasive infrastructure is the fact that it is almost totally transparent to users. The vast majority of users of the communications infrastructure need not know about IP headers or Ethernet packets; similarly, the vast majority of users of the electric power infrastructure need not know about voltage levels or current ratings. How the services of an infrastructure are delivered can, and should, be a complete "black box" to the users of the infrastructure. A properly designed security infrastructure must have the same characteristic: Virtually all the security should be hidden from the user so that there is no extra manual intervention needed, there is no requirement for user awareness of keys and algorithms, and there is little danger of user error compromising security.

The idea that the end-user should not have to know the mechanics of how the infrastructure provides security can also be expressed in this way: Security should present no impediment to the user in terms of hindering him/her from doing the tasks that need to be done. Security should require of the user no special knowledge, should demand of the user no special procedures, and should burden the user with no special delays. Other than the initial sign-on event, the infrastructure should perform all security-related tasks in a way that is completely transparent to the user.

There are, however, two exceptions to this rule. As with any infrastructure, users need to be made aware of it the first time they come into contact with it (that is, during some kind of initialization procedure) and when the security infrastructure is unable to deliver its services. Just as the user needs to know when a remote machine is not accepting IP packets and needs to know when the power is off in the house, he/she needs to know when authentication has failed or when a secure communications channel cannot be established with a remote server. Simply put, the transparency provided by the infrastructure implies a level of trust on the part of the user that the infrastructure is operating correctly and is able to deliver its services. Whenever this fails to be true, the user must be notified immediately because the lack of security will typically necessitate a change in user behaviour.

Comprehensive Security

Arguably, the most important benefit of a pervasive security infrastructure is that it ensures that a single, trusted, security technology (for example, public-key technology) is available throughout the environment. This enables unlimited numbers of applications, devices, and servers to work together seamlessly to secure the transfer, storage, and retrieval of data, to secure transaction processing, to secure server access, and so on. Electronic mail applications, Web browsers, firewalls, remote access devices, application servers, file servers, databases, and more, are all able to understand and make use of the security infrastructure in a unified way. Such an environment greatly simplifies not only the end-user's dealings with these various devices and applications, but also the complex job of administering these devices and applications, ensuring that they adhere to a particular level of security policy (which may be increased as needed for specific applications or devices).

One of the primary mechanisms that achieves this comprehensive security within the infrastructure is the ability to ensure that keys are used, understood, and processed in a consistent manner across the broad range of organizational entities and devices. Without a pervasive security infrastructure, it would be almost impossible to provide the same level of operational consistency.

Business Drivers

Business drivers are actual (though not always quantifiable), or perceived, benefits to an organization that will influence decision-making in one direction or another. A comprehensive security infrastructure, as opposed to a collection of point-to-point solutions between specific applications or devices, offers a number of significant benefits to the organizational environment. These include the following:

- *Cost savings*—Implementing a single security solution throughout a large organization will inevitably be less expensive than implementing several, more limited solutions because the incremental cost of adding new users or applications is very modest in the former situation. With multiple solutions, additional users or applications can be difficult or impossible to incorporate, and integration of a new solution with an existing collection of solutions can be a very complex and expensive activity. The cost of deploying, maintaining, and operating multiple point-to-point solutions is also likely to be high, compared with deploying, maintaining, and operating a single infrastructural solution.

- *Interoperability (intra-enterprise)*—Multiple, point-to-point solutions can prohibit interoperability because these solutions are developed independently and have incompatible operating paradigms and underlying assumptions. An infrastructure, on the other hand, ensures interoperability because each application or device accesses and uses the infrastructure in an identical manner.

- *Interoperability (inter-enterprise)*—Early adopters of any technology typically desire some confidence that their enterprise will be able to interoperate with other enterprises that will deploy solutions in the future. A recognized infrastructural technology based on open, international standards is more likely to instill this confidence than a proprietary, point-to-point technology that is not designed to handle the complexities of multiple domains.

- *Uniform solution*—A security infrastructure provides a consistent, uniform solution to all using applications and devices. Such uniformity is much easier to install, manage, and maintain across an organization than a collection of incompatible solutions. Administration cost and complexity, therefore, strongly favours the infrastructure solution.

- *Possibility of actually achieving security*—A security infrastructure offers the possibility that interactions between various applications and devices will actually be secure because all interactions are handled in a consistent manner. Furthermore, the operation and interactions of the infrastructure may have been validated for correctness (for example, by a professional, independent validation agency). Security between independent point-to-point solutions is much less likely, even if each solution has been rigorously validated, because the interaction between these solutions is largely untested.

- *Choice of provider*—The provider of the infrastructure may be a particular group within the organization, or may be selected from a list of external candidates. In either case, however, the choice of provider can be made based on expertise, price, functionality, reputation, longevity, and a number of other factors. With point-to-point solutions, the security functionality comes incorporated within the individual application or device so that it is very difficult for an organization to make a purchasing decision based purely on the security offered (because the application may be highly desirable for any of the other features it offers).

The business drivers for a pervasive security infrastructure are many and varied; the preceding list represents a handful of perhaps the most common arguments. However, the uniformity of the solution (which can lead to interoperability and significant cost savings in administration) and the security offered are probably the primary drivers for an infrastructural solution in many environments.

Public-Key Infrastructure Defined

Having gained an understanding of public-key cryptography in the previous chapter and an understanding of an infrastructure in this chapter, we are now ready to contemplate the notion of a *public-key infrastructure (PKI)*. The seed idea, of course, is very simple:

> A *PKI* is a pervasive security infrastructure whose services are implemented and delivered using public-key concepts and techniques.

Exploring this rudimentary definition further (that is, thinking about it in terms of practical operational consequences) leads to a slightly broader and more realistic definition, whose many parts we discuss briefly here and more fully in the following chapters.

Certification Authority

The fundamental premise in the original formulation of public-key cryptography was that two strangers should be able to communicate securely. For example, when George wants to send a confidential message to Lisa (whom he has not met previously), he will somehow be able to associate a public key with Lisa so that he can encrypt the message for her. With a potential user population of hundreds of thousands or millions of entities, the most practical way to achieve this is to appoint a relatively small number of authorities. These authorities are trusted (refer to Chapter 9, "Trust Models," for a working definition of trust as it is used throughout this book) by a large segment of the population (or, perhaps, the entire population) to perform the function of binding a public key pair to a given identity. Such authorities are called *Certification Authorities (CAs)* in PKI terminology; they *certify* the key pair/identity binding by digitally signing a data structure that contains some representation of the identity and a corresponding public key. This data structure is called a *public-key certificate* (or, more simply, a *certificate*) and will be discussed in some detail in Chapter 6, "Certificates and Certification."

Although not an essential element of every conceivable PKI (especially those that are very limited in size or those that operate in relatively closed environments where users can effectively act as their own authorities), the CA is a critical component of many large-scale PKIs and, therefore, forms a part of our expanded PKI definition. See Chapter 6 for further discussion on the role and function of a CA.

Certificate Repository

It will readily be recognized that a CA solves only part of the problem mentioned in the previous section (that is, that George needs to associate a public key with Lisa in order to encrypt data for her). The certificate issued by the CA associates a public key with Lisa's identity, but unless George is able to locate this certificate easily, he is effectively no further ahead than if the certificate had never been created.

Some sort of robust, scalable, on-line repository system must be in place for George to locate the certificates he needs to communicate securely. A *certificate repository*, therefore, forms a part of our expanded PKI definition (since a large PKI would effectively be useless without it). For a discussion regarding various repository technologies and choices (including X.500, LDAP, Web servers, FTP servers, DNS, corporate databases, and others), see Chapter 11, "PKI Information Dissemination: Repositories and Other Techniques."

Certificate Revocation

The CA signs a certificate binding a public key pair to a user identity. In real-world environments, however, there will be events that necessitate the breaking of that binding.

Commonly cited examples include the changing of an identity (such as the transition from a maiden name to a married name) or the compromise (that is, discovery by a hacker) of a private key. There must be a way of alerting the rest of the user population that it is no longer acceptable to use *this* public key for *that* identity. This alerting mechanism in a PKI is called *Certificate Revocation*.

An analogy for PKI Certificate Revocation may be drawn as follows. A driver's license is a form of certificate: a binding of an identity (name and picture) to a driver's license number (that is, a permission to drive) by a trusted authority. When a police officer pulls over a car, the officer does not simply check the expiration date on the license of the driver; he or she also calls an authority to see if the license has been revoked. A revocation check is necessary because sometimes circumstances dictate that the identity/permission binding present in the (unexpired) certificate should no longer be trusted.

Unless certificates have such a short lifetime that they are effectively for one-time use only (that is, they are issued, used immediately, and never used again), some form of revocation is required for those situations in which a certificate must be declared to be invalid. Single-use certificates are impractical in many PKI environments for a number of reasons, including the tremendous load this would place on the CA and the fact that the CA certificate (which holds the public key used to sign the end-user certificates) is necessarily not single-use. Thus, we find that revocation also forms a part of our expanded PKI definition. Certificate Revocation is discussed further in Chapter 8, "Certificate Revocation."

Key Backup and Recovery

In any given operational PKI environment, some percentage of users may be expected to lose the use of their private key each fixed time period (for example, each month or each year). This may be due to numerous situations, including

- Forgotten passwords (so that a given user's encrypted private key is still physically there but inaccessible to him/her)

- Destruction of a medium (such as a hard disk crash or a broken smart card)

For many environments (particularly corporate environments), the loss of data protected by the now-inaccessible key would be totally unacceptable. A business may have critical documents encrypted under a symmetric key that, in turn, is encrypted under a particular user's public key. If the corresponding private key is lost, those documents are rendered unrecoverable, which may severely hinder, or even halt, the functioning of the business.

One solution to this problem is to encrypt all data for multiple recipients, but this may not always be practical (for example, for highly sensitive data). A much more practical and commonly accepted solution is to implement backup and recovery of private decryption keys (but not private signing keys; see Chapter 2, "Public-Key Cryptography," for a discussion of different key types). The necessity of this approach for many environments means that key backup and recovery will form part of our expanded PKI definition; see Chapter 7, "Key and Certificate Management," for further discussion on this topic.

Automatic Key Update

A certificate has a finite lifetime. This may be for theoretical reasons, such as the current state of knowledge in cryptanalysis with respect to asymmetric algorithms and key lengths. Alternatively, it may be for reasons based on practical estimations ("We change keys with this frequency to limit the amount of data typically protected by a single key to x megabytes"). Whatever the reason, however, it is clear that in many PKI environments, a given certificate will need to "expire" and be replaced with a new certificate. This procedure is called *Key Update* or *Certificate Update* (see Chapter 7 for the distinction).

Most PKI users will find it cumbersome and annoying to go through a manual update procedure on a periodic basis for each of their certificates. Users will not typically remember the date on which their certificate is due to expire, and so they will find this out only when it is too late (that is, when the certificate fails to validate). Therefore, until they complete the update procedure, they will be out of service with respect to the PKI. Furthermore, when the user is in this state, the update procedure is slightly more complicated, requiring an out-of-band exchange with the CA (similar to the initialization process).

The solution is to implement the PKI in such a way that key or certificate update is handled in a totally automated way by the PKI itself, with no user intervention whatsoever. Whenever the user's certificate is about to be used for any purpose, its validity period is checked. When the expiration date is approaching, a renewal operation occurs, and a new certificate is generated. Then, the new certificate is used in place of the old, and the user-requested transaction continues.

Because automatic key update is so vital to an operational PKI in many environments, it will form part of our expanded definition of a PKI. See Chapter 7 for further discussion on key update.

Key History

The concept of key update (whether manual or automatic) implies that, over the course of time, a given user will have multiple "old" certificates and at least one "current" certificate. This collection of certificates and corresponding private keys is known as the user's *key history* (perhaps more properly called *key and certificate history*, but typically the shorter name is used). Keeping track of this entire key history is very important because data that George encrypted for himself (or data that was encrypted by someone else *for* George) five years ago cannot be decrypted with his current private decryption key. (Note that re-encrypting all data whenever a key is updated is a completely impractical solution in most environments.) George needs his key history so that the correct decryption key can be found to decrypt the required data. Similarly, some of the certificates in this key history will be needed to verify George's five-year-old signatures.

Like key update, the management of key histories must be automatic and totally handled by the PKI. Users will not typically tolerate any system in which they need to somehow select the appropriate private key themselves or (worse yet) try each private key in turn until the data decrypts to something intelligible. The PKI must hold on to all the keys in the history, perform backup and recovery where appropriate, and find the appropriate key that corresponds to any protected data.

The importance of key history causes it to form a part of our expanded definition of a PKI. See Chapter 7 for further discussion on key history.

Cross-Certification

The concept of a single, global PKI that every user in the world joins is unlikely to become a reality. Rather, what we see today is a model that seems likely to persist: multiple PKIs, independently implemented and operated, serving different environments and user communities.

Given this set of independently developed PKIs, however, it is inevitable that at least some of them will need to be interconnected. Changing business relationships or other reasons will necessitate secure communication between the user communities of some PKIs, even if secure communication was not previously a requirement.

The concept of *cross-certification* has arisen in the PKI environment to deal with precisely this need for forming trust relationships between formerly unrelated PKI installations (see Chapter 9, "Trust Models," for a discussion of trust models and trust relationships). In the absence of a single, global PKI, cross-certification is the accepted mechanism for enabling users of one PKI community to validate the certificates of users in another PKI community. The importance of satisfying this business requirement means that cross-certification will form a part of our expanded PKI definition. See Chapter 9 for details regarding cross-certification.

Support for Non-Repudiation

Users of a PKI frequently perform actions intended to be irrevocably associated with their identity (for example, George digitally signs a document, thereby making the claim that the document came from him). For the smooth and uninterrupted flow of business, there is a requirement that users cannot arbitrarily break this association (especially for their own advantage) at any time in the future. Therefore, for example, months after signing the document, George must not be able to deny that the signature really came from him by claiming that someone else had acquired his private signing key and used it on the document without his knowledge or approval.

Such a denial is referred to as *repudiation* of an action, so a PKI must provide support for avoiding or preventing repudiation—a property known as *non-repudiation*. A PKI cannot, by itself, provide true/full non-repudiation; there will typically be a human element needed to apply discretion and judgment in weighing the evidence and to provide the final decision. However, the PKI must *support* this process by providing some of the technical evidence required, such as data origin authentication and a trusted attestation of the time the data was signed. Support for non-repudiation, therefore, forms part of our extended definition of a PKI. Chapter 10, "Multiple Certificates per Entity," provides further discussion of this topic.

Time Stamping

One of the critical elements in the support for non-repudiation services is the use of *secure time stamping* (that is, the time source must be trusted, and the time value must be securely conveyed) within the PKI. There must be an authoritative source of time that a collection of PKI users will trust. (Ironically, the actual time supplied by this authoritative source within the PKI need not be correct; it simply needs to be accepted by this collection of users as the "reference time" for their PKI-related transactions (for example, Event B followed Event A). There is no dispute, however, that the use of time that is as close as practicable to the world's official time sources would be preferable.)

The authoritative source of time for the PKI (that is, the secure time stamping server whose certificate is verifiable by the relevant community of PKI users) need not exist solely for the purposes of non-repudiation; there are many situations in which an authoritative time stamp on a document may be useful. But support for non-repudiation services will perhaps be the primary driver for proper time stamping in many environments. In any case, time stamping forms part of our extended PKI definition. See Chapter 5 for further discussion on PKI time stamping services.

Client Software

A PKI may be viewed, at least at some level, as a collection of PKI servers that will "do things" for a user, such as the following:

- The CA will provide certification services.

- The repository will hold certificates and revocation information.

- The backup and recovery server will enable the proper management of key histories.

- The time stamp server will associate authoritative time information with documents.

However, as anyone who understands client-server architecture knows, servers cannot typically do anything for the client unless the client asks for service (that is, makes a request). The same principle holds true for a PKI. The client on the user's local platform must request certification services. The client must ask for certificates and process relevant revocation information. The client must understand key histories and know when to ask for a key update or a key recovery operation. The client must know when it requires a time stamp on a document. On the receiving end of secure communications (where, from an application point of view, a "server" process may be executing), it is still PKI client software that will need to understand policy, will need to understand if, when, and how revocation status is to be determined, will need to understand certificate path processing, and so on.

Client software is an essential component of a full-featured, fully operational PKI. Without it, the many services offered by the PKI are effectively impotent, because nothing is available to enable them or to make use of them. It is critical to note that this is *not* application software, not PKI-aware code that resides within an application (such as a browser or an e-mail package). Such an architecture would fundamentally violate the concept of the PKI as a true *infrastructure*, providing security in a consistent manner across all applications and platforms. Rather, client software is code that exists outside every application and implements the required client end of the PKI services. Applications connect to this client software through standardized entry points (as with any infrastructure), but the applications themselves do not interact with the various PKI servers (that is, applications *use* the infrastructure; they are not *part of* the infrastructure).

Our expanded definition of a PKI includes client software as an essential component. See Chapter 12, "PKI Operational Considerations," for further discussion on this topic.

Summary

This chapter has discussed the concept and benefits of a pervasive infrastructure for security services. Like a communications infrastructure or an electric power infrastructure (as two of many examples), the security infrastructure offers uniformity and consistency to all using applications and devices.

The benefits that flow from an infrastructural approach to security are varied and numerous. The infrastructure makes security readily available to individual applications, strengthens and simplifies the sign-on process, provides end-user transparency, and offers comprehensive security throughout the environment. Business drivers include cost savings, interoperability, simplified administration, the possibility of real security, and the opportunity to choose a provider with significant security experience and expertise.

A fully functional PKI, because it is a security infrastructure, encompasses a large number of components and services:

- Certification Authority

- Certificate repository

- Certificate Revocation

- Key backup and recovery

- Automatic key update

- Key history management

- Cross-certification

- Support for non-repudiation

- Time stamping

- Client software

This definition of a PKI (which is more comprehensive than simply *security infrastructure services implemented using public-key techniques*) describes the major areas of functionality required in an operational PKI.

It may be correctly argued that some specific environments do not need all this functionality to meet actual security requirements (a PKI used to enable secure e-mail between friends over the Internet likely has little need of extensive support for non-repudiation, for example). However, a true PKI—conceptually designed as an independent infrastructural entity—may conceivably be deployed in any environment. Thus, it makes sense to define the PKI as an infrastructure with all these components and features, and build the PKI according to this definition. In any given deployment, any unnecessary services then can easily be turned off (that is, not used) or not installed at all.

Given the concepts of a PKI conveyed in this chapter, two primary needs must be addressed to fill out the understanding of this technology:

- A need to understand in more detail the security services that a PKI can offer

- A need to discuss each of the aspects of the PKI definition in more depth

The first need is covered in Chapters 4 and 5; the second need is the focus of Chapters 6 through 12.

4

Core PKI Services: Authentication, Integrity, and Confidentiality

The previous chapter looked at the concept of a security infrastructure and gave a definition of a comprehensive PKI. Now, consider the services a PKI offers an organization. This chapter examines the fundamental, or core, security services associated with a PKI; the next chapter examines a number of additional services a PKI can enable for various business purposes.

Definitions

A PKI is generally considered to be associated with three primary services:

- *Authentication*—The assurance to one entity that another entity is who he/she/it claims to be.

- *Integrity*—The assurance to an entity that data has not been altered (intentionally or unintentionally) between "there" and "here," or between "then" and "now."

- *Confidentiality*—The assurance to an entity that no one can read a particular piece of data except the receiver(s) explicitly intended.

The following subsections explore these brief definitions in greater detail.

Authentication

Authentication, the assurance that an entity is who he/she/it claims to be, typically finds application in two primary contexts.

Entity identification, by itself, serves simply to identify the specific entity involved, essentially in isolation from any other activity that the entity might want to perform. Clearly this is of limited value (because the entity will typically want to perform other activities on the basis of its identity). Therefore, in practice, entity identification generally produces a concrete result that is then used to enable other activities or communications. For example, the process of entity identification may result in (or unlock) a symmetric key that can subsequently be used to decrypt a file for reading or modification, or to establish a secure communications channel with another entity. The identity itself, once authenticated, may also be associated with a set of privileges on an Access Control List for the purpose of making access control decisions.

Data origin identification identifies a specific entity as the source or origin of a given piece of data. This is not entity identification in isolation, nor is it entity identification for the explicit purpose of enabling some other activity. Rather, this is identification with the intent of statically and irrevocably binding the identified entity to some particular data, regardless of any subsequent activities in which the entity might engage. Such a process can provide support for a non-repudiation service (see Chapter 5, "PKI-Enabled Services," for a discussion on non-repudiation).

Entity Identification: Local Versus Remote

The area of authentication known as entity identification can be divided into two categories:

- Initial entity identification to the local environment (that is, to the entity's personal, physically proximate device with no communications to other devices on the network)

- Entity identification to a remote device, entity, or environment

Local authentication—initial authentication of an entity to the local environment—almost always involves the user directly and explicitly (a password or PIN must be entered; a thumbprint scan must be taken). By contrast, *remote authentication*—authentication of an entity to some remote environment—may or may not involve the user directly. In fact, the more sophisticated remote authentication systems do not explicitly involve the user for two reasons:

- It is hard to defend an authentication system that takes sensitive authenticating information, such as a password or thumbprint, and passes it over insecure lines (where it may be copied for later reuse by an unscrupulous party) to a remote location.

- It is inconvenient for users to have to re-enter authenticating information each time that they want to make a remote network connection.

Thus, a preferable solution is for the result, or the *effect*, of the local authentication process to be conveyed to the remote location without passing the actual authenticating value itself. For example, when the entity needs to access a remote environment, a secure communications session could be established between the two environments so that the local environment can essentially say, "Here is the identity; I have already ensured it is correct." Therefore, the password, PIN, or thumbprint does not need to be sent to the remote environment. Note that such a solution can also be used for *subsequent authentication* (that is, after a successful initial authentication) to other applications within the local environment to achieve secure single sign-on; see Chapter 3, "The Concept of an Infrastructure."

Entity Identification: Single-Factor Versus Multi-Factor

There are many ways of proving an identity. These can be divided into four categories:

- Something you *have* (such as a smart card or a hardware token)

- Something you *know* (such as a password or a PIN)

- Something you *are*, or something intrinsic to your body (such as a thumbprint or a retinal scan)

- Something you *do* (such as your typing characteristics or handwriting style)

The concept of *single-factor authentication* is that only a single method among the preceding options is used. *Multi-factor authentication* uses more than one of the options simultaneously during the authentication process (two-factor uses two, three-factor uses three, and so on). A familiar example of two-factor authentication is the "sign-on" process at a banking machine where the user presents a magnetic-stripe card ("something you have") and enters a PIN ("something you know") to gain access to his/her bank account. Clearly, multi-factor systems are more burdensome for the user (more tasks need to be completed before the authentication process is finished). However, the security benefit is that impersonation attacks become much more difficult (the would-be impersonator needs, for example, to know your password, imitate your typing style, and borrow your thumb without you knowing about it—all at the same time!).

Authentication as a PKI Service

One reason to distinguish between local and remote authentication (and between initial and subsequent authentication) is to distinguish between where a PKI can be helpful and where it cannot. Specifically, a PKI would rarely, if ever (one might go so far as to say "never"), be used for initial authentication of a human entity to the local environment. This is because a user is unlikely to *know* a private key (due to its length) and, even if it were known, the user would be highly unlikely to be able to do cryptographic calculations with it.

Also, nothing intrinsic to the user (such as a thumbprint or retinal scan) could be said to *be* the private key of a signing key pair. Similarly, nothing the user *does* (such as typing characteristics or handwriting style) is deterministic enough (in a strict sense) to be usable for generating a key pair. Finally, although the user may *have* something that contains a key pair and is able to do cryptographic calculations (such as a smart card), such devices are so easily lost or stolen that they are almost never allowed to function without the user entering a password or a PIN.

Thus, initial authentication to the local environment, whether single-factor or multi-factor, does not use the services of a PKI. Authentication to a remote environment (or subsequent authentication within the local environment), on the other hand, can. When remote authentication does not use a PKI, there are two possibilities:

- The user must authenticate explicitly to the remote environment.

- The proof of authentication from the local environment must somehow be conveyed to the remote environment.

In either case, the communication between the local and remote environments must be properly protected; otherwise, an eavesdropper can simply copy the relevant data and later replay it, thereby successfully masquerading as the original, legitimate entity. Properly protecting the communications may mean employing mechanisms that are difficult to administer or that do not scale well to large environments, such as pre-establishing shared symmetric keys between the respective communicating processes (see Chapter 6, "Certificates and Certification," for a discussion on scalability issues).

For these reasons, the benefits in using a PKI for remote authentication can be attractive. The complexity of pre-establishing shared keys between processes is eliminated, as is the security risk of transmitting sensitive authenticating information (such as a password or a thumbprint) over a network. Rather, public-key technology is used to achieve the authentication using sophisticated challenge-response protocols and signed messages.

The distinct advantage of public-key-based remote authentication over mechanisms that mimic authentication to the local environment is that sensitive authenticating information, such as a password, is never sent over the network. If server Alice holds a copy of client Bob's password or thumbprint, Bob must authenticate himself by proving that he knows or has this information; this is typically accomplished by Bob conveying this information to Alice upon sign-on (see Figure 4.1).

By contrast, if Alice holds a copy of Bob's verification public key, she can ask Bob to sign a one-time challenge message with the corresponding signing private key (which only Bob knows); if the signed response is returned, Bob has authenticated himself without having

Figure 4.1 Bob authenticates to Alice using an ID/password pair.

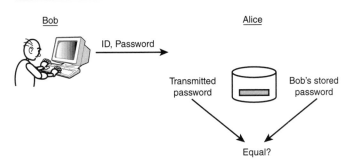

to reveal any sensitive information (see Figure 4.2). Nothing travels over the network that can be used by an eavesdropper to later impersonate Bob. Furthermore, Alice and Bob do not need to engage in a costly and inconvenient process to pre-establish shared secret information (for example, to pre-load Alice with a copy of Bob's password or thumbprint). Alice may simply retrieve a copy of Bob's public key from his verification certificate, which, for example, may be stored in a publicly known and publicly accessible repository or may have been sent directly to Alice from Bob (see Chapter 6 for a discussion on certificates).

Figure 4.2 Bob authenticates to Alice using public-key-based remote authentication.

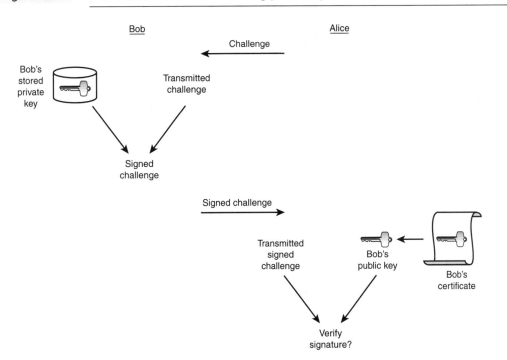

One very appealing benefit of the authentication service associated with the PKI is the possibility of single sign-on to PKI-enabled devices (and perhaps, through gateway servers, to other types of devices as well). Specifically, a user may sign-on initially to the local environment (using single-factor or multi-factor authentication, as appropriate). This process results in the user gaining local access to his/her private key(s). The signing private key can then be used to authenticate the user automatically and transparently to other servers and devices around the network whenever he/she wants to establish a connection with them. The user may freely roam both the local and remote environments without the need to enter a password, or place a thumb on the biometric print scanner, again (see Chapter 3 for a discussion on secure single sign-on).

The PKI, therefore, offers an authentication service with a number of definite advantages over non-PKI-based authentication mechanisms. Entity identification is possible with PKI authentication, in which case the entity's signing private key is used to authenticate the entity to other entities in the local or remote environment. It also can be used for data origin authentication. In this case, the entity's signing private key is used to bind the entity to a particular piece of data (perhaps as non-repudiable evidence that can be used subsequently to prove to a third party that this entity did originate—or at least possess—this data).

Integrity

Data integrity is the assurance of *non-alteration*: The data (either in transit or in storage) has not been undetectably altered. Clearly, such assurance is essential in any kind of business or electronic commerce environment, but it is desirable in many other environments as well. A level of data integrity can be achieved by mechanisms such as parity bits and *Cyclic Redundancy Codes (CRCs)*. Such techniques, however, are designed only to detect some proportion of accidental bit errors; they are powerless to thwart deliberate data manipulation by a determined adversary whose goal is to modify the content of the data for his or her own gain.

To protect data against this sort of attack, cryptographic techniques are required. Thus, appropriate algorithms and keys must be employed and commonly understood between the entity wanting to provide data integrity and the entity wanting to be assured of data integrity. The PKI service of integrity can be extremely useful in meeting the needs of both entities because it is the framework through which algorithm selection and key agreement can take place. Furthermore, such negotiations can occur in a way that is completely transparent to the entities involved so that integrity can be assumed in all PKI-related data transactions. (This situation changes only when integrity verification fails for some specific piece of data, in which case the user must be notified so that appropriate action can be taken.)

Confidentiality

Confidentiality is the assurance of data privacy: No one may read the data except for the specific entity (or entities) intended. Confidentiality is a requirement

- When data is stored on a medium (such as a computer hard drive) that can be read by an unauthorized individual.

- When data is backed up onto a device (such as a tape) that can fall into the hands of an unauthorized individual.

- When data is transmitted over unprotected networks.

Furthermore, given the sophistication and power of determined adversaries today, cryptographic techniques for providing confidentiality must be employed for all sensitive data. As with integrity, this necessitates a common understanding between entities of appropriate algorithms and keys. The PKI confidentiality service is the framework through which such a common understanding can be reached in a way that is transparent to the actual entities involved. Other non-PKI-based confidentiality services require explicit entity interaction at some level and, therefore, are more error prone and more cumbersome to use.

Mechanisms

This section gives a brief overview of the cryptographic mechanisms used to enable the PKI services of authenticity, integrity, and confidentiality. See the *Handbook of Applied Cryptography* [MvOV97] for further discussion.

Authentication

The PKI service of authentication (as opposed to the non-PKI operation of initial authentication to the local environment, which may involve single- or multi-factor authentication including passwords or biometric devices) employs the cryptographic technique of a digital signature. The signature may be computed over the hash of one of the following three values:

- Some data to be authenticated

- Some request that the user intends to send to a remote device

- A random challenge issued by a remote device

The first issue supports the PKI service of data origin authentication; the latter two support the PKI service of entity authentication.

> **Note**
>
> Whether entity authentication is done through a signature on a user request or through a signature on a random challenge depends upon the operational characteristics and requirements of a particular environment. Typically, environments in which entities have access to a common, trusted source of time will use the first alternative, whereas environments in which nonce values will be used (instead of time stamps) to provide replay protection will use the second alternative.

A good cryptographic hash function is required to reduce the data or the request message to a size suitable for a single computation of the signature function. It is also helpful in preventing an attacker from getting the decryption of a random-looking value (in certain signature algorithms such as RSA [RSA78]), which may yield valuable information in some circumstances [KR95]. Digital signatures and hash functions are introduced in Chapter 2, "Public-Key Cryptography."

Integrity

The PKI service of integrity may employ one of two techniques. First, a *digital signature*, while it serves the purpose of providing authenticity (that is, entity authentication), simultaneously provides integrity over the signed data. This is a consequence of a necessary property of cryptographic hash algorithms and signature algorithms; any change in the input data leads to a large, unpredictable change in the output with very high probability. In other words, if the data has changed (either by accident, or by deliberate manipulation) between "there" and "here" or between "then" and "now," the signature will fail to verify, and the loss of integrity will be obvious to the recipient. If, on the other hand, the signature verifies, the recipient is very likely to be in possession of the original (that is, unaltered) data.

The second technique that can be employed for integrity is a *Message Authentication Code*, or *MAC*. This technique typically uses a symmetric block cipher (for example, DES-CBC-MAC [FIPS113]) or a cryptographic hash function (for example, HMAC-SHA-1 [RFC2104]); see Chapter 2 for a discussion of ciphers and hash functions. Although these are both symmetric solutions (as opposed to public-key solutions), it is important to note that they are both keyed mechanisms; in particular, they depend on a key that must be shared between the sender of the integrity-protected data and the "consumer" (for example, receiver) of the integrity-protected data. In some environments, the shared key can be derived from a PKI (see IPsec [RFC2401, RFC2411] for example).

The PKI service of integrity for this second technique, then, is that of putting in place the mechanisms to achieve this key sharing when necessary. If Alice wants to send to Bob some integrity-protected data and Bob has an encryption public key, Alice can employ the following sequence of steps:

1. Generate a fresh symmetric key.

2. Use the symmetric key to generate a MAC for the data.

3. Encrypt the symmetric key for Bob using his encryption public key.

4. Send the data to Bob along with the encrypted key.

Alternatively, if Bob has a key exchange public key (such as a Diffie-Hellman public key—see Chapter 2), Alice can instead use the following procedure:

1. Use Bob's key-exchange public key in combination with her key-exchange private key to generate a symmetric key.

2. MAC the data using that symmetric key.

3. Send the data to Bob along with her public key certificate.

Bob can then regenerate the symmetric key using Alice's public key and his own private key to verify the integrity of the data.

If a digital signature is not used to provide data integrity, a good cryptographic MAC function is required. Digital signatures and MAC functions are introduced in Chapter 2.

Confidentiality

The PKI service of confidentiality uses a mechanism similar to one of the alternatives of the integrity service. That is:

- Alice generates a symmetric key (perhaps by using her key-exchange private key in combination with Bob's key-exchange public key).

- The symmetric key is used to encrypt the data (using a symmetric block cipher such as CAST-128 [RFC2144]).

- The encrypted data is sent to Bob either along with Alice's key exchange public key, or with a copy of the symmetric key encrypted with Bob's encryption public key.

Chapter 2 introduces key exchange and key transfer mechanisms to establish a symmetric key between the entities, Alice and Bob.

Operational Considerations

A number of operational considerations must be taken into account when a PKI is associated with its core services of authentication, integrity, and confidentiality. These include the following:

- Performance

- On-line versus off-line operation

- Commonality of underlying algorithms

- Entity naming

Each of these is described further in the following subsections.

Performance

Public-key operations are significantly slower than symmetric key operations. Thus, although an encryption public key theoretically can be used to encrypt large quantities of data, in a practical system it is virtually never used for this purpose. Rather, the data is encrypted using a symmetric key, and that key is encrypted in a single operation using an encryption public key. Similarly, a symmetric-key-based MAC will typically be a preferred data integrity mechanism unless a digital signature is already required for the purpose of data origin authentication.

The PKI services of integrity and confidentiality, therefore, consist of the less-performance-intensive key sharing (or key establishment) aspects, rather than the more-performance-intensive signature (or data encryption) aspects. This combination of public key and symmetric key mechanisms provides the required services at a performance cost that is acceptable for many environments.

On-Line Versus Off-Line Operation

One of the significant advantages of a PKI over a purely symmetric-key-based infrastructure is the possibility of off-line operation. That is, Alice can sign data, integrity-protect data, or encrypt data for Bob, or she can verify Bob's signature on data, verify Bob's integrity-protection on data, or decrypt data from Bob, all while she is working off-line (for example, on her laptop, which is not connected to the network). Alice will not have access to the most current revocation status information (see Chapter 8, "Certificate Revocation") when she works in this mode, but in some circumstances and for some types of communication this may be acceptable.

The desire for off-line operation may determine the key establishment mechanisms available for use. For example, real-time, peer-to-peer key exchange using an algorithm such as *ephemeral-ephemeral Diffie-Hellman (DH)* would not be possible. However, non-real-time key exchange using *ephemeral-static DH* or *static-static DH* is entirely possible, as well as key exchange using an algorithm such as *Rivest-Shamir-Adleman (RSA)*. Thus, although every mechanism choice may not be available, the core PKI services are available and operational during off-line mode.

DH Communication Configurations

In *ephemeral-ephemeral DH*, each party in the key establishment protocol generates an ephemeral key pair (that is, one that has never been used before and is never to be used again) solely for the purposes of this protocol. In *ephemeral-static DH*, one of the parties, Bob for example, generates an ephemeral key pair for this protocol, and the other party, Alice, uses a pre-existing key pair. In particular, Alice's pre-existing public key can be contained in a certificate that Bob can hold locally or obtain from a public repository prior to engaging in the protocol. In *static-static DH*, both Alice and Bob use pre-existing key pairs.

Commonality of Underlying Algorithms

A fundamental requirement for the PKI to operate is that a common understanding of algorithms can be achieved between PKI entities. This understanding may be limited and rigid in that a fixed, single algorithm for providing each PKI service is hard-coded into each entity upon start-up (that is, a digital signature algorithm, a hash algorithm, a key transfer algorithm, a key exchange algorithm, a MAC algorithm, and a symmetric cipher algorithm).

Much more often, however, this understanding is fluid and dynamic in that an entity, Alice, will "discover" the algorithm(s) acceptable to Bob at the time she needs to communicate with Bob. Alice will, therefore, use the algorithm appropriate for both the circumstances of the communication and the intended recipient(s) of the communication. Algorithm discovery can be accomplished through the use of certificates (that is, Bob's preferred algorithms are encoded within his public-key certificate; see Chapter 6 for a discussion on certificates).

Alternatively, algorithm discovery can be accomplished through the use of authenticated negotiation ("hand shaking") protocols (such as IKE [RFC2409], for example), out-of-band communications, or some other means. Whatever the mechanism, a commonality of underlying algorithms must be achieved so that communication between PKI entities and, therefore, the set of security services offered by the PKI can occur.

Entity Naming

An assumption implicit in much of the preceding discussion is that entity Bob has an identity that is known to and understood by entity Alice. Alice somehow knows, prior to sending data to Bob, that this is *the particular Bob* to whom she wants to send this data. This problem is typically known as the entity naming problem: How can names be assigned to entities in a way that is unique and meaningful to other relevant entities?

Many, varied techniques exist for solving this problem, and they include the extreme suggestion that there is no solution and that the use of entity naming should be avoided entirely. This topic is discussed in more detail in Chapter 9, "Trust Models"; for the time being, note that Alice must have some way of knowing with whom she is communicating for that communication to be meaningful and relevant.

Summary

Authentication (both entity authentication and data origin authentication), integrity, and confidentiality are the core security services provided by a PKI. These services enable entities to prove that they are who they claim to be, to be assured that important data has not been altered in any way, and to be convinced that data sent to another entity can be read only by that entity. Organizations can derive tremendous benefits from these services by using them to ensure, for example, that highly sensitive information only gets into the hands of those with an explicit "need-to-know."

Two needs must be addressed to make these core security services fully available to PKI entities. First, it must be possible for entity Alice to associate a public key unambiguously and correctly with Bob, the entity with whom she wants to communicate. This is the fundamental purpose for the concept of a *certificate*; this topic is discussed in Chapter 6. Second, to deal with the relatively common situation in which Alice does not already have Bob's certificate, Alice must have the capability to retrieve that certificate from a public repository. In this way, she can communicate securely with him. (Recall that the underlying premise of public-key cryptography is that secure communication between strangers can be achieved precisely through the use of such public repository concepts.) The description and use of public repositories for certificate information is the topic of Chapter 11, "PKI Information Dissemination: Repositories and Other Techniques."

References

[FIPS113]   Federal Information Processing Standards Publication 113. "Computer Data Authentication." U.S. Department of Commerce, National Bureau of Standards, National Technical Information Service. Springfield, Virginia, 1985.

[KR95]   Kaliski, B. and M. Robshaw. "The Secure Use of RSA." *RSA Laboratories' CryptoBytes* 1, no. 3 (Autumn 1995).

[MvOV97]   Menezes, A., P. van Oorschot, and S. Vanstone. *Handbook of Applied Cryptography.* Boca Raton: CRC Press, 1997.

[RFC2104]   Krawczyk, H., M. Bellare, and R. Canetti. "HMAC: Keyed Hashing for Message Authentication." Internet Request for Comments 2104. (February 1997).

[RFC2144]   Adams, C. "The CAST-128 Encryption Algorithm." Internet Request for Comments 2144. (May 1997).

[RFC2401]   Kent, S. and R. Atkinson. "Security Architecture for the Internet Protocol." Internet Request for Comments 2401. (November 1998).

[RFC2409]   Harkins, D. and D. Carrel. "The Internet Key Exchange (IKE)." Internet Request for Comments 2409. (November 1998).

[RFC2411]   Thayer, R., N. Doraswamy, and R. Glenn. "IP Security Document Roadmap." Internet Request for Comments 2411. (November 1998).

[RSA78]   Rivest, R., A. Shamir, and L. Adleman. "A Method for Obtaining Digital Signatures and Public-Key Cryptosystems." *Communications of the ACM.* 21 (1978): 120–126.

CHAPTER 5

PKI-Enabled Services

The previous chapter discussed the core security services offered by a PKI: authenticity, integrity, and confidentiality. This chapter looks at security services that in some way can be *enabled* by a PKI. That is, these are not services inherent in or fundamental to any PKI, but rather services that can build on the core PKI services. Some PKIs may support these auxiliary services, and others may not.

Secure Communication

Secure communication can be defined as the transmission of data from a sender to a receiver with one or more of the properties of authenticity, integrity, and confidentiality. This service clearly relies on the core PKI services, but it uses them in conjunction with traditional networking and communications protocols to create an expanded, PKI-enabled service. A number of important examples of secure communication can be cited, including the following:

- Secure e-mail (using, for example, a protocol such as Simple/Multi-purpose Internet Mail Extensions Version 2 (S/MIMEv2) [RFC2311, RFC2312])

- Secure Web server access (using, for example, a protocol such as Transport Layer Security (TLS) [RFC2246])

- A secure Virtual Private Network, or VPN (using, for example, a protocol such as IPsec/IKE [RFC2401, RFC2411])

Secure e-mail, for example, can be implemented as a PKI-enabled service simply by having the e-mail package access the core security services of the PKI (to encrypt and sign messages) and format the result using the S/MIME protocol. Messages can then be transported across an untrusted network without compromising their authenticity, integrity, or confidentiality.

Secure Time Stamping

Secure time stamping involves a trusted time authority associating a time stamp with a particular piece of data with the properties of authenticity and integrity. What is important is not so much the actual time format itself, but rather the security of the time/data association. In particular, for some applications the time stamp need not explicitly represent time at all; a simple sequence number demonstrating that this document was presented to the authority *before* document *x* and *after* document *y* may be sufficient. However, any interested parties must be able to verify that the time stamp associated with this document is authentic and has integrity.

The time stamp authority is also not strictly required for this service. An alternative is to have secure (that is, trusted) time available at every entity's local environment; each entity can then securely associate a time stamp with its own data as needed. In practice, however, it is typically difficult to get secure time to every local environment (for example, every user desktop). Thus, the approach often taken is to get secure time only to a very small number of locations in the network (perhaps only one)—these then become the trusted time stamp authorities—and to have entities request time stamps on data from these authorities when required.

The secure time stamp service makes use of the core PKI services of authentication and integrity. In particular, the time stamp on a document involves a digital signature over the combination of some representation of time and a cryptographic hash of the document itself (the signature of the authority provides both authenticity and data integrity).

Note

Although secure time stamping can be implemented as a PKI-enabled service, it is entirely possible to implement a secure time stamp service without exclusive reliance on an underlying PKI (see, for example, "How To Time-Stamp a Digital Document" [HS91]).

For this scheme to work, all relevant PKI entities need to know and trust the time stamp authority verification public key so that the signature on the time stamp can be verified and trusted. If such a public key becomes untrusted (for example, through compromise of the time stamp authority's signing private key), the PKI entities need to be informed of this and then reinitialize with another trusted key for that authority using some secure out-of-band process. All time stamps signed using that untrusted key will be recognized as invalid.

Notarization

The term *notarization* (that is, the primary service of a notary) can be a source of confusion in some environments because it means different things in different legal frameworks. For the purposes of this book, the PKI-enabled service of notarization is defined to be synonymous with "data certification." That is, the notary *certifies* that data is valid or correct, where the meaning of "correct" is necessarily dependent on the type of data being certified. For example, if the data to be certified is a digital signature over some hashed value, the notary may certify that the signature is "valid" in the following sense:

- The signature verification computation with the appropriate public key is mathematically correct.

- The public key is still validly associated with the entity purporting to have signed the value.

- All other data required in the validation process (such as additional certificates to form a complete path; see Chapter 9, "Trust Models," for details) is accessible and trustworthy.

The *PKI notary* is an entity trusted by some collection of other PKI entities to perform the notarization service properly. It certifies the correctness of data through the mechanism of a digital signature; the other PKI entities, therefore, need a trusted copy of the notary's verification public key so that the signed data certification structure can be verified and trusted.

The PKI-enabled service of notarization relies on the core PKI service of authentication. It will typically also rely on the PKI-enabled service of secure time stamping because the notary will need to include the time at which the notarization was done in the data certification structure.

Non-Repudiation

Non-repudiation is the term used for the service that assures, to the extent technically possible, that entities remain honest about their actions. The most commonly discussed variants are *non-repudiation of origin* (in which a user cannot falsely deny having originated a message or document) and *non-repudiation of receipt* (in which a user cannot falsely deny having received a message or document). However, a number of other variants have been defined, including *non-repudiation of creation*, *non-repudiation of delivery*, and *non-repudiation of approval*. The basic idea is that a user is cryptographically bound to a specific action in such a way that subsequent denial of that action, to some extent, constitutes an admission of malice or negligence.

As a particular example, if Bob sends a digitally signed receipt to Alice claiming that he received a specific message from her, he cannot later deny having received the message without, in effect, admitting one of the following:

- He knowingly gave his signing private key to a third party to allow the possibility of repudiating the message receipt.

- His signing private key was compromised without his knowledge (and, therefore, he was somewhat negligent in protecting it properly).

The "non-repudiation of receipt" service gives Alice some assurance that Bob will honestly stand by the digitally signed receipt that he sent.

Connection with Other Services

Non-repudiation is necessarily a PKI-enabled service; it cannot be based on a symmetric infrastructure. This is because to communicate in a symmetric-key-based environment, Alice and Bob must share a symmetric key. Bob creates a receipt, protects it with the symmetric key, and sends it to Alice. However, Alice could instead have created the receipt to implicate Bob (since both Alice and Bob know the symmetric key). Bob can repudiate his actions simply by claiming that Alice created the incriminating evidence. As a PKI-enabled service, this avenue is closed to Bob because the incriminating evidence (the signed receipt) employs a key known to Bob alone; Alice cannot be blamed for the creation of the receipt unless Bob's private key has been compromised by some means.

Non-repudiation is not a stand-alone PKI-enabled service, however; it relies on the existence of other PKI-enabled services to function. In particular, non-repudiation requires the secure time stamp service to provide evidence that a specific event occurred at a specific point in time, or that a specific piece of data existed prior to a specific date. In addition, non-repudiation can benefit from the data certification (notarization) service as a convenient method for "packaging" evidence into structures suitable for storage. These services also necessarily rely on the core PKI services of authentication, integrity, and confidentiality.

Need for a Secure Data Archive

Another service required for non-repudiation is *archival*: Evidence in the form of expired certificates, old CRLs, time stamp tokens, data certification structures, and other related data must be securely stored (archived) in preparation for a potential need when they may be required for dispute resolution.

It is important to note, however, that a "simple" archive service will not be sufficient in many environments. The stored evidence must be cryptographically protected for authenticity and integrity using a digital signature (to allow easy public verification of the archive contents). Furthermore, as the signing key expires and is replaced by a new key (see Chapter 7, "Key and Certificate Management," for a discussion on key/certificate life cycle management), the associated evidence must be re-signed with the new key. This produces, in effect, an unbroken trail of keys leading back in time to the date at which the evidence was initially created. In practice, the unbroken trail of signing keys will be associated with the corresponding trail of verification certificates as well as a statement attesting to the time of each successive signature.

Complexity of this Service

In some ways, non-repudiation is the most difficult and complex of all the PKI-enabled services. Perhaps the biggest reason for this is that its primary purpose is to gather evidence attesting to the validity of an event that will be convincing to an unbiased, external third party. Clearly there are no hard and fast rules here. How much evidence is enough? What will a third party require at some indeterminate time in the future? How can it be proven that the evidence has never been manipulated or tampered with? How can a third party be assured that all due diligence was taken to gather as complete a set of evidence data as possible at the time of evidence creation?

These and other questions demonstrate the difficulties and intricacies involved in properly implementing a non-repudiation service.

The Human Factor

Regardless of the best intentions of those involved in designing and implementing the technical aspects of the PKI-enabled non-repudiation service, there will almost always be a need for non-automated (that is, human) judgment in the eventual dispute resolution. Yes, the receipt to Alice was signed with Bob's private key, but Bob makes a convincing case that it was only three days *after* the purported signing event that he discovered his key had been compromised two weeks *prior* to the signing event. The (human) judge will have to weigh all evidence (including this new non-cryptographically-protected claim) and rule either in favor of Bob or in favor of Alice.

For this reason, it is incorrect to say that a PKI can *provide* non-repudiation; this can never be done if humans must be involved in the dispute resolution phase. Rather, a PKI can be said to provide or implement a service that *supports* non-repudiation (in that it creates, maintains, and archives some of the evidence that will be needed when dispute resolution is performed).

Privilege Management

Privilege management is a generic term for what is variously called authorization, access control, rights management, permissions management, capabilities management, and so on. Specifically, this topic addresses what an entity is allowed to see and do within a particular environment. This topic also encompasses questions such as the following:

- Is Alice allowed to read this record in the database?

- Can Bob execute this application program?

- Should Christine be granted remote access to this network?

- Must David be prevented from seeing pages in this portion of the Web server?

- Are purchase orders for over $10,000 from Erica to be accepted?

Policies (sometimes referred to as *rules*) must be defined for individual entities, for particular groups of entities, or for designated entity roles within an environment. These policies specify what these entities, groups, and roles are allowed to do and (either explicitly or implicitly) what they are not allowed to do. Privilege management is the creation and enforcement of these policies for the purpose of enabling day-to-day business while maintaining a desired level of security.

Authentication and Authorization

It is important to note the distinction, and yet the synergy, between the concepts of *authentication* and *authorization*. Authentication is concerned with who an entity is; it is the association of an identity with an entity. Authorization is concerned with what that identity is allowed to see and do. Authorization does not prove that the entity requesting remote access to the network is Bob; it merely says that if it *is* Bob, he should be allowed in.

Authentication and authorization, then, must necessarily work together in many circumstances. Authentication without authorization is useful for some purposes (for example, for data origin identification, see Chapter 4, "Core PKI Services: Authentication, Integrity, and Confidentiality"). On the other hand, authorization without authentication has virtually no value (because the privileges of an identity, group, or role are of no help unless it can be determined that a specific entity has a particular identity or belongs to a particular group or role).

Authorization Authorities

In the physical world, the concept of *authorization authorities* is widely recognized and well understood. When Bob is a child, his mother, father, baby-sitter, teacher, and so on tell him what he can and cannot do. When he is an adult, he is still granted and denied specific privileges by his boss, his doctor, his financial institution, and his government.

In the electronic world, authorization authorities must still exist, though their presence may or may not be explicit. One or more entities will still have the authority to associate specific privileges with specific identities, groups, or roles within a given environment. Ideally, this association will be made using cryptographic techniques to prevent malicious tampering, but this may not be necessary in all environments (for example, where secure local storage of privilege information can be assumed for some particular entity locations).

Authorization authorities may be established in a centralized or distributed manner (that is, there may be a single authorization authority for all entities in the environment, or there may be a collection of authorities with varying needs for communication among them). The distributed scheme perhaps more closely models the physical world with which we are familiar, but both schemes have their utility.

Delegation

The notion of privilege quickly leads to the notion of *delegation*. If Alice has a certain privilege, is she able to pass that privilege on to another entity, such as Bob (perhaps with some restrictions or limitations)? For example, if Alice has unrestricted access to a certain Web site in order to perform a specific job function, can she arrange that her colleague Bob will be able to access that site to do that job while she is out of the office next Tuesday? For a number of environments, such functionality can be very useful.

Delegation comes in two flavors: *blinded* and *non-blinded*. Blinded delegation occurs when Alice has delegated some privilege to Bob and the entity verifying Bob's authorization is unable to determine that this delegation has occurred. That is, from the entity's point of view, Bob was granted this privilege directly by a trusted authorization authority, and Alice had no role whatsoever in this process. With non-blinded delegation, it is obvious to the entity that Alice originally had this privilege and has passed it on to Bob for some period of time. This is sometimes called *auditable delegation* (delegation with an audit trail), or power-of-attorney delegation, because the complete delegation path from authorization authority to final privilege holder is obvious to the verifying entity.

Both types of delegation may have their uses and benefits, but it can be argued that non-blinded delegation more closely suits the business requirements of corporate and financial environments (because, for example, there is more certainty with respect to liability in case of malicious use that causes financial loss).

Connection with the PKI

As discussed in the section on authentication and authorization earlier, privilege management requires authentication in order to be useful. In theory, any authentication mechanism can be used, although the benefits inherent in using the authentication service associated with a PKI can be very attractive in some environments. In particular, the strength of public-key-based authentication (compared with typically weak user passwords) and the convenience of secure single sign-on, coupled with the added features of a good authorization infrastructure, brings comprehensive security to an organization.

Mechanisms Required to Create PKI-Enabled Services

A number of mechanisms are required to create the PKI-enabled services discussed in this chapter. Some of the most important mechanisms are discussed in the following subsections.

Digital Signatures, Hashes, MACs, and Ciphers

Secure communication, because it relies on the core PKI services, requires the mechanisms that make the core services possible. These include digital signatures, cryptographic hash functions, MAC algorithms, and symmetric block ciphers. See Chapter 2, "Public-Key Cryptography," for a discussion of such mechanisms.

Trusted Time Sources

Secure time stamping can be implemented in such a way that it requires the presence of one or more trusted time sources for the environment. That is, there may need to be a way to get a trusted representation of the current time (synchronous with the global clock, to some high level of accuracy) to one or more devices/entities in the local environment.

As discussed in the previous "Secure Time Stamping" section, getting trusted time to a small number of devices can be easier in practice than getting trusted time to every device in the network. However, getting trusted time to even a single device can be a non-trivial task. This can be one of the desirable features of the concept of a *time stamp authority (TSA)*: If every entity in the environment trusts the TSA's assertion of time, then (within this closed environment) it does not matter whether or not the TSA's time is accurate. However, to support non-repudiation (in which evidence may need to be brought to an external third party for arbitration), the TSA should have as accurate a value of time as possible.

Privilege Policy Creation Mechanism

The PKI-enabled service of privilege management depends on the existence of policies that map identities, groups, or roles to specific privileges (a simple example of this is the well-known Access Control List (ACL), which lists access grant or deny decisions corresponding to entity names or roles).

In general, privilege policies can be complex Boolean expressions specifying precise conditions under which a claimant can invoke an object method under the control of a verifier. These expressions can include arbitrarily complicated time restrictions (for example, the second Tuesday of every fourth month from noon until 1 p.m.), as well as any other conditions on the validity of the privilege.

The potential for such complex expressions for privilege policy demands that a suitably general creation and editing mechanism exist. This is primarily a user interface design issue, although a module for translating human user policy input into a precise, machine-readable privilege policy expression can require some delicate engineering as well.

Privilege Policy Processing Engines

The privilege policy construct discussed in the preceding section does not simply need to be created and edited, it also needs to be processed and understood by some sort of verification engine at the time when an entity is requesting access to some resource. The fact that this policy needs to be machine-readable and yet flexible seems to necessitate a formal language for policy specification. Mechanisms that can understand and act on encoded policies are an important requirement of general privilege management infrastructures.

Privilege Management Infrastructure Mechanisms

A number of mechanisms exist to support the implementation of a *privilege management infrastructure (PMI)*. They tend to fall broadly into three categories:

- Mechanisms based on Kerberos [RFC1510], such as DCE [DCE] and SESAME [AV99].

- Mechanisms based on the concept of a Policy Server (a central server that creates, maintains, and verifies privilege policy for identities, groups, and roles).

- Mechanisms based on *Attribute Certificates (AC)*. An AC is similar in concept to a public-key certificate, but it does not contain a public key; it is a signed structure from an Attribute Authority binding some privilege or permission information to an identity (or perhaps to a public-key certificate, which contains the identity).

All three mechanisms have their proponents and their detractors because (not surprisingly) all have their advantages and disadvantages. Briefly, Kerberos schemes are symmetric-key-based, and so they have very attractive performance characteristics but somewhat unattractive key management and single-point-of-failure characteristics. Policy Server schemes are highly centralized, and so they have attractive single-point-of-administration benefits but somewhat unattractive communications overhead. Attribute Certificate schemes can be fully distributed, and so they have attractive failure resistance but somewhat unattractive performance characteristics (due to the public-key operations).

Each of the privilege management mechanisms may be more suited to some environments than others. For example, a Kerberos-based technology may be the best choice for authorization in a high-volume, real-time transaction environment. A policy-server-based architecture may be most appropriate for geographically localized environments with strong central administrative control. Finally, an attribute certificate technology may be the ideal choice for inter-organizational authorization activities that need to support a non-repudiation service. Note, however, that cooperation between mechanisms is sometimes possible, whereby one mechanism is used for some aspects in the PMI and another mechanism is used for other aspects.

Of the three PMI mechanisms listed here, the AC technology makes most direct use of the PKI (because the AC is digitally signed for authenticity and integrity, and it may possibly contain attributes that are encrypted for confidentiality, all through the use of public-key technology). All three mechanisms can be implemented as PKI-enabled services, however, because authorization must be tied to authentication and each of these technologies is able to work with a PKI authentication service.

Operational Considerations

A number of operational considerations must be taken into account if some of the PKI-enabled services discussed in this chapter are to be offered in a given environment. Some of these are discussed in the following subsections.

Trusted Time Delivery Mechanism

For the secure time stamping service (and, consequently, for the notarization and non-repudiation services that rely on it), there must be a way of delivering trusted time to (at least) the time stamp authority (or authorities) in the network.

Work has been done to transform the well-known Network Time Protocol, NTP [RFC1305], to a Secure Network Time Protocol by cryptographically authenticating the identity of the sender and verifying the integrity of the data included in an NTP message. Such work may prove to be very valuable as more PKI deployments begin to implement the PKI-enabled service of secure time stamping.

Secure Protocols

Many of the PKI-enabled services discussed in this chapter incorporate the concept of a server that will communicate with other PKI entities (for example, the time stamp authority, the notary, and the authorization authority). Such communication relies on the existence of secure protocols; otherwise, tampering with the messages passed back and forth could invalidate the intended service provided.

The PKI, therefore, must incorporate secure client-server and peer-to-peer protocols wherever necessary (that is, employing authenticity, integrity, and confidentiality) to maintain the trustworthiness of the services being offered. Examples of on-line protocols that can be used for this purpose include TLS [RFC2246] and Simple Public Key GSS-API Mechanism (SPKM) [RFC2025].

Server Redundancy

Servers are a critical architectural element in many of the PKI-enabled services discussed in this chapter. Therefore, the loss of a server (due to network segment outages or server crashes) can have a significant impact on the PKI entities in the environment.

For this reason, it may be required to have redundant servers available on warm- or hot-standby mode in the network. The time stamp authority may be particularly critical in this regard, but for some environments, other authorities may provide a vital service that cannot be dysfunctional for any period of time as well.

Physically Secure Archive Facilities

For the PKI-enabled service of non-repudiation, it is a requirement to have archival facilities (to hold old copies of CRLs at least, but perhaps to hold notarized documents and other data as well). See Chapter 8, "Certificate Revocation," for a discussion of Certificate Revocation Lists (CRLs).

Such archival facilities must be physically secure (for example, from damage due to fires, earthquakes, hurricanes, and other acts of nature; as well as from theft, bombs, and other acts of human nature). In many cases, it will be prudent to archive the data in physically redundant archive facilities as well.

Real Life

Real life may be considered to be the most important operational consideration of all. Both the core services and the PKI-enabled services offered by the infrastructure will be subject to unpredictable behavior, incorrect operation, or unreliable results if the PKI has not been implemented properly or if users and administrators have not had some minimal level of security training.

For example, if PKI entities are not careful to keep their private keys hidden from other entities, the core service of authentication and the PKI-enabled service of non-repudiation are completely compromised. If the underlying S/MIME or IKE protocol is badly implemented, the PKI-enabled service of secure communications cannot be trusted.

In real life, humans occasionally make mistakes. Such errors can find their way into PKI implementation, deployment, and use; when this occurs, the errors can lead to PKI vulnerabilities (or at least to operational uncertainties). Reputable software and hardware vendors, rigorous testing, continuous monitoring, and user training can all help and should all be used to deal with the problems that real life may introduce.

"Comprehensive PKI" and Current Practice

Chapters 3 and 4, along with this chapter, have described an architecture for what may be called the *comprehensive PKI* (see Figure 5.1). That is, components, functions, and services have been defined for a PKI that would, in some abstract sense, be "perfect" because it would satisfy the requirements of virtually every environment. Specific environments would "turn off" (or not install) the pieces they did not need in order to tailor this generic solution to their particular problems of interest.

Figure 5.1   Comprehensive PKI.

Certification Authority	Certification Repository	Certificate Revocation
Key Backup	Key Recovery	Automatic Key Update
Key History Management	Cross-Certification	Client Software
Authentication	Integrity	Confidentiality
Secure Time Stamping	Notarization	Non-Repudiation Support
Secure Data Archive	Privilege/Policy Creation	Privilege/Policy Verification

The comprehensive PKI is a vision of what the future may hold; it does not describe current practice (in particular, at the time of writing, no known PKI product implements every aspect of the PKI as described in Chapters 3-5). PKIs today are often implemented or deployed to solve only a particular problem or set of problems. However, these specific architectures may be viewed simply as proper subsets of the comprehensive architecture.

Consider, for instance, four example PKI usage scenarios that may be found in real-world environments today. In Figure 5.2, the *Internet PKI* encompasses such activities as casual e-mail between friends and Web browsing using SSL server authentication. In such usage, a CA is needed to issue the required public-key certificates, and the core services of authentication, integrity, and confidentiality may be used. However, there is no repository (certificates are sent via the communications protocol itself), revocation status of the e-mail recipient (or even of the server certificate) is not checked, key/certificate life cycle management is unavailable, cross-certification is unnecessary (browser and server have at least one root key in common), client software (as a separate module called by the browser) does not exist, and none of the PKI-enabled services are required.

Figure 5.2   Internet PKI.

Certification Authority	Certification Repository	Certificate Revocation
Key Backup	Key Recovery	Automatic Key Update
Key History Management	Cross-Certification	Client Software
Authentication	Integrity	Confidentiality
Secure Time Stamping	Notarization	Non-Repudiation Support
Secure Data Archive	Privilege/Policy Creation	Privilege/Policy Verification

In Figure 5.3, the *Extranet Security* still uses a browser as the access mechanism, but employs SSL client authentication for greater control over who may enter the corporate network. In such usage, Certificate Revocation checking is likely to be employed, as is some level of privilege and policy creation/verification (perhaps in the form of an Access Control List). Due to current browser limitations, life cycle management, cross-certification, and other PKI-enabled services are not available.

In Figure 5.4, the enterprise uses a standard mail package and secures the messages using a PKI. Because this is a single enterprise environment, key/certificate life cycle management may be required, but cross-certification may still be unnecessary. Client software will likely be employed (as a plug-in) because the standard e-mail package may not natively support PKI-based security. PKI-enabled services are not available because they are typically unnecessary for e-mail.

Figure 5.3   Extranet Security (via SSL Client Authentication).

Certification Authority	Certification Repository	Certificate Revocation
Key Backup	Key Recovery	Automatic Key Update
Key History Management	Cross-Certification	Client Software
Authentication	Integrity	Confidentiality
Secure Time Stamping	Notarization	Non-Repudiation Support
Secure Data Archive	Privilege/Policy Creation	Privilege/Policy Verification

Figure 5.4   Enterprise secure e-mail.

Certification Authority	Certification Repository	Certificate Revocation
Key Backup	Key Recovery	Automatic Key Update
Key History Management	Cross-Certification	Client Software
Authentication	Integrity	Confidentiality
Secure Time Stamping	Notarization	Non-Repudiation Support
Secure Data Archive	Privilege/Policy Creation	Privilege/Policy Verification

Finally, in Figure 5.5, inter-enterprise signed transactions may require much of the functionality of the comprehensive PKI. In particular, the care that must be taken to ensure proper authentication and authorization necessitates proper revocation checking, privilege and policy creation/verification, and so on. Cross-certification is likely to be required if the different enterprises have independently-deployed PKIs. Some aspects of non-repudiation support may be required (particularly, support for multiple key pairs, levels of commitment with respect to signed documents, and signed receipts), but for this usage scenario, time stamping, notarization, and data archiving may not be implemented.

Figure 5.5   Inter-enterprise signed transactions.

Certification Authority	Certification Repository	Certificate Revocation
Key Backup	Key Recovery	Automatic Key Update
Key History Management	Cross-Certification	Client Software
Authentication	Integrity	Confidentiality
Secure Time Stamping	Notarization	Non-Repudiation Support
Secure Data Archive	Privilege/Policy Creation	Privilege/Policy Verification

It should be apparent from the above figures that current PKI usage scenarios are often subsets of the comprehensive PKI architecture. This suggests that understanding the principles and concepts of the comprehensive architecture is helpful in understanding the more specific architectures available today.

More than this, however, it also suggests that as this field continues to mature, many PKI vendors will begin to implement comprehensive PKI products, rather than single-use PKI products. It may prove to be simpler and more cost-effective to tailor a comprehensive product to a specific problem than to build and maintain several separate products, each solving only one or two specific problems.

Finally, it may be argued that in many environments PKIs will make the inevitable transition from a *particular tool to solve a particular problem* to a *pervasive substrate that solves security-related problems for a wide variety of applications*. Only the comprehensive PKI has the generality and capability to meet the demanding requirements of a true infrastructure.

This book espouses and discusses the comprehensive PKI architecture for all the reasons given above. Therefore, other architectures, being subsets of the comprehensive architecture, are implicitly (if not explicitly) included in the discussion, as appropriate.

Summary

PKI-enabled security services build on the core PKI services to add more useful, business-oriented functionality to an environment. Secure communication, secure time stamping, notarization, non-repudiation support, privilege management, and others provide important benefits to an organization and greatly enhance the overall value of the public-key infrastructure.

Together, the components, core services, and PKI-enabled services described in this and the previous two chapters define a *comprehensive PKI*. Many currently deployed PKIs and so-called "single-use" PKIs may be seen to be subsets of this comprehensive architecture.

Two needs must be addressed to fully realize the PKI-enabled services discussed in this chapter. First, there must be a good understanding of the breadth of PKI concepts and terminology. This is the purpose of most of the remaining chapters in this part of the book: Chapters 6 through 12 discuss the important concepts of PKI, from the idea of a certificate to PKI operational considerations. Second, an understanding of the legal framework for PKI operation is important, especially with respect to responsibilities and mitigation of risk. This discussion is the topic of Chapter 13, "Legal Framework."

References

[AV99]   Ashley, P. and M. Vandenwauver. *Practical Intranet Security: Overview of the State of the Art and Available Technologies.* Boston: Kluwer Academic Publishers, 1999.

[DCE]   The Open Group. *DCE Today.* Upper Saddle River, NJ: Prentice Hall, 1998.

[HS91]   Haber, S. and W.S. Stornetta. "How To Time-Stamp a Digital Document." *Journal of Cryptology* 3.2 (1991): 99–111.

[RFC1305]   Mills, D. "Network Time Protocol (Version 3): Specification, Implementation, and Analysis." Internet Request for Comments 1305. (March 1992).

[RFC1510]   Kohl, J. and C. Neuman. "The Kerberos Network Authentication Service (V5)." Internet Request for Comments 1510. (September 1993).

[RFC2025]   Adams, C. "The Simple Public-Key GSS-API Mechanism (SPKM)." Internet Request for Comments 2025. (October 1996).

[RFC2246]   Dierks, T. and C. Allen. "The TLS Protocol Version 1.0." Internet Request for Comments 2246. (January 1999).

[RFC2311]   Dusse, S., P. Hoffman, B. Ramsdell, L. Lundblade, and L. Repka. "S/MIME Version 2 Message Specification." Internet Request for Comments 2311. (March 1998).

[RFC2312]   Dusse, S., P. Hoffman, B. Ramsdell, and J. Weinstein. "S/MIME Version 2 Certificate Handling." Internet Request for Comments 2312. (March 1998).

[RFC2401]   Kent, S. and R. Atkinson. "Security Architecture for the Internet Protocol." Internet Request for Comments 2401. (November 1998).

[RFC2411]   Thayer, R., N. Doraswamy, and R. Glenn. "IP Security Document Roadmap." Internet Request for Comments 2411. (November 1998).

Certificates and Certification

As Chapter 2, "Public-Key Cryptography," discussed, *public-key cryptography* involves the use of public/private key pairs to facilitate digital signature and key management services. The fundamental principle that enables public-key technology to scale is the fact that the public component of the public/private key pair may be distributed freely among the entities that need the public component to use the underlying security services. (See Chapter 4, "Core PKI Services: Authentication, Integrity, and Confidentiality," and Chapter 5, "PKI-Enabled Services," for more information regarding security services enabled through the use of a PKI.)

However, distribution of the public component without some form of integrity protection would defeat the very foundation for these security services. Thus, the public-key component must be protected—but in such a way that it will not impact the overall scalability that public-key cryptography techniques offer.

Thus, a data integrity mechanism is required to ensure that the public key (and any other information associated with that public key) is not modified without detection. However, a data integrity mechanism alone is not sufficient to guarantee that the public key belongs to the claimed owner. A mechanism that binds the public key to the claimed owner in a trustworthy manner is also required. In the end, the goal is to provide a single mechanism by which a relying party (that is, the "user" of the certificate as defined in RFC2527) is assured that

- The integrity of the public key (and any other associated information) is sound.

- The public key (and any other associated information) has been bound to the claimed owner in a trusted manner.

The purpose of this chapter is to explain how using public-key certificates accomplishes this goal.

Certificates

Kohnfelder first introduced the concept of using a signed data structure or *certificate* to convey the public key to a relying party in his 1978 bachelor's thesis entitled "Towards a Practical Public-Key Cryptosystem" [KOHNFELDER]. Thus, even two decades ago, it was recognized that a scalable and secure method (from an integrity perspective) would be required to convey the public keys to the parties that needed them. Simply stated, *public-key certificates* are used to bind an entity's name (and possibly additional attributes associated with that entity) with the corresponding public key.

When discussing the concept of a "certificate," it is important to recognize that a number of different types of certificates exist, including

- X.509 Public-key certificates

- Simple Public Key Infrastructure (SPKI) certificates

- Pretty Good Privacy (PGP) certificates

- Attribute certificates

The certificate types listed here have separate and distinct formats. In some cases, one type of certificate may be defined in several different versions, and a single version may be instantiated in a number of different ways. For example, there are three versions of an X.509 public-key certificate. Version 1 is a subset of Version 2, and Version 2 is a subset of Version 3. Because a Version 3 public-key certificate includes numerous optional extensions (as discussed further later), it can be instantiated in a number of application specific ways; for example, Secure Electronic Transaction (SET) certificates are X.509 Version 3 public-key certificates with specific extensions defined solely for SET exchanges.

To complicate matters further, there seem to be multiple terms commonly used to denote the same thing. For example, in many environments the terms *certificate* and *digital certificate* are synonymous with an X.509 public-key certificate.

For the purposes of this book, a *certificate* is synonymous only with a *Version 3 public-key certificate* as defined in the X.509 Recommendation [X.509]. Any other type of certificate will be further qualified to avoid any confusion with this usage. This chapter discusses the structure and content of a certificate.

Note

Three versions of an X.509 public-key certificate are defined. The original Version 1 public-key certificate, defined in the 1988 X.509 Recommendation, suffers from inherent inflexibility because there is no way to extend this version to support additional attributes. The

Version 2 public-key certificate did little to correct this shortcoming because it simply augments Version 1 with the addition of two optional fields. Because the demand for these fields was (and continues to be) negligible and the same inability to support extensions also applies, the Version 2 public-key certificate has failed to gain widespread acceptance. Not surprisingly, Version 3 public-key certificates, as specified in the 1997 X.509 Recommendation [X.509], were introduced to correct the deficiencies associated with the Version 1 and Version 2 definitions. Specifically, Version 3 offers significant improvements over Version 1 and Version 2 through the addition of optional extensions.

In the enterprise domain, it is fair to say that Version 3 public-key certificates are the preferred choice as they are the most flexible, and many of the extensions are required to fully support the requirements of the enterprise.

Digital Certificate

The term *digital certificate* is sometimes used to denote a certificate in electronic form. However, this term can be somewhat confusing in some circumstances because a number of quite different certificates (for example, an X.509 public-key certificate, an attribute certificate, a PGP certificate, and so on) are "digital." For that matter, even a digitized birth certificate is a "digital certificate." Thus, unless the term is either explicitly defined or further qualified, it is not precise enough to convey any intended meaning.

The use of this term has also introduced confusion when describing the relationship between "digital certificates" and "digital signatures." In particular, a common mistake is to assume that Alice can authenticate herself by simply supplying a "digital certificate" without the corresponding "digital signature." Further, while "digital signature" is meaningful in itself (that is, a digital signature is distinguished from a handwritten signature or an electronic signature), "digital certificate" does not offer the same connotation—especially when referring solely to a public-key certificate.

To be perfectly precise, any reference to a "certificate" should be fully qualified to avoid unnecessary confusion. However, in accordance with common practice in the PKI industry, we will simply use the term *certificate* as a shorthand notation for an *X.509 Version 3 public-key certificate*. We will explicitly identify all other types of certificates where appropriate—even the generic use of "certificate" will be qualified wherever any doubt may arise.

Certificate Structure and Semantics

Although X.509 defines certain requirements associated with the standard fields and extensions of a certificate, a number of issues still must be further refined in specific profiles to fully address interoperability considerations. The Internet Engineering Task Force (IETF) Public Key Infrastructure X.509 (PKIX) Working Group has introduced such a profile, RFC2459 (informally referred to as *PKIX Part 1*). Although RFC2459 is targeted for the

Internet community, a number of useful recommendations could apply in the enterprise environment and consistency should be maintained wherever possible. Therefore, we will provide references to some of the recommendations made in RFC2459 where appropriate.

Figure 6.1 shows the generic structure of a Version 3 certificate.

Figure 6.1   Version 3 certificate structure.

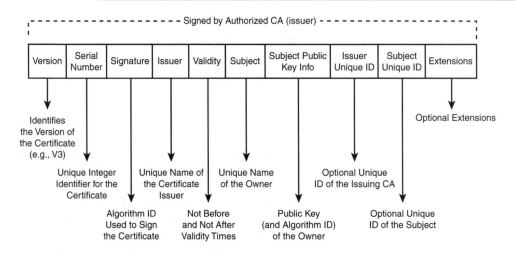

The following list defines the fields represented in Figure 6.1:

- *Version*—Indicates the version of the certificate (either Version 1, Version 2, or Version 3).

- *Serial Number*—Unique identifier for this certificate relative to the certificate issuer.

- *Signature*—Indicates the algorithm identifier (that is, the object identifier plus any associated parameters) of the algorithm used to calculate the digital signature on the certificate. For example, the object identifier for SHA-1 with RSA might be present, indicating that the digital signature is an SHA-1 hash encrypted using RSA.

- *Issuer*—The *Distinguished Name (DN)* of the certificate issuer—must always be present.

- *Validity*—The window of time that this certificate should be considered valid unless otherwise revoked (refer to Chapter 8, "Certificate Revocation," for more information on revocation). This field is comprised of *Not Valid Before* and *Not Valid After* dates/times that may be represented in UTC Time or in Generalized Time (however, RFC2459 has specific rules associated with the use of these time representations).

- *Subject*—The DN of the certificate owner—must be non-null unless an alternate name form is used (refer to the Extensions field later).

- *Subject Public Key Info*—The public key (and algorithm identifier) associated with the subject—must always be present.

- *Issuer Unique Identifier*—An optional unique identifier of the certificate issuer present in Version 2 and Version 3 only; this field is rarely used in implementation practice, and it is not recommended for use by RFC2459.

- *Subject Unique Identifier*—An optional unique identifier of the certificate owner present in Version 2 and Version 3 only; this field is rarely used in implementation practice, and it is not recommended for use by RFC2459.

- *Extensions*—Optional standard and private extensions (present in Version 3 only), including

  - *Authority Key Identifier*—Unique identifier of the key that should be used to verify the digital signature calculated over the certificate—used to distinguish between multiple keys that apply to the same certificate issuer. RFC2459 mandates the inclusion of this field for all but self-signed certificates (Chapter 9, "Trust Models," discusses self-signed certificates).

  - *Subject Key Identifier*—Unique identifier associated with the public key contained in this certificate—used to distinguish between multiple keys that apply to the same certificate owner. RFC2459 mandates this field for Certification Authority (CA) certificates, and it is recommended for end-entity certificates.

  - *Key Usage*—A bit string used to identify (or restrict) the functions or services that can be supported by using the public key in this certificate—can be used to indicate support for digital signature, non-repudiation, key encipherment, data encipherment, key agreement, certificate signature, CRL signature, encipher only, and decipher only. A profile typically specifies allowable combinations (for example, the U.S. Federal PKI profile [FPKI] explicitly identifies permitted key usage combinations).

  - *Extended Key Usage*—A sequence of one or more *object identifiers (OIDs)* that identify specific usage of the public key in the certificate. Although X.509 does not explicitly define identifiers for this purpose, RFC2459 identifies several *Extended Key Usage* OIDs, including *Transport Layer Security (TLS)* server authentication, TLS client authentication, code signing, e-mail protection, and time stamping. It is likely that the list of OIDs specified in RFC2459 will be augmented over time as needs dictate, and so this should not be considered an exhaustive list.

  - *CRL Distribution Point*—Indicates the location of the CRL partition where revocation information associated with this certificate resides (refer to Chapter 8 for more information regarding revocation techniques and CRL Distribution Points).

  - *Private Key Usage Period*—Indicates the time window that the private key associated with the public key in this certificate can be used—intended for use with digital signature keys/certificates. Like the certificate validity period, this window is specified in terms of *Not Valid Before* and *Not Valid After* dates/times (although only Generalized Time is permitted here). Judicious use of this extension can establish a buffer between the time the signing private key expires and the time the corresponding public key used to verify the digital signatures created with that private key expires. This should help to eliminate many instances where perfectly valid digital signatures needlessly come into question because the key lifetimes of both the private and public key were too close together (or even identical).

Note that when this extension is absent, the validity periods of the public key and the private key are identical. As Chapter 7, "Key and Certificate Management," discusses, a new key pair should be issued before the private key expires to avoid any unnecessary downtime. It is interesting to note that RFC2459 recommends against the use of this extension. One reason for recommending against the use of this extension is that the interpretation of this field is not universally agreed, which could give rise to inconsistent implementations.

- *Certificate Policies*—Indicates a sequence of one or more policy OIDs and optional qualifiers associated with the issuance and subsequent use of the certificate. If this extension is marked critical, the processing application must adhere to at least one of the policies indicated, or the certificate is not to be used. Although RFC2459 recommends that policy qualifiers should not be used in order to promote interoperability, it does define two possible qualifiers: the *Certification Practice Statement (CPS)* qualifier and the *User Notice* qualifier. The CPS qualifier is a *Uniform Resource Identifier (URI)* where one can find the CPS that applies to this certificate. A notice reference, an explicit notice (up to 200 characters), or both can comprise the User Notice qualifier.

- *Policy Mappings*—Indicates one or more policy OID equivalencies between two CA domains—only present in CA certificates. The "Certificate Policies" section in this chapter provides additional information related to policy mappings.

- *Subject Alternative Name*—Indicates alternative name forms associated with the owner of the certificate (for example, e-mail address, IP address, URI, and so on). Alternative name forms are to be considered just as binding as the subject DN, if present. RFC2459 further specifies that if the subject DN is null, one or more alternative name forms must be present, and this extension must be marked critical.

- *Issuer Alternative Name*—Indicates alternative name forms associated with the issuer of the certificate (for example, e-mail address, IP address, URI, and so on). RFC2459 specifies the same processing rules as specified under Subject Alternate Name extension with the exception that the issuer's DN must always be present in the Issuer field. One of the reasons for this requirement is to maintain compatibility with the S/MIME specification.

- *Subject Directory Attributes*—Indicates a sequence of attributes associated with the owner of the certificate. Although this extension is not currently in widespread use, several known applications exist where this extension is used to convey access control information. However, we recommend exercising caution when using a certificate to convey privilege-related information, because any change in those privileges would force the revocation of the existing certificate, and a new certificate would have to be issued. RFC2459 also recommends against the use of this extension.

Certificate Perishability

Any change to the information contained within a given certificate before it naturally expires necessarily means that the existing certificate must be revoked, and a new certificate must be issued. Therefore, care must be exercised to ensure that the attributes placed within the certificate are fairly static in order to avoid wasteful certificate revocation and (re)issuance. Attributes associated with an end-entity that will tend to be fairly dynamic in nature should be conveyed through some other means (for example, via attribute certificates, which are briefly discussed later in this chapter as well as in Chapter 5).

- *Basic Constraints*—Indicates whether or not this is a CA certificate. Typically, this field is absent in end-entity certificates. If it is present in an end-entity certificate, the value of the CA attribute in the Basic Constraints field must be `false`. For CA certificates, the Basic Constraints field should always be present, and the CA attribute in the Basic Constraints field must be set to a value of `true`. Note that X.509 [X.509] recommends (but doesn't mandate) that this extension be marked critical. RFC2459 mandates that this extension be present and marked critical for all CA certificates.

- For CA certificates, the Basic Constraints extension can also include a *Path Length Constraint*. In accordance with X.509 [X.509], the Path Length Constraint indicates "the maximum number of CA-certificates that may follow this certificate in a certification path." (Chapter 9 describes certification path processing.) A value of zero indicates that the CA can issue only end-entity certificates. The Path Length Constraint must not be present in end-entity certificates (or if it is, it should be ignored). The absence of the Path Length Constraint in a CA certificate indicates that there is no restriction on the length of the certification path (that is, the length of the certification path between an end-entity and the subject CA is unbounded).

- *Name Constraints*—Present only in CA certificates, this extension indicates required and/or excluded subtree names through the use of the *Permitted Subtrees* and/or *Excluded Subtrees* attributes, respectively. The specified names can take the form of a DN, a URI, an e-mail address, or any other name form that lends itself to a hierarchical structure. The idea is to qualify the name space restrictions that apply to all subject names in a given certification path. If present, this extension should be marked critical [X.509]. RFC2459 mandates that this extension be marked critical. Chapter 9 provides additional information regarding Name Constraints in relation to certification path validation.

- *Policy Constraints*—Present only in CA certificates, this extension indicates required policy identifiers and/or prohibited policy mappings through the use of the *Require Explicit Policy* and/or *Inhibit Policy Mapping* attributes, respectively. A value of zero for either attribute indicates that the restrictions apply to the entire certification path. A non-zero value for either attribute indicates where the restrictions begin (that is, the value is an offset in the certification path). If present, this extension should be marked critical [X.509]. RFC2459 simply states that this extension may be critical or non-critical.

Private extensions (that is, extensions not defined in any standards document and not intended for general interoperability) can also be defined in accordance with X.509. Private extensions are typically defined for domain specific use. For example, RFC2459 defines a private extension for Internet use. This extension, referred to as the *Authority Information Access extension*, is designed to identify alternative methods (and locations) that can be used to retrieve revocation status information associated with the certificate. One of the primary reasons behind the introduction of this extension is to help deal with the fact that there is no ubiquitous directory service available in the Internet, and so alternative methods for obtaining revocation information must be established.

Note

As noted earlier, extensions can be marked critical or non-critical. An extension that has been marked critical must be processed and understood by the relying party, or the certificate is not to be used. Non-critical extensions may be gracefully ignored if the relying party does not understand them.

Certificate Validation

As the beginning of the chapter discussed, a scalable method is required to disseminate public-key certificates to the relying parties that need them. Certification introduces a mechanism to ensure that the integrity of the certificate is sound and that a trusted party issued the certificate. (Chapter 9 provides a discussion on the somewhat controversial topic of trust relationships.)

As you might expect, other requirements are involved when considering the validity or usability of a certificate in a specific context other than simple integrity checks. Specifically, a number of additional questions must be resolved before a given certificate should be considered appropriate for use. The process of determining whether or not a given certificate can be used in a given context is referred to as *certificate validation*. Certificate validation includes determining that

- A trusted CA has digitally signed the certificate (that is, the CA's signature verifies correctly). Note that this may include certificate path processing, as discussed in Chapter 9.

- The integrity of the certificate is sound; that is, the digital signature on the certificate corresponds to the independently-calculated hash value of the certificate itself and the signer's public key (see Chapter 2).

- The certificate is within its established validity period (as indicated by the Not Valid Before and Not Valid After parameters in the certificate).

- The certificate has not been revoked (refer to Chapter 8 for more information on certificate revocation).

- The certificate is being used in a manner that is consistent with any indicated policy and/or intended use restrictions (as indicated in specific extensions such as the Certificate Policy extension or Key Usage extension).

While the order in which these operations should be performed is not universally agreed, many implementations are designed to perform the more intensive operations after the less intensive operations have successfully completed.

Alternative Certificate Formats

As discussed previously in this chapter, there are a number of certificate types other than the X.509 Version 3 public-key certificate. The following subsections discuss some of these further.

SPKI

In contrast to the IETF PKIX Working Group that focused on X.509 issues for the Internet (see Chapter 16, "Major Standards Activities"), a separate IETF working group was formed to address a (potentially) simpler public-key infrastructure for the Internet referred to as the *Simple Public Key Infrastructure (SPKI)*. Specifically, the charter of the IETF SPKI Working Group (see `http://www.ietf.org/html.characters/spki-charter.html`) was to

develop Internet standards for an IETF sponsored public-key certificate format, associated signature and other formats, and key acquisition protocols. The key certificate format and associated protocols are to be simple to understand, implement and use.

The IETF SPKI Working Group produced a number of technical and informational documents, including

- SPKI certificate format

- SPKI certificate theory

- SPKI requirements

- SPKI examples

You can retrieve the relevant SPKI documents from `http://www.ietf.org/html.charters/spki-charter.html`.

Because the focus of the SPKI work was on authorization rather than on identity, the SPKI certificate is referred to as an *authorization certificate*. The primary purpose of the SPKI authorization certificate is to convey permissions. It also includes the ability to delegate permissions to others.

Although the SPKI authorization certificate has a number of things in common with a X.509 public-key certificate (for example, issuer, validity, and so on), the syntax and, in many cases, the semantics of these fields is not the same. Further, a number of fields are defined for one type of certificate that do not correspond to an equivalent mapping in the other. In addition, the naming conventions (and assumptions) are completely different, as the SPKI work adopted the naming conventions as defined in "SDSI—A Simple Distributed Security Infrastructure" [SDSI].

The IETF work on SPKI has concluded. However, the extent to which this work will be used in practice still remains to be seen. There is currently very little demand for SPKI-based certificates, and in the absence of market demand, CA and PKI vendors are not likely to implement a completely different certificate syntax in addition to X.509 Version 3 public-key certificates.

Chapter 16 provides additional information regarding the role and status of the SPKI work.

PGP

Essentially, *Pretty Good Privacy (PGP)* is a method for encrypting and digitally signing e-mail messages and files. Phil Zimmermann introduced the first version of PGP in the early 1990s [Zim 95]. Version 2.x of PGP was published a number of years later as an IETF standards-track specification entitled "PGP Message Exchange Formats" [RFC1991]. The latest version of PGP, referred to as *OpenPGP*, has been published as an IETF standards-track specification entitled "OpenPGP Message Format" [RFC2440]. There is also a document on the Internet standards track that incorporates MIME with PGP entitled "MIME Security with Pretty Good Privacy" [RFC2015].

PGP specifies packet formats that are used to convey messages and files from one entity to another. PGP also includes packet formats that are used to convey *PGP keys* (sometimes referred to as *PGP certificates*) from one entity to another.

A number of significant differences exist between PGP keys (or certificates) and X.509 Version 3 public-key certificates, and the trust models they embody are also completely different. (Chapter 9 discusses the PGP trust model further.) The significant differences between PGP keys and the X.509 Version 3 public-key certificate have created interoperability barriers between the PGP user community and other communities that base their certificate formats on X.509 (for example, the S/MIME user community). This is much more than a protocol incompatibility issue because the very foundation for the underlying public-key-enabled security services is different and incompatible. One possible solution is for PGP (or OpenPGP) to adopt X.509 Version 3 public-key certificates in addition to (or perhaps in lieu of) the PGP certificate. In fact, Version 6.5 of OpenPGP has pursued this direction and is now capable of supporting X.509 certificates. While this will allow OpenPGP users to tap into X.509-based PKIs, it should be noted that this still does not solve the basic protocol incompatibilities between OpenPGP and S/MIME. Another possibility might be for PKI vendors to offer products that support both PGP and X.509 Version 3 public-key certificates, but this can lead to other difficulties due to the significant differences in the trust models (for example, it would introduce significant administrative and control issues).

Although PGP enjoys a significant amount of use over the Internet, it does not make a good candidate for the corporate intranet (that is, the enterprise domain) because all trust decisions rest with individuals rather than with the enterprise. Because many CA and PKI vendors seem to have concentrated their product development efforts on the enterprise domain, it is unclear that they have any motivation to offer PGP-compatible (or OpenPGP-compatible) products.

Chapter 16 provides additional information regarding the role and status of the PGP/OpenPGP work.

SET

The *Secure Electronic Transaction (SET)* specifications [SET1, SET2, and SET3] define a standard to support credit card payment transactions over distributed communications networks such as the Internet. Essentially, SET defines a standard payment protocol and specifies requirements that the supporting PKI is expected to meet.

SET adopts the X.509 Version 3 public-key certificate format, and it defines specific private extensions that have meaning only in a SET context. SET also levies certain profile requirements on the standard extensions. Figure 6.2 illustrates a SET certificate. Note that

Figure 6.2 does not represent all the possible extensions (for example, it does not represent the Hashed Root Key extension present in a SET root CA certificate).

Figure 6.2   SET certificate structure.

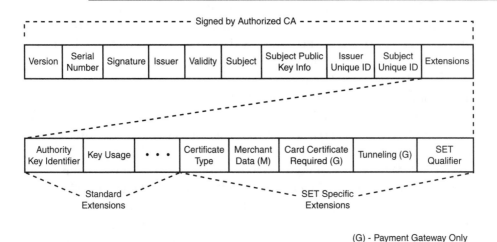

(G) - Payment Gateway Only
(M) - Merchant Only

Because non-SET applications will not understand the private extensions SET defines, one cannot expect a non-SET application (for example, S/MIME-based e-mail) to accept a SET certificate for use. This is true even though the SET certificate format is compliant with an X.509 Version 3 public-key certificate. Although one might suggest that a non-SET application could ignore the SET extensions, the *Certificate Type* extension is critical; therefore, by definition a non-SET application must reject a SET certificate. Note that it is accepted practice to intentionally mark certain extensions critical so that a certain type of certificate can be used only in the context of a specific application to minimize liability concerns.

Although it is not necessarily the case that end-users will require a separate certificate for each and every application, this example helps illustrate that multiple certificates per end-entity will be required. Chapter 10, "Multiple Certificates per Entity," provides additional discussion regarding the requirements for multiple certificates.

Attribute Certificates

Although the X.509 Recommendation [X.509] defines the basic ASN.1 constructs for an attribute certificate, it should be recognized that attribute certificates are not public-key certificates. Attribute certificates are designed to convey (potentially short-lived) attributes about a given subject to facilitate flexible and scalable privilege management. The subject of the attribute certificate may be identified through "pointers" to the associated public-key certificate. Chapter 5 provides additional information regarding privilege management.

Certificate Policies

As indicated in the "Certificate Structure and Semantics" section earlier, a number of policy-related extensions may be present in a given certificate. The policy-related extensions are extremely important in the sense that they help to govern the acceptable use of the certificate in terms of policy compliance—potentially across multiple PKI domains.

The policy-related extensions refer either directly or indirectly to a certificate policy. The X.509 Recommendation [X.509] defines a *certificate policy* as

> A named set of rules that indicates the applicability of a certificate to a particular community and/or class of application with common security requirements. For example, a particular certificate policy might indicate applicability of a type of certificate to the authentication of electronic data interchange transactions for the trading of goods within a given price range.

The Internet X.509 Public Key Infrastructure Certificate Policy and Certification Practices Framework [RFC2527] also adopts this definition.

Unfortunately, this somewhat nebulous definition of a certificate policy has created some degree of uncertainty with respect to the content and role of a certificate policy. Further, the relationship between a certificate policy and a *Certification Practice Statement (CPS)*, where a CPS is defined to be

> A statement of the practices which a certification authority employs in issuing certificates [ABA]

is also not universally agreed.

The U.S. Federal PKI document entitled "Model Certificate Policy" [MCS] provides an interesting treatment of this topic. Additional sources of information related to certificate policies and CPSs include

- "The Internet X.509 Public Key Infrastructure Certificate Policy and Certification Practices Framework" [RFC2527]

- CARAT Guidelines [CARAT] sponsored by the National Automated Clearing House Association (NACHA)

- The American Bar Association (ABA), Digital Signature Guidelines, Legal Infrastructure for Certification Authorities and Electronic Commerce [ABA]

- The Automotive Network eXchange (ANX) Certificate Policy [ANX]

From a high-level perspective, most of this documentation reflects a common theme. In particular, a Certificate Policy is expected to be a higher-level document than a CPS, and it is typically concerned with *what* will be supported, rather than *how* it will be supported. Conversely, a CPS is expected to be a fairly detailed and comprehensive technical and procedural document regarding the operation of the supporting infrastructure. As discussed in RFC2527, CPSs

> may be quite comprehensive, robust documents providing a description of the precise service offerings, detailed procedures of the life-cycle management of certificates, and more—a level of detail which weds the CPS to a particular (proprietary) implementation of a service offering.

Role of Certificate Policies and CPSs

The role of certificate policies and CPSs is not universally agreed. One point of view is that a Certificate Policy should be a high-level statement of requirements and restrictions associated with the intended use of the certificates issued under that policy and that a CPS is an extremely detailed (and potentially extremely sensitive) document that describes the internal operating procedures of the CA and/or PKI that issues those certificates. In this case, it is the Certificate Policy that makes a natural and logical vehicle for formalizing cross-certification agreements, not a CPS.

From this perspective, a CPS will not make a good candidate for cross-certification. (Chapter 9 describes concepts associated with cross-certification.) This is because it may be considered too sensitive or too detailed (and potentially too voluminous) to be useful in a cross-certification context (that is, using CPS as a basis for cross-certification will not scale). Thus, an enterprise-specific CPS will not be subject to review by external sources—although the CPS may be used to support internal (and confidential) audits. From this point of view, the notion of supplying a pointer to a CPS in a certificate as defined in RFC2459 makes little sense; a pointer to a Certificate Policy would be more appropriate.

An alternative point of view is that the CPS is a public domain document that comes under the scrutiny of anyone with an interest in the CPS. Further, it is the CPS that forms the foundation for any cross-certification agreements. The notion of supplying a pointer to a CPS in a certificate as defined in RFC2459 is appropriate in this model.

Yet another view is that only a CPS is required for a CA service provider, and only a certificate policy is required for an organization.

It is unclear at this point which view will become the most dominant in the industry, if any. The first point of view seems to be prevalent in the enterprise domain. On the other hand, the second point of view seems to be favoured in the Web environment. All these viewpoints may be valid and may continue to be implemented, depending on the target environment in question.

Object Identifiers

To easily distinguish one Certificate Policy from another, each Certificate Policy is assigned a globally unique Object Identifier (OID). One or more OIDs can be specified in the Certificate Policies certificate extension, which can be further qualified as appropriate. For example, RFC2459 defines two optional Certificate Policy qualifiers: a User Notice and a pointer to a CPS. Certificate Policies can be placed in end-entity certificates as well as CA certificates. Cross-certificates may also contain the Policy Mappings extension, which permits a policy OID in one domain to be designated equivalent to a policy OID in another domain. Thus, if two PKI domains have each defined a Certificate Policy for the exchange of their own internal e-mail and the two policies are deemed to be equivalent by each domain, there is no need to define yet a third policy OID to allow e-mail exchanges between the two domains.

Note

An Object Identifier, or OID, is simply a unique representation for a given object. When expressed verbally or in writing among human beings, an OID is represented as a sequence of integers, which are separated by decimal points or dots (much the same as an Internet Protocol address is expressed in the familiar dotted decimal notation). OIDs are hierarchical in nature, and they are registered with international, national, or organizational registration authorities in order to ensure that the allocated OID for a given object is unique. As an example, the OID for SHA-1 with RSA (which might be present in the Signature field of a certificate) is 1.2.840.113549.1.1.5.

Policy Authorities

Policy authorities (sometimes referred to as *policy management authorities*) establish Certificate Policies. The policy authority itself may vary from one organization to another. For example, each organization may establish its own policies under the authority of the internal *Information Technology Security (ITS)* department (or equivalent). Alternatively, this authority may emanate from a policy advisory board made up of members from each major department in an organization. In concert with the internal authority (or perhaps in lieu of such an authority), there may be an external policy authority that establishes the Certificate Policies for a number of PKI domains that belong to the same community of interest. In any event, the applicable policy authority is responsible for registering Certificate Policies with the appropriate registration authority (for example, a national registration authority) so that the certificate policy OIDs can be assigned appropriately.

Certification Authority

In the context of a PKI, *certification* is the act of binding an identity (and potentially other attributes) with a public key. As discussed previously in this chapter, this binding occurs in the form of a signed data structure referred to as a *public-key certificate*. A *Certification Authority (CA)* is responsible for issuing these public-key certificates. These certificates are digitally signed with the private key of the issuing CA.

Certificate Authority Versus Certification Authority

A CA is sometimes referred to as a *certificate authority* rather than a *certification authority* in much of today's literature. Although it may be too late to stop the growing use of this term, we would like to point out that the use of this term to denote a CA is technically (and logically) incorrect. There is no such thing as a "certificate authority" in X.509, and the implication that a CA is an authority on certificates is somewhat misleading. Specifically, a policy authority (or policy management authority) is the authority on certificates; the CA is simply an instrument that issues certificates in accordance with the certificate policy dictated by the policy authority. The term certification authority is used throughout this book.

Because the issuing CA digitally signs certificates, they are self-protected from an integrity perspective. Thus, the certificates can be freely disseminated—assuming that they do not contain any sensitive information. Chapter 11, "PKI Information Dissemination: Repositories and Other Techniques," discusses difficulties associated with the dissemination of certificates that might be considered sensitive in nature.

The CA can take on a number of different representations, depending on the trust model to be embodied by that CA. For example, in an enterprise domain, one can expect one or more CAs to be responsible for issuing certificates to the employees of the enterprise. The employees essentially place their "trust" in the enterprise CA(s). A completely different architecture is reflected in the PGP "web of trust" model where individuals can act as their own CA, and all trust decisions lie with the individual rather than a remote CA. Chapter 9 provides a more detailed discussion regarding trust models and the role a CA plays in relation to those trust models.

Note

We recognize that the interpretation of the word *trust* is often the subject of lively debate. Chapter 9 provides the definition of *trust* as it applies in the context of this book.

Registration Authority

Although the registration function can be implemented directly with the CA component, it sometimes makes sense to offload the registration function to a separate component referred to as a *Registration Authority (RA)*. For example, as the number of end-entities in a given PKI domain increases and/or the end-entities are widely dispersed geographically, the notion of centralized registration becomes problematic. Judicious deployment of multiple RAs (sometimes referred to as *Local Registration Authorities*, or *LRAs*) helps to solve this problem. The primary purpose of the RA is to offload certain functions from the CA to enhance scalability and decrease operational costs.

Although the functions implemented by the RA may vary, it can be designed to support one or more of the following:

- Establish and confirm the identity of an individual as part of the initialization process

- Distribute shared secrets to end-users for subsequent authentication during an on-line initialization process

- Initiate the certification process with a CA on behalf of individual end-users (including the registration of certain attributes to be associated with the end-user)

- Generate keying material on behalf of an end-user

- Perform certain key/certificate life cycle management functions, such as to initiate a revocation request or a key recovery operation on behalf of an end-entity

Regardless of the set of functions implemented in the RA, it should be noted that a RA is never allowed to issue certificates or CRLs. These functions rest solely with the CA.

End-entity registration requirements may vary significantly from one domain to another, between distinct applications in a given domain, or between distinct contexts in a given application in a given domain. Chapter 7 discusses specific registration issues and procedures further.

> **Note**
>
> Chapter 7 discusses in detail all aspects associated with key/certificate life cycle management (for example, registration and initialization, revocation, key recovery, and so on).

Summary

The primary focus of this chapter has been the structure and semantics of the X.509 Version 3 public-key certificate, and the need for certification in order to maintain the integrity and trustworthiness of the certificate itself. This chapter notes that the X.509 public-key certificate is by far the preferred choice for the enterprise domain, and it is quickly becoming widely accepted in other environments such as the Internet. It also has discussed a number of other certificate types (which may or may not be encountered in wide-scale implementation practice).

This chapter has also addressed the importance and role of the CA and RA components. A CA is responsible for issuing certificates in accordance with one or more certificate polices. The CA may also be responsible for end-entity registration, although one or more RAs can implement this function separately. The advantage to deploying one or more RAs is to reduce cost and to enhance the overall scalability of a large-scale PKI.

A full understanding of certificates and certification requires familiarity with two related topics: the details regarding key/certificate life cycle management discussed in Chapter 7, and the proper legal framework around the process of certification and the business/financial use of certificates as discussed in Chapter 13, "Legal Framework."

References

[ABA]   American Bar Association (ABA). Digital Signature Guidelines: Legal Infrastructure for Certification Authorities and Electronic Commerce, 1995.

[ANX]   Automotive Network eXchange (ANX) Certificate Policy. Automotive Industry Action Group. Southfield, Michigan U.S., undated.

[CARAT]   CARAT Guidelines—Guidelines for Constructing Policies Governing the Use of Identity-Based Public Key Certificates, National Automated Clearing House Association (NACHA)—The Internet Council Certification Authority Rating and Trust (CARAT) Task Force, DRAFT Version 1.0 (21 September 1998).

[FPKI]   Federal Public Key Infrastructure (PKI) X.509 Certificate and CRL Extensions Profile, Booz-Allen and Hamilton Inc. (4 January 1999).

[KOHNFELDER]   Kohnfelder, L. "Towards a Practical Public-key Cryptosystem." MIT S.B. Thesis (May 1978).

[MCS]   "Model Certificate Policy." Government Information Technology Services—Federal PKI Steering Committee—Legal/Policy Working Group, Discussion Draft. (25 March 1998; revised 8 July 1998).

[RFC1991]   Atkins, D., W. Stallings, and P. Zimmermann. "PGP Message Exchange Formats." Internet Request for Comments 1991. (August 1996).

[RFC2015]   Elkins, M. "MIME Security with Pretty Good Privacy." Internet Request for Comments 2015. (October 1996).

[RFC2440]   Callas, J., L. Donnerhacke, H. Finney, and R. Thayer. "OpenPGP Message Format." Internet Request for Comments 2440. (November 1998).

[RFC2459]   Housley, R., W. Ford, W. Polk, and D. Solo. "Internet X.509 Public Key Infrastructure Certificate and CRL Profile." Internet Request for Comments 2459. (January 1999).

[RFC2510]   Adams, C. and S. Farrell. "Internet X.509 Public Key Infrastructure Certificate Management Protocols." Internet Request for Comments 2510. (March 1999).

[RFC2511]   Myers, M., C. Adams, D. Solo, and D. Kemp. "Internet X.509 Certificate Request Message Format." Internet Request for Comments 2511. (March 1999).

[RFC2527]   Chokhani, S. and W. Ford. "Internet X.509 Public Key Infrastructure Certificate Policy and Certification Practices Framework." Internet Request for Comments 2527. (March 1999).

[SDSI]   Rivest, R. and B. Lampson. "SDSI—A Simple Distributed Security Infrastructure." (undated—work in progress).

[SET1]   SET Secure Electronic Transaction Specification. Book 1: Business Description, Visa and MasterCard, Version 1.0 (31 May 1997).

[SET2]   SET Secure Electronic Transaction Specification. Book 2: Programmer's Guide, Visa and MasterCard, Version 1.0 (31 May 1997).

[SET3]   SET Secure Electronic Transaction Specification. Book 3: Formal Protocol Definition, Visa and MasterCard, Version 1.0 (31 May 1997).

[X.509]   ITU-T Recommendation X.509. "Information Technology—Open Systems Interconnection—The Directory: Authentication Framework." June 1997 (equivalent to ISO/IEC 9594-8, 1997).

[Zim95]   Zimmermann, P. *The Official PGP User's Guide*. Cambridge, MA: MIT Press, 1995 (second printing).

Key and Certificate Management

As discussed in Chapter 2, "Public-Key Cryptography," asymmetric cryptography is based on the use of public/private key pairs. A public key is typically distributed in the form of a certificate, whereas a private key is a separate and distinct data structure always protected from unauthorized disclosure (either in transit, in use, or in storage). The term *key/certificate life cycle management* denotes the life cycle management functions associated with the creation, issuance, and subsequent cancellation of public/private key pairs and their associated certificates.

> **Note**
>
> The key/certificate life cycle management functions are considered separate and distinct from the actual *usage* of the public/private keying material. As discussed in Chapter 2, *usage* is related to performing cryptographic operations. This includes applying the signing private key to generate a digital signature and applying the corresponding verification public key to perform digital signature verification. Similarly, usage includes applying the encryption public key to encrypt data and applying the corresponding decryption private key to decrypt the data.

The purpose of this chapter is to discuss the various phases of key/certificate life cycle management that must be offered as part of any comprehensive PKI. Where appropriate, the relationship this has to the actual usage of the keying material will also be discussed.

It is important to recognize that the discussion provided within this chapter is based on a fundamental separation between the *identity* of the end-entity (that is, an end-user, process, or component) and the *keying material* associated with that end-entity. In other words, the key/certificate life cycle management process described herein is associated with the generation, issuance, and subsequent cancellation of the keying material, not with the identity of the individual, process, or component associated with that keying material.

A few of the underlying assumptions regarding a comprehensive key/certificate life cycle management to keep in mind are as follows:

- End-entity management of key and certificate life cycle is not practical.

- The key/certificate life cycle management must be as automated as possible.

- The key/certificate life cycle management must be as unobtrusive to the end-entity as possible.

- Comprehensive key/certificate life cycle management requires the secure operation and cooperation of trusted entities such as Registration Authorities (RAs) and Certification Authorities (CAs), as well as client-end software that interacts with these components when necessary.

Key/Certificate Life Cycle Management

The various phases of the key/certificate life cycle management are illustrated in Figure 7.1. These phases are discussed further in the following sections.

> **Note**
> As mentioned in Chapter 3, "The Concept of an Infrastructure," not all environments will necessarily require each and every facet of the key/certificate life cycle management as discussed within this chapter. Further, some environments may require certain aspects that are not required in others. To meet these varying demands, a comprehensive PKI must offer each of the services described in this chapter.

> **Note**
> A similar term, *key management* or *key exchange*, is often used to denote the method in which encryption/decryption keys are securely conveyed to the appropriate parties. This interpretation should not be confused with key/certificate life cycle management as it is being used within this chapter.

Initialization Phase

Before end-entities can engage in services supported by the PKI, they must *initialize* into the PKI. Initialization is comprised of the following:

- End-entity registration

- Key pair generation

- Certificate creation and key/certificate distribution

- Certificate dissemination

- Key backup (if applicable)

Figure 7.1   Key/certificate life cycle management.

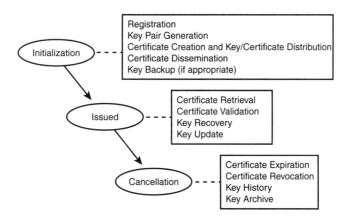

The registration process can be achieved in a variety of ways. Figure 7.2 illustrates one possible scenario where end-entity initialization involves both a RA and a CA (the RA and CA components are introduced in Chapter 6, "Certificates and Certification"). Note that other possible scenarios are also available. For example, all the transactions could flow through the RA, or the RA component may not exist at all, and the transactions would flow directly between the end-entity and the CA.

Figure 7.2   End-entity initialization scenario.

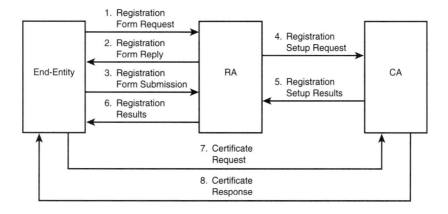

The aspects that comprise the initialization phase are discussed further in the subsections that follow.

End-Entity Registration

End-entity registration is the process wherein the identity of an individual user or process is established and verified. The level of verification associated with assessing the identity of a given end-entity will depend on the Certificate Policy and/or Certification Practice Statement (CPS) that applies to that particular end-entity's security domain. (Certificate Policies and CPSs are addressed in Chapter 6.)

In Figure 7.2, the end-entity registration is performed on-line, as illustrated by the exchange of the registration form. Note that this on-line registration process should be authenticated and protected. The actual registration requirements will vary based on the environment as well as the associated privileges implied by the issuance of a given certificate.

For example, one might expect the registration process for an end-user authorized to approve multi-million dollar transactions to be rather rigid, including physical presence at the appropriate RA or CA coupled with several forms of photographic identification such as a passport and employee identification badge, plus any requisite authorization forms. On the other hand, the registration procedures associated with credentials that will be used solely for non-committal e-mail applications are expected to be much less stringent.

In any case, the registration process typically includes assigning one or more shared secrets to the end-entity in order to authenticate that end-entity to the CA later in the initialization process. The type(s) of shared secret(s) and the complexity of the authentication step(s) is likely to vary from one domain to another. For example, an RA or CA might assign a reference value and initial authentication key to the end-entity through some trusted out-of-band mechanism [RFC2510]. Another alternative might be to use pre-existing shared secrets when the relationship between the end-entity and the certificate issuer is already established. This latter method is expected to be prevalent where an existing customer relationship exists (for example, in the case of a pre-existing client/bank relationship).

Key Pair Generation

Key pair generation consists of the generation of a public/private key pair as described in Chapter 2. The keying material may be generated in advance of the end-entity registration process or in direct response to the end-entity registration process.

In the comprehensive PKI model, it is possible to generate the keying material within the end-entity's client system (for example, within a browser), within the RA, or within the

CA. Alternatively, a trusted third-party key generation facility may be appropriate in some environments. The location of the key pair generation is an important consideration, and it is often the topic of some lively debate. Factors that may have an impact on this location include capability, performance, assurance, legal ramifications, and intended key usage.

Much of the controversy associated with the location of the key pair generation function centers around key usage. In particular, multiple key pairs per end-entity can be used to support separate and distinct services (refer to Chapter 10, "Multiple Certificates per Entity," for more information regarding the use of multiple key pairs). For example, one key pair might be used to support non-repudiation services while another key pair might be used to support confidentiality or key management functions.

While it is not necessarily universally agreed, it can be argued that the location of the key generation must be within the client if the keys are to be used for non-repudiation purposes. This is due to the assertion that possession of the signing private key by any other entity makes non-repudiation much more difficult to achieve. Alternatively, the view can be taken that the CA should be the most trusted entity within the PKI, so knowledge of the signing private keys of individual users should not jeopardize the ability to support non-repudiation as long as that keying material is adequately protected by that CA.

Note

Regardless of the level of trust that a given PKI entity places in the CA (and in those that operate the CA), true PKI support for non-repudiation requires the CA—or any other key backup facility that may be in place—to prove to the *satisfaction of a third party* that the private key could not possibly have been used by anyone other than the owner of the private key. In practice, this will often be very difficult to achieve. Therefore, for keys that may be used to authenticate transactions that are intended to have the property of non-repudiation, the simplest and most prudent course of action appears to be to never have such keys generated or stored by anyone other than the owner of the private key.

Dual-Key Pair Model

The notion of using distinct key pairs to separate non-repudiation services from confidentiality services is referred to as the *dual-key pair model*. This orientation has existed since the earliest PKI systems were available, and it is now a widely recognized paradigm to be supported in any comprehensive PKI.

continues

In the dual-key pair orientation, the private key used to support digital signatures is referred to as the *signing private key*, and the corresponding certificate is referred to as the *verification certificate*. Similarly, the certificate used for encryption purposes is referred to as the *encryption certificate*, and the corresponding private key is referred to as the *decryption private key*.

More generally, the concept of three key pairs has been introduced by the Swedish-based association *Secured Electronic Information in Society (SEIS)*, which explicitly identifies an even finer degree of service separation between authentication and non-repudiation.

Chapter 10 provides additional details regarding multiple key pairs.

Another factor that may have an impact on the location of the key generation is performance. Anyone who has requested a certificate using standard Web browser technology knows that the key generation process on a typical PC or laptop is very slow. Although this is likely to improve as the performance of the underlying technology improves, some would suggest that it might make more sense to relegate the key generation to the more powerful systems, such as a CA. (However, as discussed earlier, the authors suggest that this recommendation does not hold true for key pairs that are to be used for non-repudiation purposes.) Alternatively, a counter argument can be made that centralized key generation will not scale because a single component (or limited number of components) will be required to perform CPU intensive key generation for a large number of end-entities. Given that there is no universally agreed position regarding this topic, it seems clear that both scenarios should be supported by the PKI. This flexibility is reflected in certain PKI-related protocols [RFC2510].

Another factor that may have an influence on the location of the key generation is related to *assurance*. It may be a requirement, for example, to have a trusted and independently evaluated cryptographic module generate the keying material. This would be in response to a requirement that the keying material must be generated in accordance with specific cryptographic guidelines. Also that the software or hardware module that is used to generate the keying material may be required to meet some minimum set of criteria to provide a sufficient level of assurance that the keying material is generated properly. The (U.S.) Federal Information Processing Standard (FIPS) 140-1 [FIPS] is an example of evaluation criteria associated with cryptographic modules.

Yet another consideration would be based on legal and/or liability ramifications. For example, it may be a requirement to assert a certain amount of reliability in the key generation process. A PKI entity may not be capable of meeting the minimum criteria associated with this requirement, or it may not be willing to take responsibility for such a liability.

Certificate Creation and Key/Certificate Distribution

The purpose and structure of a certificate is described in Chapter 6. Regardless of where key generation occurs, the responsibility for *certificate creation* lies solely with an authorized CA. If the public key was generated by an entity other than the CA, that public key must be securely conveyed to the CA so that it can be placed within a certificate.

Once the keying material and related certificate have been generated, they must be distributed appropriately. The specific *key and certificate distribution* requirements depend on several factors, including where the keying material was generated, the intended use of the certificate, and any other considerations such as operational and/or policy constraints. For example, a given certificate may be distributed directly to the owner, to a remote repository, or both; this will depend on the intended key usage and operational considerations. Further, the distribution requirements associated with the private keying material is dependent on where the keying material was generated and whether or not key backup is required.

Note

If the keying material was generated at the client system, the private key is already stored with the owner of the private key and no further key distribution is required (this does not apply to key backup, which is addressed in the "Key Backup" subsection). However, if the keying material was generated elsewhere, the private key must be securely distributed to the owner of that key. Various mechanisms can be used to accomplish this, including RFC2510.

As a reminder, it is recommended that keying material intended for non-repudiation purposes should be generated at the client end. Therefore, the requirement to securely distribute private keys to their owner is typically associated with confidentiality keys (although these can be generated at the client as well).

The requirement to request a certificate and to receive a certificate (and the associated private key, if applicable) back from a trusted entity (that is, the CA) requires the definition of a secure protocol mechanism. The IETF PKIX working group (see Chapter 16, "Major Standards Activities," for further details) has a pair of specifications on the standards-track that addresses this requirement in both on-line and off-line modes as follows:

- The Internet X.509 Public Key Infrastructure Certificate Management Protocols [RFC2510]

- The Internet X.509 Certificate Request Message Format [RFC2511]

For some environments, other mechanisms, such as the Public Key Cryptography Standards (PKCS) 7 [PKCS7] and 10 [PKCS10], are a popular alternative (see also extensions to these protocols, such as *Certificate Management Messages over CMS* [CMC]).

Certificate Dissemination

Once the private key and corresponding public key certificate have been distributed, one or more methods for conveying the certificate to other end-entities must be adopted. Possible methods for disseminating this information include

- Out-of-band distribution

- Posting certificates in a public repository or database to facilitate on demand and on-line retrieval

- In-band protocol distribution; for example, include the applicable verification certificate with a secure e-mail message (S/MIME)

Which of these alternatives is the most appropriate will depend on a number of factors, including the key usage restrictions, privacy issues, scalability, and other operational considerations. Some of the more conventional methods are discussed in the "Certificate Retrieval" section later in this chapter.

The important point is that certificates must be readily available to fully realize the benefits of public-key cryptography. When a digital signature is verified, the verification certificate that corresponds to the signing private key used to create the digital signature must be available in order to verify the authenticity of that digital signature. Similarly, when a message originator is encrypting an e-mail message destined for one or more recipients, the encryption certificates for each of those recipients must be available so that the one-time symmetric key used to encrypt the e-mail message can be encrypted for each recipient.

As an example, certificates used for digital signature purposes may need only to be disseminated to their owners, because any digitally signed document (such as an e-mail message) may include the certificate necessary to validate the digital signature on the recipient end as part of the protocol exchange. On the other hand, certificates used for confidentiality purposes must be readily available to originators in order to facilitate scalable key management. Of course, variations of these examples are possible (for example, certificates used for digital signature purposes may be posted to a central repository in addition to, or in lieu of, distributing the certificate directly to the owner).

Certificate dissemination alternatives are discussed further in Chapter 11, "PKI Information Dissemination: Repositories and Other Techniques."

Key Backup

If the public/private key pair is to be used for confidentiality, the initialization phase may also include key and certificate backup by a trusted third party. Whether or not a given key pair is backed up by a trusted third party is the function of the governing policy for the environment under consideration. It should also be possible to indicate whether or not backup is requested during the initialization process [RFC2510].

Note

Again, it is the opinion of the authors that private keys designated for digital signature purposes in support of a non-repudiation service should never be backed up by a third party.

Also note that this section addresses trusted third-party backup, which is a completely separate issue from any backups that might be performed directly by the end-entities. Although there are certain circumstances where end-entities should be capable of backing up their own keying material, this is not always possible, nor is it something that is easily controlled at an organizational level. Backups performed by end-entities simply cannot be relied on as a fool-proof mechanism for recovering corporate data.

The location of the backup facility may vary from one PKI domain to another. Factors that may have an impact on the specific choice include the dictates of the governing security policy and the liability model associated with each of the PKI components. In particular, the key backup function might be carried out by the CA that issues the corresponding certificate or it might be supported by a separate key backup and recovery facility.

Key Backup versus Key Escrow

The notion of *key backup* as discussed here should not be confused with *key escrow*. The necessity for key backup in a comprehensive PKI is based on sound and practical business requirements, which has nothing to do with law enforcement or government access to encrypted data. Specifically, it is inevitable that a certain percentage of encryption keys will be rendered inaccessible to the owner of those keys for any number of reasons. This could be a result of a forgotten password, a corrupted disk (where the keys are stored), a malfunctioning smart card (where the keys are stored), or due to employee dismissal. A process for recovering encryption keys must be available under these circumstances, or there would be no way to recover the encrypted data. The inability to recover this data could have severe financial and operational consequences, especially in a corporate setting.

Issued Phase

Once the private key and the public-key certificate have been generated and appropriately distributed, the *issued* phase of the key/certificate life cycle management begins. This phase includes

- *Certificate Retrieval*—Retrieval of a certificate from a remote repository.

- *Certificate Validation*—Determining the validity of a certificate (including certificate path validation as described in Chapter 9, "Trust Models").

- *Key Recovery*—Retrieval of keying material from a CA or trusted third party when normal access to that material is no longer possible.

- *Key Update*—Automatic generation of a new public/private key pair and issuance of the corresponding certificate when a legitimate key pair is about to expire.

Certificate Retrieval

Certificate retrieval is concerned with the ability to readily access an end-entity certificate when and as required. As discussed in the "Certificate Dissemination" section earlier, the need to retrieve an end-entity certificate can be driven from two separate usage requirements:

- The need to encrypt data destined for another end-entity

- The need to verify a digital signature received from another end-entity

When encrypting data for one or more recipients, it is necessary to retrieve the encryption certificate of each recipient. The most common application of this requirement is to support key management between the originator of the protected data and the intended recipient(s). This allows for symmetric encryption of the data (for example, an e-mail message) using a newly generated secret key; and this secret key can then be encrypted in the public key of each recipient (which is extracted from each recipient's encryption certificate). As a reminder, both symmetric and asymmetric cryptographic techniques are discussed in Chapter 2.

In the case of digital signature verification, the verification certificate of the originator is typically sent with the signed data as part of the protocol exchange. This avoids the need to look up the requisite verification certificate from a remote repository. However, it is also possible that retrieval of verification certificates from a remote repository might be preferred in some environments (for example, when the originator is forced to use an extremely low bandwidth communication channel).

Certificate Validation

Certificate validation is concerned with assessing the legitimacy of a given certificate. Certificate validation is performed before cryptographic operations based on that certificate are permitted. At a minimum, the validation logic includes the following:

- Verification of the certificate's integrity (as described in Chapter 6).

- Assurance that the certificate was issued by a trusted CA (including certificate path validation, as described in Chapter 9).

- The validity period of the certificate is appropriate (that is, the time of use is between the Not Before and Not After dates/times as specified within the certificate).

- The certificate is being used in compliance with any intended usage and/or policy restrictions.

Key Recovery

As discussed under the "Key Backup" section earlier in this chapter, it is extremely important to provide for an automated key backup and recovery facility in a comprehensive PKI. Inevitably, some number of end-users will lose access to the private keying material that is used for encryption purposes. Without a key backup and recovery capability, this could result in the permanent loss of enterprise-critical information. Thus, the key management life cycle includes the ability to recover private encryption keys from a remote backup facility such as a trusted key recovery center or a CA.

Note
The discussion related to the key backup and recovery capability is reserved for encryption/decryption key pairs only. Signing private keys should not be backed up because this will inhibit the ability to provide non-repudiation. However, verification certificates should be archived as discussed under the "Key Archive" section later in this chapter.

For reasons of scalability and to minimize the burden on both the PKI administrator and the end-user, this process must be automated to the maximum extent possible. Any comprehensive life cycle management protocol must include support for this capability [RFC2510].

Key Update

Certificates are assigned a fixed lifetime (based on the applicable certificate policy and/or CPS) when they are issued. When a certificate "nears" expiration, it is necessary to issue a new public/private key and the associated certificate. This is referred to as *key update*.

Although there is no universally agreed definition for what constitutes "near" in this context, it is suggested that key updates should occur automatically once 70 to 80 percent of the key lifetime has been exhausted, and the new keying material should then be used for all subsequent cryptographic operations. This should allow a reasonable transition time for relying parties to acquire the new certificate so as to avoid service outages related to possession of the expired certificate.

As discussed in Chapter 6, private keys used for signing purposes may also have a specified lifetime. The specified validity period may be less than or equal to the expiration time of the associated verification certificate. If the private key expires before its companion certificate, the threshold established for the key update should be based on the private key expiration rather than the verification certificate expiration so that the end-entity is always in possession of a valid signing key.

> **Note**
>
> We emphasize the fact that key (and certificate) update should occur *before* the current certificate (or associated private key, if applicable) expires. This is to avoid any delays or gaps in the ability of the end-entity to conduct business without any unnecessary interruption. Certificate update *after* the previously issued certificate expires essentially forces a reset to the initialization phase, which will involve direct user interaction that could have otherwise been avoided.

For reasons of scalability, this process must be automated, and any comprehensive life cycle management protocol must include support for this capability [RFC2510]. In addition, this process should be totally transparent to the end-user.

Cancellation Phase

The key/certificate life cycle management concludes with the *cancellation phase*. This phase includes the following:

- *Certificate Expiration*—Natural expiration of a certificate.

- *Certificate Revocation*—Asserting that an otherwise legitimate certificate (and associated private key) is no longer valid.

- *Key History*—Maintaining a record of relevant keying material (typically with the end-entity) so that data encrypted by keying material that has subsequently expired can be decrypted.

- *Key Archive*—Secure third-party storage of keying material for key history recovery, audit, and dispute resolution purposes.

Certificate Expiration

As discussed in Chapter 6, certificates are assigned a fixed lifetime at the time of issuance (as indicated by the Not Valid After date/time within the certificate). Eventually, the established validity period of a given certificate will expire.

When a certificate expires, the following three things can occur with respect to the end-entity associated with that certificate:

- *No action*—The end-entity is no longer enrolled in the PKI.

- *Certificate renewal*—The same public key is placed into a new certificate with a new validity period.

- *Certificate update*—A new public/private key pair is generated, and a new certificate is issued (although this step should take place before the certificate expires, as discussed in the "Key Update" section earlier in this chapter).

Certificate Renewal versus Certificate Update

The notion of *certificate renewal* is different than *certificate update*. The specific difference is that certificate renewal preserves the original public/private key pair, whereas certificate update does not (that is, a new public/private key pair is generated). Presumably, certificate renewal is used when the circumstances associated with the issuance of the original certificate have not changed, and the cryptographic strength of the public/private key pair is still thought to be sound.

However, it is dangerous to renew certificates unless certain precautions are taken. Specifically, you must be careful to ensure that digital signatures produced under the auspices of one set of certificate attributes can be distinguished from digital signatures produced under another set of certificate attributes. It has been suggested that one method for achieving this is to always (securely) couple the appropriate verification certificate with the digital signature.

Certificate Revocation

As discussed in Chapter 8, "Certificate Revocation," certificate revocation is concerned with the timely cancellation of a given certificate before it might naturally expire. The requirement to revoke a certificate can stem from a number of factors, including suspected private key compromise, a change in job status, or termination of employment. The specific reason codes are defined in the X.509 Recommendation [X.509], and they are described further in Chapter 8.

Under certain circumstances, an end-user may personally initiate the revocation of his/her own certificate (for example, due to suspected compromise of the corresponding private key). Such a request may be initiated on-line directly to a RA or CA. Alternatively, the end-user may need to contact the RA or CA through some other means (for example, via telephone or through physical presence). For example, this would be necessary when the end-user's laptop or smart card has been lost or stolen. In either case, the RA can be used to initiate the Certificate Revocation on the end-user's behalf (the functionality of a RA is not limited to registration). Figure 7.3 illustrates these two scenarios. Of course, authorized administrators will also have the capability to revoke end-entity certificates when circumstances warrant.

Figure 7.3   Certificate revocation sample scenarios.

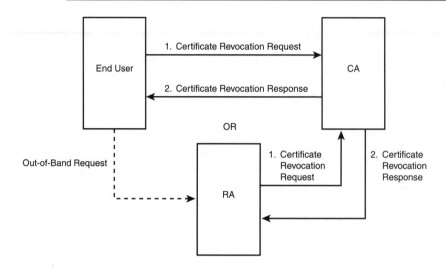

Key History

Because encryption keys eventually expire, there is a danger that encrypted data could become unrecoverable if the appropriate steps are not taken. Specifically, it is necessary to reliably and securely store keying material even though it has expired. This is referred to as *key history*.

The requirement for this service is mainly for confidentiality keys. Specifically, private keying material used for decryption must be stored so data that has been encrypted using the corresponding encryption public key can be recovered in the future. Some would argue that key history also applies to keys used for digital signature purposes, although this is more appropriately satisfied through key archive (as discussed in the next subsection).

Key history information is typically stored local to the owner for easy retrieval when necessary. However, it could also be stored with a CA or other trusted party, assuming that an automated mechanism is available to securely retrieve the necessary keying material when and as required.

Key Archive

Key archive is the long-term storage of keying material (including encryption and verification certificates) typically supported by a CA or other trusted party. Key archive differs from key history in the sense that archival can be used for audit purposes as well as to help resolve disputes, especially when coupled with trusted time stamp and notarization services. These concepts are discussed further in Chapter 5, "PKI-Enabled Services."

Note

Key history is typically directly coupled with the end-entity to provide easy access to that end-entity's expired keying material when attempting to access data that has been encrypted in a key that has since expired. *Key archive* is a service typically provided by a third party, and it involves the storage of keying material associated with many end-entities. The services provided by the key archive may include (or be coupled with) notarization and time stamp services, audit trails, and/or restoration of an end-entity's key history. The latter service would be necessary when the local key history of an end-entity is lost or destroyed. The key history of a given end-entity can be restored by the key archive facility in response to a request from the owner of the key history, or in response to a request from someone authorized to access that keying material in the absence of the end-entity.

Finally, a key archive facility may be necessary when attempting to verify a digital signature created by what is now expired keying material. Retrieval of the expired public key certificate is required in this case (assuming that the public key certificate is not available with the digitally signed data). This may also be coupled with a notarization service that could be used to prove that the signing private key was valid at the time the digital signature was created (even though that key has since expired).

Summary

This chapter has addressed the various phases that comprise the comprehensive key/certificate life cycle management. Each of these phases was discussed in detail, and various issues associated with each phase have been identified.

The importance of a comprehensive key/certificate life cycle management has been addressed, and various pointers to additional information within this book have been provided. In particular, the details regarding certificate revocation can be found in Chapter 8, the certificate dissemination mechanisms are described in Chapter 11, and the requirements associated with client-side software are discussed in Chapter 12, "PKI Operational Considerations."

References

[CMC]   Myers, M., X. Liu, J. Schaad, and J. Weinstein. *Certificate Management Messages over CMS*. Internet Draft. <draft-ietf-pkix-cmc-04.txt>. (Subject to update; refer to www.ietf.org for latest edition).

[FIPS]   National Institute of Standards and Technology. *Federal Information Processing Standard (FIPS) 140-1, Security Requirements for Cryptographic Modules*. (11 January 1994).

[PKCS7]   Kaliski, B. *PKCS#7: Cryptographic Message Standard*. Version 1.5. RSA Laboratories.

[PKCS10]   Kaliski, B. *PKCS#10: Certification Request Syntax Standard*. Version 1.5. RSA Laboratories.

[RFC2510]   Adams, C. and S. Farrell. Internet X.509 Public Key Infrastructure Certificate Management Protocols. Internet Request for Comments 2510 (March 1999).

[RFC2511]   Myers, M., C. Adams, D. Solo, and D. Kemp. Internet X.509 Certificate Request Message Format. Internet Request for Comments 2511 (March 1999).

[X.509]   ITU-T Recommendation X.509. "Information Technology—Open Systems Interconnection—The Directory: Authentication Framework." June 1997 (equivalent to ISO/IEC 9594-8, 1997).

CHAPTER 8

Certificate Revocation

As discussed in Chapter 6, "Certificates and Certification," certificates are used to bind an identity with their corresponding public key. Normally, this binding is valid for the full lifetime of the issued certificate. However, there are circumstances when an issued certificate should no longer be considered valid, even when the certificate has not yet expired. Reasons for revocation vary, but they may involve anything from a change in job status to a suspected private key compromise. Therefore, an efficient and reliable method must be provided to revoke a public key certificate before it might naturally expire.

Note that the frequency with which revocation information is updated and posted is an extremely important consideration. The acceptable delay associated with knowing that a certificate should be revoked and actually disseminating this information to the relying parties who are processing that certificate must be established. In some environments, this delay may be relatively generous (say on the order of hours or perhaps even days). In other environments, even minimal delay could be considered intolerable. The delay between the knowledge that the certificate should be revoked and actually posting the revocation information in a form that can be retrieved by a relying party is referred to as *revocation delay*. Revocation delay must be specified as part of the governing Certificate Policy, and the revocation techniques used within a given domain must adhere to that policy.

Certificate Revocation can be implemented in a number of ways. One method is to use periodic publication mechanisms such as *Certificate Revocation Lists (CRLs)*, which can be instantiated in a number of different forms or variations. There are also alternative on-line query mechanisms such as the *Online Certificate Status Protocol (OCSP)*. It is the purpose of this chapter to explore the various options that have been, or are being, defined. Circumstances where the traditional notion of revocation information may not be required or desired will also be explored in this chapter.

> **Note**
>
> This chapter does not address specific retrieval mechanisms or protocols unless it is an explicit part of the revocation method itself (as in the case of OCSP). In general, any number of protocols can be used to retrieve the revocation information described in this chapter, including the Lightweight Directory Access Protocol (LDAP), the File Transfer Protocol (FTP), and the Hypertext Transfer Protocol (HTTP). These retrieval mechanisms are addressed in Chapter 11, "PKI Information Dissemination: Repositories and Other Techniques."

Periodic Publication Mechanisms

The purpose of this section is to describe the various periodic publication mechanisms available. The periodic publication mechanisms discussed within this section are

- Complete Certificate Revocation Lists (CRLs)

- Authority Revocation Lists (ARLs)

- CRL Distribution Points (also known as Partitioned CRLs)

- Delta CRLs

- Indirect CRLs

- Enhanced CRL Distribution Points and Redirect CRLs

- Certificate Revocation Trees (CRTs)

Generally, these periodic publication mechanisms can be considered "pre-publication" techniques characterized by issuing the revocation information on a periodic basis in the form of a signed data structure. All but one of these techniques (CRTs are the exception) are based on the same basic data structure referred to as a *Certificate Revocation List* or *CRL*, as discussed in the following section, "Certificate Revocation Lists (CRLs)." The remaining subsections are devoted to the periodic publication mechanisms listed earlier.

Certificate Revocation Lists (CRLs)

Simply stated, *CRLs* are signed data structures that contain a list of revoked certificates. The integrity and authenticity of the CRL is provided by the digital signature appended to the CRL. The signer of the CRL is typically the same entity that signed the issued certificate. However, the CRL may be signed by an entity other than the certificate issuer, as discussed in the subsection, "Indirect CRLs," later in this chapter.

Note

Given that the CRL is protected when issued, the protocol exchanges used to convey the revocation information to the relying party need not be signed. This is due to the fact that the integrity of the CRL is already provided through the digital signature on the CRL itself.

CRLs can be cached to enhance performance. Caching of CRLs also facilitates the ability to verify certificates while working off-line. Of course, the ability to cache CRLs and the reliance placed in a cached CRL must be in accordance with the applicable Certificate Policies.

Currently two different versions of a CRL are defined. Version 1 was defined in the original X.509 specifications (circa 1988). Note that Version 1 CRLs are inherently flawed for several reasons:

- Scalability concerns (that is, the size of a Version 1 CRL could easily grow beyond acceptable limits)

- Functionality limitations specifically related to the inability to extend the CRL with additional features when needed

- The fact that Version 1 CRLs are subject to CRL substitution attacks (that is, it is possible to maliciously substitute one CRL for another without detection)

Version 2 CRLs solve these problems by introducing the notion of *extensions*—much the same as the introduction of extensions with Version 3 X.509 public key certificates as discussed in Chapter 6. Certain extensions have been defined on a per-revoked-certificate-entry basis, and others are defined on a per CRL basis, as described in the following subsections. Note that extensions may be marked critical or non-critical. An extension marked critical should be processed and understood by the relying party, although X.509 does provide for some degree of flexibility that can be applied under certain circumstances [X.509, Section 11.2, Note 4]. Non-critical extensions may be gracefully ignored if they are not understood by the relying party (that is, the extension can be ignored without any further action on the part of the relying party).

Note

Although X.509 defines certain requirements associated with the standard fields and extensions of a certificate, a number of details must be further specified. As discussed in Chapter 18, "Standards: Necessary but Not Sufficient," this is due to the fact that many standards tend to be general in nature, and additional levels of specificity are required to realize interoperability. As an example, RFC2459 has been introduced by the Internet

continues

Engineering Task Force (IETF) Public Key Infrastructure X.509 (PKIX) Working Group to address specific certificate and CRL profiles associated with the Internet.

Although RFC2459 is targeted for the Internet community, a number of useful recommendations could apply in the Enterprise environment, and consistency should be maintained wherever possible. Therefore, references to some of the recommendations made within RFC2459 will be provided where appropriate.

RFC2459 was formerly known as PKIX Part 1.

The generic structure of a Version 2 CRL is represented in Figure 8.1.

Figure 8.1   Version 2 CRL structure.

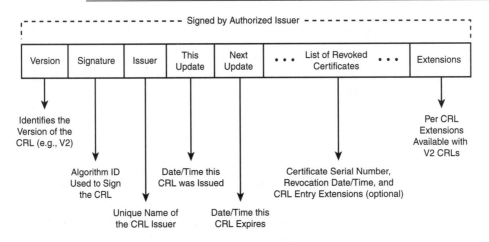

The fields represented within Figure 8.1 are defined as follows:

- *Version*—Indicates the version of the CRL (either the value is 2, or the field is not present indicating that it is a Version 1 CRL; that is, this field was not defined as part of the Version 1 CRL syntax).

- *Signature*—Indicates the object identifier of the algorithms used to calculate the digital signature on the CRL. For example, the object identifier for Message Digest 5 (MD5) with RSA might be present, indicating that the digital signature is an MD5 hash encrypted using RSA.

- *Issuer*—The Distinguished Name (DN) of the CRL issuer (that is, the signer of the CRL)—must always be present and unique.

- *This Update*—The time that this CRL was issued, which may be represented in UTC Time or in Generalized Time (however, RFC2459 has specific rules associated with the use of these time representations).

- *Next Update*—Optionally, the time that the next CRL will be issued (note that the same time representations for This Update also apply here and that RFC2459 actually mandates the use of this field even though it is designated as Optional in X.509).

- *Revoked Certificates*—The list of revoked certificates, where each certificate is referenced by a unique identifier (that is, it contains the unique serial numbers of the revoked certificates, not the actual certificates). Each entry also includes the time that the certificate was no longer considered valid and, optionally, it may include per entry extensions as discussed further in the following "Per-Entry Extensions" section.

Per-Entry Extensions

The X.509 standard defines four extensions that can be used on a per-entry basis. This allows additional information to be conveyed with each individual revocation, which was not possible with Version 1 CRLs. The per-entry extensions are

- *Reason Code*—The reason the certificate was revoked. Reason Codes include key compromise, CA compromise, affiliation change, superseded, cessation of operation, certificate hold, remove from CRL, and unspecified.

- *Certificate Issuer*—The name of the certificate issuer, which is only required for Indirect CRLs as described in the "Indirect CRLs" section later in the chapter. If the Certificate Issuer extension is present, it must be marked critical in accordance with X.509.

- *Hold Instruction Code*—Used to support the temporary suspension of a certificate. The suspended certificate can be subsequently reinstated or permanently revoked. The specific action to be taken when this extension is encountered is identified by an OID present in this extension.

- *Invalidity Date*—The known (or suspected) time that the certificate was no longer considered valid.

Note

The utility of the Hold Instruction Code has been the topic of some debate. Some have questioned the usefulness of temporarily suspending the use of a certificate while others see legitimate business reasons for implementing this capability. RFC2459 does define several OIDs that can be used in the Internet. Specifically, three hold instruction codes have been defined representing None, Call Issuer, and Reject. However, there are currently no known implementations of this capability.

Per-CRL Extensions

There are also a number of CRL extensions that have been defined on a per CRL basis. The standard CRL extensions are

- *Authority Key Identifier*—Unique identifier of the key that should be used to verify the digital signature calculated over the CRL. The Authority Key Identifier is used to distinguish between multiple keys that apply to the same CRL issuer (the generation of this field is mandated by RFC2459). Multiple (unexpired) keys may exist for the same CRL issuer for a number of reasons, including during overlapping periods of time to facilitate CA key rollover (see Chapter 7, "Key and Certificate Management," for additional information regarding key rollover or update).

- *Issuer Alternative Name*—One or more alternative name forms associated with the CRL issuer. The Issuer Alternative Name is used to identify the CRL issuer using something other than the DN designated in the Issuer Name field (for example, an IP address, DNS name, RFC-822 e-mail address, and so on).

- *CRL Number*—Unique serial number relative to the issuer for this CRL. It is a monotonically increasing integer that allows the detection of missing CRLs for any given CRL issuer. Although this extension is always marked non-critical, the generation of this field is mandated by RFC2459.

- *Issuing Distribution Point*—Indicates the name of the CRL distribution point (if any) and the types of certificates contained within the CRL (for example, end-user certificates only, CA certificates only, and/or certificates revoked for this reason only). When applicable, it is also used to indicate that the CRL is an Indirect CRL (additional information on Indirect CRLs is provided in the section, "Indirect CRLs," later in the chapter). Note that this extension, if present, must be marked critical in accordance with X.509.

- *Delta CRL Indicator*—When applicable, indicates that this CRL is a delta CRL as opposed to a base CRL (as discussed in the section, "Delta CRLs," later in the chapter). This extension, if present, must be marked critical in accordance with X.509.

Private Extensions

Private extensions can also be defined in accordance with X.509 on both a per-entry and per-CRL basis. Private extensions are typically defined for domain specific use. As recommended in RFC2459, care should be exercised to avoid interoperability problems with other domains that do not recognize any privately defined extensions. Specifically, private extensions should not be marked critical unless it is absolutely essential to meet the operational requirements within a specific domain. Of course, this is true regarding any extension, standard or private.

Note

Certificates are not actually recorded in the CRL; only a reference to the revoked certificate is included (for example, the unique serial number). Further, when the revoked certificate eventually expires (that is, when the "not valid after" date/time has been reached), it is no longer necessary to retain the serial number of that certificate on any subsequently issued CRLs. However, if a certificate is revoked, it should appear on at least one CRL (even if the certificate validity period has subsequently expired between the time revocation first occurred and the time the next CRL was issued). This is to ensure that evidence that a given certificate was revoked before it actually expired can be recorded and archived appropriately.

However, the information associated with that certificate (that is, when it was revoked, revocation reason, and so on) must be securely archived for future reference. This will help in any dispute resolution that may be encountered in the future.

Complete CRLs

It is possible to create complete CRLs so that all revocation information associated with a particular CA domain is posted on a single CRL. Complete CRL postings may be appropriate for some CA domains, particularly where the number of end-entities is relatively small.

However, there are two primary criticisms levied against the use of complete CRLs:

- First is the issue of scalability. Given that revocation information must survive throughout the life of an issued certificate, it is conceivable that full CRL postings can become quite voluminous in some domains. While this is not a concern for relatively modest sized communities, it is easy to see that this can become an issue in the larger domains.

- The second concern is related to the timeliness of the posted Certificate Revocation information. As the CRL size grows, it is reasonable to expect that the CRL validity period would be fairly generous, because continual downloading of new, voluminous CRLs every time a certificate is validated would represent unacceptable performance degradation with respect to network resources.

Although it is difficult to pinpoint the exact threshold where complete CRL postings would become too voluminous for a given CA domain, it is possible to identify the primary factors likely to dictate this threshold. Specifically, the number of end-entities, the probability of revocation, the validity period of the issued certificates, and the certificate serial number size will all have an impact on the size of a given CRL.

Given that it is reasonable to conclude that there will be a significant number of environments where this threshold will be exceeded, it is fair to conclude that complete CRL postings will not be a viable alternative in many instances. Fortunately, a number of standard alternatives exist to help alleviate this problem, as discussed throughout the remainder of this chapter.

Authority Revocation Lists (ARLs)

An *ARL* is actually a CRL devoted exclusively to revocation information that is associated with CAs. Thus, by definition, ARLs do not contain end-user Certificate Revocation information. An ARL is identified using the Issuing Distribution Point extension, as described earlier.

ARLs are used to revoke the public key certificates of other CAs. The issuer of an ARL is typically either a superior CA (that is, it is responsible for revoking any subordinate CAs), or the issuing CA is revoking a cross-certificate issued by that CA. (The concepts associated with superior, subordinate, and cross-certified CAs are discussed further in Chapter 9, "Trust Models.") Support for Indirect ARLs is also possible. When validating a certificate path, a valid ARL must be available for each CA that has signed one or more certificates in that path.

Note

Revocation of CA certificates is expected to be quite rare. Generally, a CA certificate need only be revoked when it is decommissioned, or when compromise of the CA's private key is known or suspected. Note also that in a strict rooted hierarchy, revocation of any given superior CA impacts all subordinate CAs and all end-entities that fall under any of the affected CAs. The "higher" in the tree the revocation occurs, the more widespread the effect. Cross-certification has the distinct advantage that revocation of any given CA does not impact the internal operation of any other CA domain. These concepts are discussed further in Chapter 9.

CRL Distribution Points

CRL Distribution Points (sometimes referred to as *Partitioned CRLs*) allow revocation information within a single CA domain to be posted in multiple CRLs. CRL Distribution Points have two significant benefits over complete CRLs:

- The revocation information can be subdivided or partitioned into more manageable pieces to avoid the proliferation of voluminous CRLs.

- The certificates can point to the location of the CRL Distribution Point, so there is no need for the relying party to have prior knowledge of where the revocation information for a particular certificate might reside.

Thus, the syntax of the CRL Distribution Point extension enables one to identify the specific location of the corresponding CRL partition. For example, a CRL Distribution Point can identify a specific server (for example, using a DNS name or IP address), as well as the specific location within that server where the CRL partition can be found. (For example, a specific location within a Directory Information Tree of a public repository or the name of a file resident on a Web server.)

In summary, CRL Distribution Points offer a much more scalable alternative as compared to complete CRL postings. They can also be used to alleviate the performance issue when combined with proper partitioning and caching. However, one of the criticisms levied against the use of CRL Distribution Points is that the CRL partitions are fixed or static. The notion of a more dynamic partitioning scheme, which can be exploited through the use of CRL Distribution Points, is discussed in the following section, "Enhanced CRL Distribution Points and Redirect CRLs."

Enhanced CRL Distribution Points and Redirect CRLs

One drawback associated with the use of CRL Distribution Points is that once the associated certificate is issued, the CRL partition pointed to by the CRL Distribution Point is fixed for the life of that certificate. It also implies that the issuing CA has a prior knowledge regarding how the CRL information should be partitioned, and that this partitioning cannot change over time. However, it may be desirable to make this more flexible so the CRL partition sizes and storage locations may vary over time (for example, to optimize performance as the size of the PKI community fluctuates).

Further, partitioning strategies could be based on a number of elements, including certificate serial number ranges, revocation reasons, certificate types, or any other range criteria that might apply to CRL information. It is, therefore, desirable to define new CRL extensions that would permit this more flexible and dynamic partitioning capability.

The notion of dynamic partitioning was first introduced in an early Internet Draft document referred to as *Open CRL Distribution Points*. This document has evolved significantly since it was first issued, including the adoption of certain concepts related to *Redirect CRLs* as described in *A General, Flexible Approach to Certificate Revocation* [Adams]. The latest version of the aforementioned document is now referred to as *Enhanced CRL Distribution Options* [Ford], which is available on-line as an IETF PKIX Internet Draft document.

An Introduction to Redirect CRLs

Redirect CRLs can be used to indicate where each CRL partition can be found. Redirect CRLs are based on existing standards and protocols, but they allow a more flexible partitioning

continues

approach than the static orientation offered by standard CRL Distribution Points. This is accomplished through the definition of a new (but standards compliant) CRL extension that allows the relevant revocation information to be repartitioned and/or relocated over time without impacting existing certificates.

A single Redirect CRL can be used to point to multiple CRLs. This is accomplished through the use of multiple scope statements, which identify the range and/or type of certificates that can be found on a given CRL partition. The range information can be based on certificate serial numbers or some other identifier(s), as discussed within this section. Thus, a relying party would retrieve the Redirect CRL (which can be pointed to by the CRL Distribution Point in the certificate being processed or referenced by some other means), and the Redirect Pointer is then parsed to find the appropriate partition based on the applicable scope statement. This concept is illustrated in Figure 8.2.

It is possible that this redirect process could be iterative, but this must be tempered with the additional performance overhead that would be incurred through multiple retrievals of the redirect information. In general, it is expected that one level of indirection will be sufficient.

Figure 8.2   Redirect CRL orientation.

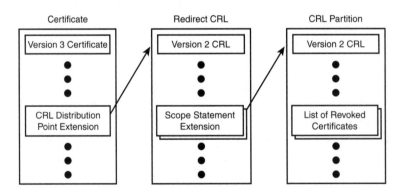

The ideas behind Redirect CRLs have been fully incorporated into the *Final Proposed Draft Amendment on Certificate Extensions* [FPDAM] through the introduction of two CRL extensions. The first extension, referred to as *CRL Scope*, defines the scope or applicability of a given CRL, and the other extension embodies the redirect or "referral" capability. This latter extension is referred to as a *Status Referral*, which incorporates everything related to the Redirect CRL as discussed earlier. The Status Referral extension also incorporates additional information, including

- Status information regarding the revocation information in question (for example, the time that the referenced CRL was last updated)

- Explicit identification of the type of referral; for example, CRL, Delta CRL, or Other (for non-CRL mechanisms).

Note

The *CRL Scope* extension syntax is similar to the existing *Issuing Distribution Point* extension syntax, but it adds several new attributes such as the name of the CA (necessary if different from the issuer of the referral), specified ranges such as serial number range or subject public key identifier range, and subtree name constraints. Given that the *Issuing Distribution Point* extension and the *CRL Scope* extension may contain overlapping fields (for example, they both can identify the *Distribution Point* name, and they both can contain the *Only Contains User Certs, Only Contains Authority Certs,* and *Only Some Reasons* flags), it is possible that the two extensions can conflict with one another. As such, these two extensions are not meant to be used together. However, as this is not explicitly prohibited, care must be exercised to ensure consistency between them if they both are used.

Delta CRLs

Delta CRLs are used to enhance timeliness without significantly impacting performance. In accordance with the 1997 version of X.509 [X.509], Delta CRLs can be used in conjunction with full CRL postings or with CRL Distribution Points. In the future, Delta CRLs are expected to afford even greater flexibility [FPDAM].

The idea behind Delta CRLs is to allow incremental postings of Certificate Revocation information, without requiring the generation of a complete, potentially voluminous CRL each time a certificate is revoked. However, Delta CRLs do not eliminate the requirement for either a full CRL posting or, alternatively, a CRL Distribution Point (although this may change in the future [FPDAM]). Delta CRLs are, by definition, based on some previously posted revocation information. This previous posting is referred to as a *base CRL*, and the Delta CRL contains revocation information that was not available when the base CRL was constructed. This allows for the publication of relatively small Delta CRLs that can be issued on a much more frequent basis than the base CRL, thus optimizing the often-competing goals of performance and timeliness.

It is possible to create and post multiple Delta CRLs against the same base CRL. Each subsequently issued Delta CRL contains the complete list of revoked certificates from the previously issued Delta CRL plus any new certificates that have been revoked. Thus, it is only necessary to retrieve the latest Delta CRL; it is not necessary to accumulate previously issued Delta CRLs.

As an example, consider an enterprise domain that needs to restrict the issuance of complete CRL postings to once a week for performance reasons. However, the security policy within this domain dictates that revocation information must be disseminated within eight hours of the time a certificate is considered to be revoked (that is, the revocation delay can be no longer than eight hours). Obviously, the performance issue and the timeliness requirement associated with the dissemination of the revocation information are at odds with one another. The solution is to issue the base CRL once a week and issue Delta CRLs every eight hours. Thus, the more voluminous CRL posting only needs to be downloaded and cached once a week, and the relatively small Delta CRLs can be downloaded as required.

Note that Delta CRLs can also be cached until the validity period associated with the Delta CRL expires. Alternatively, caching can be prohibited so that a Delta CRL would have to be retrieved every time a given certificate is validated—which may be a requirement in order to implement a near zero latency policy with respect to the dissemination of timely revocation information.

A relying party can determine if Delta CRLs are implemented through a number of ways. For example, this can be determined through a published policy statement (which may be associated with a specific policy OID contained within a given certificate). It can also be accomplished through detecting the presence of a *Freshest Revocation Information Pointer* certificate extension [Adams]. This certificate extension can be used to point directly to a Delta CRL, much the same as the CRL Distribution Point extension is used to point to a specific CRL partition. This extension has also been incorporated into the *Final Proposed Draft Amendment on Certificate Extensions* [FPDAM]; it is referred to as the *Freshest CRL* extension.

When Delta CRLs are disseminated through the use of a directory service, they are typically expected to reside under the issuing CA's directory entry under the *Delta Revocation List* attribute as defined in X.509. However, as noted earlier, the Freshest Revocation Information Pointer extension [Adams] or, more recently, the Freshest CRL extension [FPDAM] can be used as an alternative to point to a specific location where the Delta CRL resides.

Note

The wording in the 1997 X.509 Recommendation regarding the use of Delta CRLs is somewhat confusing. The *Final Proposed Draft Amendment on Certificate Extensions* [FPDAM] clarifies the intended use of Delta CRLs. (A *Proposed Draft Amendment*, or *PDAM*, is essentially a change proposal to an existing standard.) Specifically, the wording in the 1997 X.509 Recommendation implies that a full CRL posting must be generated and issued every time a Delta CRL is created.

Clearly, this is contrary to the overall intent and expected use of Delta CRLs. The FPDAM clarifies that a full CRL need not be generated and posted every time a new Delta CRL is issued. The FPDAM also includes several useful examples of how Delta CRLs are to be used in concert with their corresponding base CRL. Additional flexibility beyond that defined within the 1997 X.509 Recommendation has also been incorporated. The enhancements defined within the FPDAM are expected to be incorporated into the next version of X.509 (circa 2000).

Indirect CRLs

Indirect CRLs enable revocation information normally supplied from multiple CAs to be issued within a single CRL. Indirect CRLs can be used to reduce the number of overall CRLs that need to be retrieved by relying parties when performing the certificate validation process. For example, a single PKI domain may have several CAs. Rather than force a relying party to retrieve multiple CRLs (one for each CA), the domain may decide to improve efficiency by combining all of that domain's Certificate Revocation information into one Indirect CRL. This may also prove useful in inter-domain scenarios to reduce traffic load and cost. There is also the possibility that trusted third-party service providers may offer this capability as a "for fee" service. In all cases, the relying party must trust the Indirect CRL issuer to the same degree they trust the CA that issued the certificate in question.

The Indirect CRL is based on the same construct that defines a "normal" CRL, but there are certain extension values that distinguish an Indirect CRL from a CRL. For example, the *Indirect CRL* Boolean attribute within the Issuing Distribution Point CRL extension would be set to TRUE to indicate that this CRL contains revocation information from multiple CAs.

Given that the revocation information is originating from multiple sources, it is necessary to identify which CA is associated with the individual entries in the list of revoked certificates. Thus, there is a *Certificate Issuer field* associated with each entry. However, X.509 defines processing rules such that the Certificate Issuer field need not be set for every single entry. Specifically, if the Certificate Issuer field is empty, it can be assumed that the issuing CA is the last one that was specified. If it is the first entry and the Certificate Issuer field is empty, the issuing CA must be the same as the issuer of the CRL itself.

Although the X.509 standard does not specify how revocation information is to be conveyed between the individual CAs and the CA issuing the Indirect CRL, one can imagine that it might be reasonable for the generator of the Indirect CRL to collate revocation information based on individual CRLs issued by each CA. This would allow an existing standard mechanism to be exploited, and it would still have the benefit of reducing the number of CRLs each relying party must download. The reasonable assumption here is that the number of relying parties will far exceed the number of Indirect CRL issuers. However, the realized benefit is based on a number of factors, including assurance that the Indirect CRL does not become so large as to counter the performance benefit expected through combining revocation information from multiple sources.

Certificate Revocation Trees

Certificate Revocation Trees (CRTs) is a revocation technology developed by a U.S.-based company named Valicert. Essentially, CRTs are based on Merkle hash trees, where the tree itself represents all known Certificate Revocation information relevant to some known set of PKI communities. Although the information used to generate the CRT may be obtained from CRLs, the CRT technology is the only periodic publication mechanism discussed within this chapter that is not based on the CRL construct described under the "Certificate Revocation Lists (CRLs)" section in this chapter.

To generate the hash tree, a sequence of equations is generated for each participating CA. Each sequence represents a range, where the lower end-point on the range represents the serial number of a revoked certificate for a given CA. For example, an expression might be

$$CA_1 = CA_n \text{ and } 1138 \leq x < 2001$$

where X is the serial number of the certificate issued by CA_1 that is currently under evaluation. This expression effectively indicates that the certificate issued from CA_1 with serial number 1138 has been revoked, and that certificates issued by CA_1 with serial numbers 1139 through 2000 (inclusive) have not been revoked. The expressions are ordered sequentially relative to a given CA, and the set of expressions for a given CA is also sequentially ordered relative to all the other known CAs. The entire set of mathematical expressions represent all that is known about the certificates that have been revoked for the universe of CAs currently known to the entity generating the hash tree.

A sample CRT is represented in Figure 8.3. The nodes on the extreme left represent the hashes of each mathematical expression known to the entity generating the tree. As illustrated by the arrows in Figure 8.3, each adjacent pair of nodes at a given level within the tree is then combined into one. In the case where a pair exists, the two nodes are concatenated and hashed. The hash result is the value of the newly formed node to the right. If a pair does not exist (that is, there is an odd number of nodes at any given level), the single node is simply carried forward to the next level within the tree (as represented by Nodes $N_{2,2}$ and $N_{3,1}$ in Figure 8.3). This process occurs repeatedly until a final "root" node is calculated, as represented by the rightmost node in Figure 8.3. This final node is signed for integrity and authenticity purposes.

Figure 8.3   Sample CRT.

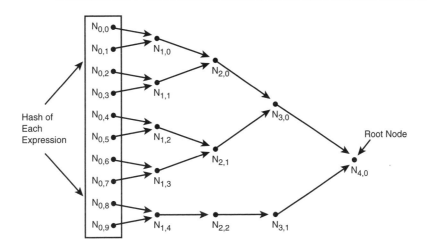

To determine if the certificate has been revoked, the relying party checks to see if the certificate serial number is the lower end-point on a range represented within the tree for a given CA. If it is, the certificate has been revoked. If not, it hasn't. This decision is based on comparing the certificate serial number being evaluated against the "nearest" equation to that value.

The integrity of this process must be verified, so the relying party must reconstruct the root node and compare it against the signed root node value. To accomplish this, the entity that generated the tree supplies the nearest range to the serial number in question, all the necessary supporting nodes, and the signed (and time stamped) root node. Again, this information is supplied by the entity that generated the tree, which is presumably a trusted third service or a service offered within a given enterprise domain. The necessary information can be supplied to the relying party so that it can perform the evaluation itself, or it can rely on a trusted server to perform the evaluation on its behalf.

The main advantage associated with CRTs is that they can represent a large amount of Certificate Revocation information in a very efficient manner. In fact, the size of a CRT is on the order of $\log_2 N$, where N is the number of revoked certificates.

On-Line Query Mechanisms

The purpose of this section is to discuss on-line query mechanisms for retrieving Certificate Revocation information. The on-line mechanisms differ from the periodic publication mechanisms in several respects—most notably because the on-line mechanisms typically require that the relying party be on-line whenever a question regarding the revocation status of a given certificate must be resolved. Periodic publication mechanisms are better suited for off-line operation because the revocation information can be cached.

The most popular on-line revocation mechanism available today is the *Online Certificate Status Protocol (OCSP)*. This is the primary topic addressed within this section. An alternative on-line mechanism that may be available in the future is also briefly discussed.

Online Certificate Status Protocol (OCSP)

The Online Certificate Status Protocol (OCSP) is documented in the proposed standard Request for Comments (RFC) entitled *X.509 Internet Public Key Infrastructure Online Certificate Status Protocol* [RFC2560]. OCSP is a relatively simple request/response protocol that offers a vehicle for obtaining on-line revocation information from a trusted entity referred to as an *OCSP responder*.

An OCSP request is comprised of the protocol version number (currently only Version 1 is defined), the service request type, and one or more certificate identifiers. The certificate identifier consists of the hash of the certificate issuer's DN, the hash of the issuer's public key, and the certificate serial number. Additional optional extensions may also be present.

Responses are also fairly straightforward, consisting of the certificate identifier, the certificate status (that is, "good," "revoked," or "unknown"), and the validity interval of the response associated with each certificate identifier specified within the original request. If the status of a given certificate is "revoked," the time that the revocation occurred is indicated and, optionally, the reason for revocation may also be included.

The validity interval consists of This Update and, optionally, Next Update. However, whether or not the OCSP response can be cached locally will ultimately be a policy decision dictated by the governing domain. Their intended use is consistent with the same fields in a CRL as described in the "Per-CRL Extensions" section earlier in the chapter. Like the request, the response may also contain optional extensions. OCSP also defines a small set of error codes that can be returned in the event that processing errors are encountered. The interaction between a relying party and an OCSP responder is illustrated in Figure 8.4. Figure 8.4 also illustrates that numerous revocation strategies can be implemented behind the OCSP responder as indicated by the dotted box labeled "Backend."

Figure 8.4   CSP component interaction.

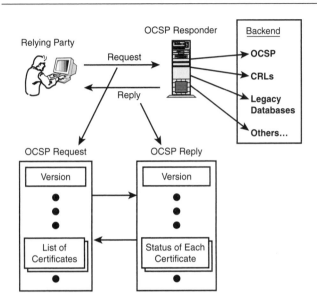

Note that the OCSP responses must be digitally signed to provide assurance that the response is originating with a trusted entity and that it is not altered in transit. The signing key may belong to the same CA that issued the subject certificate, a trusted third party, or an entity that has been approved (through delegation) by the CA that signed the subject certificate. In any case, the relying party must be able to "trust" the response, which inherently implies that the signer of the response must be "trusted" by the relying party. The relying party must, therefore, obtain a copy of the OCSP responder's public key certificate, and that certificate must be signed by a trusted source. Requests may also be signed, but this is an optional feature within the protocol.

To help a relying party discover the appropriate OCSP responder(s), OCSP embraces the Authority Information Access private certificate extension as defined within RFC2459, Section 4.2.2.1. This allows the location(s) of the OCSP responder(s) applicable to a particular certificate to be conveyed as part of the certificate itself—much the same as the standard CRL Distribution Points extension is used to point to a CRL partition. Alternatively, the locations of one or more OCSP responders can be configured locally or via some other means.

Understanding OCSP's Limitations

OCSP makes no claims whatsoever regarding the validity of the certificate other than its revocation status. In other words, OCSP is designed to indicate whether or not a given certificate has been revoked. OCSP does not verify that a certificate is within its validity period, nor does it ensure that the subject certificate is being used in the proper context as might be indicated through the Key Usage, Extended Key Usage, or any Policy Qualifier extensions that may be associated with the certificate. It is up to the relying party to perform all these checks via other means.

In addition, there seems to be some confusion regarding the utility of this protocol, especially in the sense of whether or not it can offer both real-time and up-to-date information regarding the revocation status of a given certificate. While the protocol itself offers a real-time response (assuming an appropriate OCSP responder is available on-line to service the requests), it does not necessarily mean that the reply from the OCSP responder will comprise a zero latency response regarding the current revocation status of the certificate.

Stated another way, OCSP is nothing more than a protocol. It does not specify the backend infrastructure that might be used to collect the revocation information. Thus, it does not necessarily eliminate the need for CRLs or other methods for collecting Certificate Revocation information, and the "freshness" of the information supplied by the OCSP responder will be only as up-to-date as the latency involved in obtaining the revocation information from their definitive source. This is not to say that it is impossible to implement a scheme based on OCSP that will be capable of offering near-zero latency revocation information—especially if the information is closely coupled with the OCSP service itself. However, it is inappropriate to simply assume that OCSP automatically offers fresh and up-to-date information even if it is considered to be a "real-time" service.

In addition, the responses from an OCSP responder must be digitally signed, and this may result in a significant performance impact. However, it also may be possible to preconstruct at least some subset of responses, which can be used to help alleviate some of the performance overhead. There are also issues associated with checking the revocation status of the OCSP responder's certificate that should be reviewed [RFC2560, Section 4.2.2.2.1].

Section 5 of the *X.509 Internet Public Key Infrastructure Online Certificate Status Protocol* [RFC2560] summarizes some of these concerns as well as others (for example, concerns with denial of service due to flooding or by introducing false error responses are also mentioned).

The Future: On-Line Transaction Validation Protocols

It has been noted that OCSP is limited in the sense that it can only supply information related to the revocation status of one or more certificates. It is reasonable to suggest that this does not meet the more general requirement to perform full certificate path validation or, even more generally, to authorize on-line transaction requests (for example, in association with consumer-to-business electronic commerce over the Internet).

Therefore, it can be argued that a more general and flexible protocol is required, and that such a protocol may eventually subsume the limited capabilities offered by OCSP. This protocol should provide a vehicle for validating a complete transaction, including digital signature verification, complete certification path validation, and purchase approval (based on a variety of payment methods). In any case, potential alternatives to OCSP are briefly introduced in Chapter 19.

Other Revocation Options

Circumstances exist in which the direct dissemination of revocation information to the relying party is either unnecessary or undesirable. There are at least two circumstances for this:

- There is the notion of short-lived certificates, where the validity period of those certificates is shorter than the associated need to revoke them. For example, an enterprise may decide that it can accept a revocation window of up to eight hours. If the certificates they issue were valid for eight hours or less, there would not be a requirement to revoke those certificates. However, it should be noted that this orientation is only useful in relatively closed environments where performance issues associated with continual certificate renewal can be mitigated. It also assumes that any client software acting on behalf of a relying party recognizes that there is no need to retrieve Certificate Revocation information when validating certificates originating within this particular domain. This could be achieved through a policy OID contained within the short-lived certificates. The concepts associated with Certificate Policies and the use of OIDs are discussed in Chapter 6.

- The second case is where the approval of any given transaction is always rooted with the same entity. This orientation is prevalent in the banking industry where on-line transactions are always brokered through the consumer's bank. In this case, the bank uses backend databases to map the identity of the consumer to the specific accounts the consumer is authorized to access. Because revocation information can be maintained along with the consumer account profile, and all transactions are routed through the bank, there is no need to disseminate this information to the consumer's desktop. This orientation is also popular with a number of prominent banks when it comes to authorizing consumer debit or credit card transactions over the Web. Essentially, the current "brick-and-mortar" merchant orientation is favored such that the merchant must always go to its bank to have a financial transaction authorized by that bank. The authorization process would include verification that the consumer's certificate had not been revoked, which is achieved through direct interaction with the consumer's bank.

Note that in the second case, the need to support a revocation capability has not been eliminated. It is simply that the method for facilitating the revocation need not be based on any of the methodologies described previously.

Performance, Scalability, and Timeliness

Intuitively, one can make certain assumptions (or at least ask intelligent questions) regarding the performance, scalability, and timeliness characteristics of the various revocation information dissemination techniques described in this chapter. The key is to understand the principles behind these various techniques, and to ask enough questions that will lead to solid engineering choices for a given PKI domain, or set of interoperable PKI domains.

Unfortunately, there is little operational information available with respect to performance in large-scale PKIs. There are, however, several papers available that explore performance issues associated with some of the techniques described in this chapter. One such example is *A Model of Certificate Revocation* [Cooper]. Another paper that addresses general PKI performance issues is *Limits to the Scale of a Public Key Infrastructure* [Moses].

In general, it is fair to assume that complete CRL postings will not scale in environments with a large number of end-users. The threshold where scalability becomes a factor will depend on a number of factors, including the number of end-users, the validity time of the issued certificates, and the frequency of revocation. CRL Distribution Points offer significant improvements in terms of performance and scalability, and Delta CRLs can be combined with CRL Distribution Points to achieve an efficient and timely revocation information distribution mechanism. Implementation issues associated with the dissemination of this information are explored further in Chapter 12, "PKI Operational Considerations."

On-line mechanisms such as OCSP may offer a viable service, but little is known with respect to the scalability and performance issues associated with the implementation of this type of model. For example, the number and physical distribution of OCSP responders that will be required to service a large, geographically distributed community of users requires further exploration. Further, the backend infrastructure is unspecified, and it may actually consist of a number of different revocation information distribution schemes.

It is also important to note that OCSP responses must be digitally signed to guarantee the integrity of the response. Given that these digital signature operations are required on a per transaction basis, it is likely that this will have a non-negligible impact on performance. As the number of queries increases, this impact could become rather significant. Further, OCSP is, by definition, an on-line service. An appropriate OCSP responder must be available in order to respond to a given query. This orientation is clearly not well suited for off-line operation.

In any case, timeliness is ultimately a function of policy, and it is up to the vendor community to respond to the specified requirement by selecting the appropriate revocation method(s).

Table 8.1 summarizes the various Certificate Revocation schemes and highlights specifics regarding each.

Table 8.1   Certificate Revocation Scheme Summary

Scheme	General Description	Remarks
CRLs	Signed data structure containing a list of revoked certificates; defined in [X.509].	Criticized from a performance, scalability, and timeliness perspective. However, standards-based alternatives to enhance performance and ensure scalability exist as defined in [X.509].
ARLs	A type of CRL devoted solely to revocation information associated with CAs; defined in [X.509].	Separation of end-user and CA certificate revocation information is both logical and found in common implementation practice.
CRL Distribution Points	A standard method to partition CRL information; defined in [X.509].	Offers relief in terms of performance and scalability. Timeliness still called into question.
Delta CRLs	A standard method to post timely revocation information without requiring a complete CRL or CRL Distribution Point update; defined in [X.509].	Can be used in conjunction with CRL Distribution Points to enhance performance, scalability, and timeliness.
Indirect CRLs	A standard method that allows revocation information from multiple CAs to reside on the same CRL; defined in [X.509].	Can be used to enhance performance when the performance advantage associated with concatenating Certificate Revocation information from multiple sources outweighs the requirement to otherwise retrieve that information from those multiple sources.
OCSP	An on-line capability to return the status of one or more certificates; defined in [RFC2560].	Although capable of offering real-time responses, it should be noted that the "freshness" of the response is only as good as the source of the revocation information itself, which might be subject to delays.

continues

Scheme	General Description	Remarks
Redirect and Referral CRLs	Relatively new concept to support dynamic CRL partitioning as well as multiple revocation information retrieval methods; defined in [FPDAM].	Concepts expected to filter into future releases of X.509 (circa year 2000).
CRTs	A technology that allows revocation information to be expressed in low-volume binary hash trees as defined by Valicert.	May become one of several alternatives for representing revocation information through a third-party service provider.
None of the Above	Either revocation information is not required or it is implemented in a manner other than those described earlier (for example, it might be tied into a backend legacy database).	May have a prominent role in the banking community (for example, on-line banking, where the customer interacts directly with the bank).

Summary

This chapter has identified a number of certificate revocation schemes, and it has discussed some of the pros and cons of each.

It seems clear that different techniques are well suited for some environments but not for others. It is, therefore, reasonable to assume that PKI vendors will be required to offer a number of choices with their product range to offer the best possible revocation strategy (or collection of strategies) for any given PKI domain. Therefore, it is likely that hybrids of these revocation techniques will be available in the future.

In order to understand revocation issues more fully, the reader is encouraged to review two related areas as follows:

- Certificate revocation dissemination options as discussed in Chapter 11
- Client-side software requirements as discussed in Chapter 12

References

[Adams]   Adams, Carlisle and Robert Zuccherato. *A General, Flexible Approach to Certificate Revocation*. 10 June 1998. (White paper available at www.entrust.com.)

[Cooper]   Cooper, David A. *A Model of Certificate Revocation*. National Institute of Standards and Technology. 17 August 1998.

[Ford]   Ford, Warwick and P. Hallam-Baker. *Enhanced CRL Distribution Options*. 7 August 1998. Internet Draft; <draft-ietf-pkix-ocdp-01.txt> (Subject to update—refer to www.ietf.org for latest edition).

[FPDAM]   Collaborative ITU and ISO/IEC meeting on the Directory. *Final Proposed Draft Amendment on Certificate Extensions*. Orlando, Florida. April 1999.

[Moses]   Moses, Tim. *Limits to the Scale of a Public Key Infrastructure* Proceedings of PKS '97. 27–30 April 1997.

[RFC2560]   Myers, M., R. Ankney, A. Malpani, S. Galperin, and C. Adams. X.509 Internet Public Key Infrastructure On-line Certificate Status Protocol— OCSP. Internet Request for Comments 2560. (June 1999).

[X.509]   ITU-T Recommendation X.509. "Information Technology—Open Systems Interconnection—The Directory: Authentication Framework." June 1997 (equivalent to ISO/IEC 9594-8, 1997).

9

Trust Models

This chapter discusses the concept of *trust models* in a PKI. It addresses questions such as the following:

- How is it determined which certificates an entity can trust?

- How can such trust be established?

- Under what circumstances can this trust be limited or controlled in a given environment?

An understanding of the prevalent PKI trust models is important because the trust models that might be implicitly assumed by someone new to this topic (that is, a PKI that parallels an organizational chart or an existing authorization schema in a company) are rarely used in practice.

This chapter considers the four primary trust models in use today (strict hierarchy of CAs, distributed trust architecture, Web model, and user-centric trust), along with a mechanism (cross-certification) that can, for some environments, serve an important role in extending and managing trust. This chapter also includes a brief examination of the sometimes-controversial issue of entity naming and a discussion of the difficulties and complexities that can arise during certificate path processing.

Before looking at trust models, however, it is important to clarify what is meant by *trust* in this context because different people can have quite different understandings of the word *trust*; this has led to (sometimes heated) debates in public meetings and on mailing lists. We have no intention of trying to resolve these disparate views or of trying to propose a new definition that will please everyone. Rather, we will simply state that the definition the ITU-T Recommendation X.509 specification [X.509, Section 3.3.23] gives is suitable for our purposes:

> Entity "A" trusts entity "B" when "A" assumes that "B" will behave exactly as "A" expects.

Therefore, trust deals with assumptions, expectations, and behavior. This clearly implies that trust cannot be measured quantitatively, that there is risk associated with trust, and that the establishment of trust cannot always be fully automated (for example, when "A" and "B" in preceding definition are human users). However, the concept of a trust model is useful because it shows where and how trust is initiated in the PKI, which can allow more detailed reasoning about the security of the underlying architecture as well as any limitations imposed by the architecture. In particular, in the context of a PKI, the preceding definition can be applied as follows: An end-entity trusts a CA when the end-entity assumes that the CA will establish and maintain an accurate binding of attributes to a public key (for example, will accurately represent the identity of an entity to whom it issues a certificate).

The word *trust* is frequently used in another way that is useful to us as well: PKI literature often refers to a so-called *trusted public key*. This phrase (which we adopt during certificate path processing discussions within this chapter) does not describe assumptions and expectations about behavior. Rather, a public key is said to be "trusted" by Alice when Alice is convinced that the public key corresponds to a private key that legitimately and validly belongs only to a specific named entity. Typically, this name or identifying information will appear along with the public key in a certificate, but the name may instead be known to Alice by other means (for example, it may be the identity of the root CA with which she is initialized into the PKI).

This chapter uses *trust* in both of the ways mentioned earlier. The intended meaning of the word *trust* at any given point within this chapter (that is, *trusted entity* versus *trusted public key*) should be clear from the context.

Strict Hierarchy of Certification Authorities

The strict hierarchy of Certification Authorities (CAs) is typically shown pictorially as an inverted tree with the root at the top, the branches extending downward, and the leaves at the bottom. In this inverted tree, the root represents a particular CA, commonly known as the *root CA*, which acts as a root of trust, or "trust anchor," for the entire domain of PKI entities under it. Below the root CA are zero or more layers of intermediate CAs (also known as *subordinate CAs* because they are subordinate to the root), represented by the intermediate nodes, from which further branches spring forth. The leaves correspond to non-CA PKI entities, often called *end-entities* or simply *end-users*. See Figure 9.1.

The term "root," while conveniently conjuring up the image given previously as the starting point for a large tree configuration with numerous branches and leaves, actually portrays something more fundamental. The root is not simply a starting point for a network, communications, or subordination architecture; it is a starting point for trust. All entities in this community (end-entities as well as any intermediate CAs) hold this public key as their trust anchor, their starting or ending point of trust for all certificate verification decisions. Thus, it is appropriate to refer to this key as a "root" even if the configuration has no intermediate CAs (looking more like a bush than a tree), or if the configuration is drawn in any other manner.

Note

Note that in some hierarchies an upper-level CA may certify end entities as well as other CAs. While the standards do not preclude this, discussion of hierarchies in the literature typically tends to assume that a given CA will certify *either* end entities *or* other CAs (but not both). We will follow that convention in the text below, but it should be recognized that this is not meant to be restrictive.

Figure 9.1   Strict hierarchy of CAs trust model.

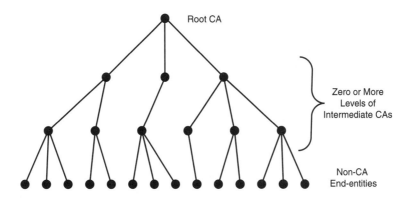

In this model, all entities in the hierarchy trust the single root CA. The hierarchy is established as follows:

1. The root CA certifies (that is, creates and signs the certificates for) zero or more CAs immediately below it.

2. Each of those CAs certifies zero or more CAs immediately below it.

3. At the second-to-last level, the CAs certify end-entities.

Each entity in the hierarchy (both intermediate CA and non-CA leaf) must be supplied with a copy of the root CA's public key. This public key installation process is the foundation for certificate processing for all subsequent communication in this model; therefore, it must be accomplished in a secure, out-of-band fashion. For example, an entity may acquire this key via a physical channel such as (paper) mail or via a telephone call. Alternatively, the key may be acquired electronically and then simply confirmed via the out-of-band mechanism (for example, the SHA-1 hash of the key—sometimes called the "fingerprint" of the key—may be sent in a letter by mail, printed in a newspaper, or read out over the telephone).

Note that in a multi-level strict hierarchy, end-entities are certified (that is, issued certificates by) the CA immediately above them, but their trust anchor is a different CA (the root). For shallow hierarchies in which there are no subordinate CAs, the root and the certificate issuer are identical for all end-entities. Such hierarchies are referred to as *trusted-issuer* hierarchies.

An end-entity, Alice, holding a trusted copy of the root CA public key, can verify the certificate of another end-entity, Bob, in the following way. Suppose that Bob's certificate is signed by CA_2, whose certificate is signed by CA_1, whose certificate is signed by the root CA. Alice (with the root's public key k_R) can verify the certificate of CA_1 and, therefore, extract a trusted copy of CA_1's public key k_1. Then, this key can be used to verify the certificate of CA_2, which similarly leads to a trusted copy of CA_2's public key k_2. The key k_2 can be used to verify Bob's certificate, leading to a trusted copy of Bob's public key k_B. Alice can now use the desired key k_B, depending on its type (see Chapter 2, "Public-Key Cryptography"), to encrypt messages for Bob, or to verify digital signatures Bob purportedly created. That is, by following a procedure such as the one outlined, secure communications between Alice and Bob can be enabled.

Note

It is interesting to note that the strict hierarchy of CAs trust model (along with interesting enhancements, such as "policy CAs" and name subordination) is the one that the failed *Privacy Enhanced Mail (PEM)* specifications [RFC1422, RFC1424] adopted. However, PEM failed not because a strict hierarchy is a fundamentally flawed model, but because the strict hierarchy is not appropriate for every environment (particularly the Internet). For some environments (for example, the U.S. Department of Defense PKI), such a model may be entirely suitable both in theory and in practice.

Distributed Trust Architecture

In contrast to strict hierarchy, in which all entities in the PKI community trust a single root CA, the *distributed trust architecture* distributes trust among two or more (perhaps many) CAs. That is, Alice may hold a copy of the public key of CA_1 as her trust anchor, and Bob may hold a copy of the public key of CA_2 as his trust anchor. Because these CA keys serve as trust anchors, it follows that each corresponding CA is the root CA for a strict hierarchy involving some subset of the total PKI community (CA_1 is the root for a hierarchy that includes Alice, and CA_2 is the root for a hierarchy that includes Bob).

If each of these hierarchies is a shallow, *trusted-issuer hierarchy*, then the resulting configuration may be referred to as a *fully-peered* architecture because all CAs are effectively independent peers (there are no subordinate CAs in the architecture). On the other hand, if each hierarchy is a *multi-level hierarchy* the result may be called a *full-treed* architecture. (Note that the root CAs are peers with each other, but each root acts as a superior for one or more subordinate CAs.) The *hybrid* architecture is also possible (with one or more *trusted-issuer hierarchies* and one or more *multi-level trees*); this configuration is illustrated in Figure 9.2.

Typically (although not always), the *fully peered* architecture is a planned deployment configuration within a single organizational domain (for example, within a single company), whereas the *fully treed* and *hybrid* architectures arise as a result of interconnecting independent, pre-existing PKIs from different organizational domains.

The point is that many enterprise domains deploy their own PKIs, and these PKIs do not necessarily emanate from a common root CA. The isolated PKI domains may be configured in a variety of ways, including a strict hierarchy, a fully peered architecture, or

Figure 9.2   Distributed trust architecture model.

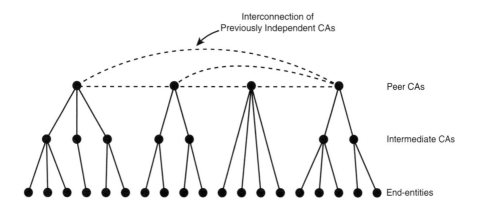

The process of interconnecting the peer root CAs is commonly known as *cross-certification*, although the term *PKI networking* is growing in use (particularly for the fully-treed and hybrid architectures). This topic, along with the related issue of certificate path processing in such an environment, is discussed later in this chapter. Note, however, that two different kinds of configuration are commonly employed for cross-certification: *mesh* and *hub-and-spoke*.

Mesh Configuration

In the mesh configuration, all root CAs are potentially cross-certified with each other. In particular, two root CAs will cross-certify whenever their respective communities need to communicate securely. In the fully connected case (sometimes called a *full mesh*), this requires roughly n^2 cross-certification agreements to be established when there are n root CAs, although in practice implementations would be expected to be somewhat less than fully connected (a *partial mesh*). Figure 9.2 illustrates a *partial mesh hybrid distributed trust architecture*. (It is not a full mesh because no direct cross-certification agreement is in place between the first and third CAs.)

Hub-and-Spoke Configuration

In the hub-and-spoke configuration, each root CA cross-certifies with a single central CA whose job is to facilitate such interconnection. This central CA is sometimes referred to as a *hub* CA with *spokes* out to the various root CAs (hence, the name of this configuration) and is sometimes referred to as a *bridge* CA, bridging communication gaps between pairs of roots. The attraction of this configuration is that the fully connected case requires only n cross-certification agreements for n root CAs (because each root CA cross-certifies only with the hub).

Note that the hub CA should not be viewed as a root for all the systems that cross-certify with it; the hub-and-spoke configuration does *not* create a hierarchy. The fundamental difference between these two trust models lies in which keys end-entities hold. In a strict hierarchy, all entities hold a trusted copy of the root CA key as an anchor (that is, a starting or ending point for certificate path processing). In the hub-and-spoke configuration, no end-entity holds a hub CA key as an anchor. Instead, each end-entity holds a trusted copy of the key of a CA in its own domain and, through certificate path processing, obtains the key of the hub CA, and then a CA in another domain, and eventually the key of the target end-entity in that domain.

Web Model

The *Web model* derives its name from its birth over the World Wide Web and its dependence on popular Web browsers such as Netscape Navigator and Microsoft Internet Explorer. In this model, a number of CA public keys are pre-installed in a standard, off-the-shelf browser. These keys define the set of CAs that the browser user will initially "trust" to act as roots for certificate verification. Note that although this set of root keys may be modified (for example, reduced or augmented) by the user, it is generally recognized that few browser users will be sophisticated enough, with respect to PKI and security issues, to understand or modify this aspect of browser behavior.

This model, similar on a cursory examination to the distributed trust architecture model, is fundamentally more similar to the strict hierarchy of CAs model. Rather than expanding the available subject community for a particular relying party, Alice, by interconnecting with the relevant domains, the Web model instantaneously makes Alice a relying party of all domains represented in the browser. For all practical purposes, each browser vendor has its own root, and it certifies the "root" CAs that are embedded in the browser. The only real difference is that the root CAs, rather than being certified by the browser vendor's root, are physically embedded in software releases as a means of effecting the secure binding between a CA name and its key. In essence, this is a strict hierarchy with an implied root (that is, the browser vendor is the virtual root CA and the first level down in the hierarchy is all the embedded CA keys). See Figure 9.3.

| Figure 9.3 | Web model. |

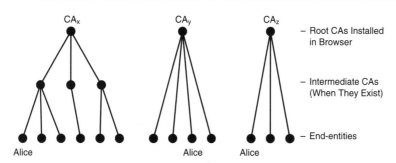

- Root CAs Installed in Browser

- Intermediate CAs (When They Exist)

- End-entities

The Web model has clear advantages in terms of convenience and simple interoperability. However, a number of security implications with this model should be taken into consideration when making deployment decisions for an environment. For example, because browser users automatically trust the full set of pre-installed public keys, security may be completely compromised if even one of those root CAs is "bad" (for example, fails to exercise any due diligence whatsoever in certifying entities). Therefore, Alice will believe that what purports to be Bob's certificate is a legitimate certificate for Bob, even if it is really Eve's public key together with Bob's name, signed by CA_{bad}, whose public key is embedded in the browser. Alice, therefore, may unintentionally divulge confidential information to Eve or accept Eve's bogus digital signature. The reason such an impersonation can succeed is that Alice is typically unaware which root key in the browser verified a given incoming certificate. Of the twenty or more root keys embedded in her browser, Alice may recognize only a handful of the CAs represented; the rest may be completely unknown to her. Yet, in this model, her software trusts *all* of them equally and implicitly so that a certificate signed by *any* of them will be accepted without question.

Note that a similar situation can occur in some of the other trust models as well. For example, in the distributed trust architecture, Alice may not recognize a particular CA, but her software will trust its key if the relevant cross-certificate is valid. The Web model is arguably worse, however. In the distributed trust architecture, Alice explicitly agrees to trust her local CA to "do the right things" with respect to PKI security (including cross-certifying with "appropriate" CAs). In the Web model, Alice may acquire a particular browser for a variety of reasons, none of which has anything to do with security. She, therefore, has no reason to assume that the browser will hold "appropriate" CA keys (from her security perspective).

If Alice is somewhat sophisticated with respect to PKI issues (and if her particular browser supports this), she may have the understanding and the diligence to check which root key verified a given incoming certificate. She can then decide, if she wishes, not to rely on a certificate signed by a CA she does not recognize. However, even this may not produce the desired result. For example, Alice may recognize and trust the root key associated with "CA Company, Inc.," but if the bad CA calls itself "CA Company, Ltd.," it is very unlikely that Alice will readily be able to distinguish between certificates that may be relied on and those that may not. Even if Alice's particular browser vendor was careful not to embed keys for two different CAs with such similar names, it may certainly happen that Alice trusts the CA named "Foo" and the company named "Bar," but not the CA named "Fred" who might issue a certificate to a rogue company calling itself "Bar." Again, without due diligence, Alice may simply see a certificate for "Bar" and think that all is well.

Another potential security consideration associated with the Web model is that there is no practical mechanism to revoke any of the root keys embedded in the browser. If it is discovered that one of the CAs is "bad" (as discussed earlier) or if the private key corresponding to any of the root (public) keys is compromised, it is effectively impossible to discontinue the use of that key in the millions upon millions of browsers around the world. This is partly because of the practical difficulty of getting an appropriate message to each of these sites and partly because the browser software itself is not written to understand such a message. Removal of the bad key from the browser, therefore, requires an explicit action on the part of each user in the world. This action would need to be taken immediately around the world; otherwise, some users would be safe while others would remain at risk. It may be asserted with a fairly high degree of confidence that such a worldwide, instantaneous user action will never occur.

Finally, for some contexts it is important to note that in the Web model there is essentially no opportunity for any kind of legal agreement or contract to be put in place between a user (relying party) and the CAs represented in the browser. The browser may be freely downloaded from a variety of Web sites, or perhaps it comes pre-installed in the operating system; a CA does not know (and has no way of determining) who its relying parties are, and users cannot, in general, be expected to be aware enough of the potential issues to contact the CAs directly. Thus, all liability, regardless of circumstances, is likely to rest with the relying party and cannot be transferred to the CA or to any other party.

User-Centric Trust

In the model typically referred to as *user-centric trust*, each user is directly and totally responsible for deciding which certificates to rely on and which to reject. This decision may be influenced by a number of factors, although the initial set of trusted keys often includes those of friends, family, or colleagues a given user knows personally. See Figure 9.4.

Figure 9.4   User-centric trust model.

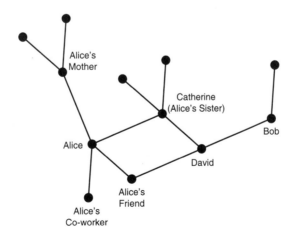

User-centric trust is probably best illustrated by the well-known security software program *Pretty Good Privacy (PGP)* [Zim95, Gar95], particularly in its more recent incarnations (version 5.0 and later). In PGP, a user builds (or effectively joins) the so-called "web of trust" by acting as a CA (signing the public keys of other entities) and by having his/her own public keys certified by others. When Alice later receives a certificate purportedly belonging to Bob, she will see that this certificate is signed by David, whom she does not know, but that David's certificate is signed by Catherine, whom she does know and trust (for example, Catherine may have a certificate signed by Alice herself). Alice may then decide to trust Bob's key (by trusting the chain of keys from Catherine to David to Bob), or she may decide to reject Bob's key (judging that the "unknown" Bob is too many links away from the "known" Catherine).

Because of its reliance on user actions and decisions, the user-centric model may be workable in a highly technical and highly interested community, but it is unrealistic for a general community (one in which many users have little or no knowledge of security or PKI concepts). Furthermore, such a model is generally inappropriate for corporate, financial, or governmental environments because these typically want or need to exercise some control over user trust (that is, such environments may want to enable or disable trust in a particular key or set of keys on an organization-wide basis). Such organizational trust policies cannot be implemented in any kind of automatic and enforceable way with the user-centric model.

Cross-Certification

Cross-certification is a useful mechanism for binding together previously unrelated CAs so that secure communications between their respective subject communities can be enabled. The actual mechanics of cross-certification (for example, the specific protocol messages exchanged) may be identical to certification (see Chapter 6, "Certificates and Certification," for a discussion of certification), except that both the subject and the issuer of the resulting cross-certificate are CAs (rather than the subject being an end-entity). When the distinction is important, the following terminology from RFC2510 can be used:

- If the two CAs belong to the same domain (for example, within an organization's CA hierarchy, where a CA at one level is certifying a CA at the next level below), the process is referred to as *intra-domain cross-certification*.

- If the two CAs belong to different domains (for example, when a CA in one company is certifying a CA in another company), the process is referred to as *inter-domain cross-certification*.

Cross-certification can occur in one or two directions. That is, CA_1 can cross-certify (that is, sign the identity and public key of) CA_2 without CA_2 cross-certifying CA_1; such *unilateral cross-certification* results in a single cross-certificate and would be the typical practice in the CA hierarchy mentioned earlier. Alternatively, CA_1 and CA_2 can cross-certify each other; such *mutual cross-certification* results in two distinct cross-certificates and can be a more common occurrence, for example, between companies wanting to enable secure communications between their respective employees.

According to the terminology given in the X.509 Recommendation [X.509], from the perspective of CA_1, a cross-certificate issued *for* it (that is, with CA_1 as the subject and some other CA as the issuer) is called a *forward cross-certificate*; one issued *by* it is called a *reverse cross-certificate*. If an X.500 directory is used as the certificate repository (see Chapter 11, "PKI Information Dissemination: Repositories and Other Techniques," on repository options), the appropriate forward and reverse cross-certificates may be stored in a *cross-certificate pair* structure in the directory entry of each relevant CA. This structure can be helpful in facilitating certificate path construction. See Figure 9.5.

Figure 9.5   Example of mutual cross-certification between CA_1 and CA_2.

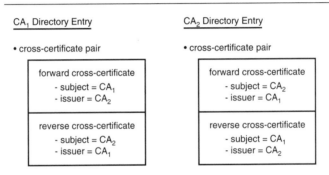

The mechanism of cross-certification can be used to extend trust between (or among) distinct relying party communities. In particular, cross-certification between two CAs is one way that a given CA can recognize that another CA is authorized to issue certificates in (typically a specified part of) a name space. (This is the fundamental trust extension mechanism for the distributed trust architecture but is equally applicable to the Web model. It can be used to characterize trust extension in the user-centric model as well, because in that model each user effectively acts as its own CA.) Thus, cross-certification allows otherwise disparate PKI domains to easily establish an interoperability path. The (undesirable) alternative would be to exchange root CA keys and to populate every end-entity's software or hardware tokens with the root CA key of the external domain.

For example, assume that Alice has been certified by CA_1 and holds a trusted copy of CA_1's public key, and that Bob has been certified by CA_2 and holds a trusted copy of CA_2's public key. Initially, Alice may trust only entities whose certificates have been signed by CA_1 because these are the certificates she is able to verify. She is unable to verify Bob's certificate (because she does not hold a trusted copy of CA_2's public key); similarly, Bob is unable to verify Alice's certificate. After CA_1 and CA_2 have cross-certified, however, Alice's trust can be extended to the subject community of CA_2—including Bob—because she can verify CA_2's certificate using her trusted copy of CA_1's public key, and then verify Bob's certificate using her now-trusted copy of CA_2's public key.

However, the distinct advantage that cross-certification brings to the concept of trust extension is *control*, using one or more of the standard extensions defined for cross-certificates, such as

- Name constraints

- Policy constraints

- Path length constraints

CA_1 may cross-certify CA_2 but limit in some desired way the subject community of CA_2 that the relying party community under CA_1 will trust. Trust can be extended, on an organization-wide basis within the domain of CA_1, only to certain individuals, only to certain groups, only for specific purposes, and so on, in the domain of CA_2. This kind of organizational control over trust extension, centrally determined by the CA_1 administrator, is difficult or impossible to achieve with the Web model or with the user-centric trust model. It also is irrelevant in a strict CA hierarchy model (because there is only one domain; there is no other domain to which trust can be extended).

In particular, through the *name constraints* certificate extension, CA_1 may stipulate that only certificates issued by CA_2 to subjects within a specified portion of the name space will be accepted as valid by the relying party community under CA_1. This portion of the name space may be constrained as required for the business purpose, encompassing a single user, a group, a department, the entire organization, or whatever naming restriction is relevant. Thus, for example, one company may use this mechanism to ensure that only certificates from the other company's purchasing department will be accepted as valid.

The *policy constraints* certificate extension provides a means to limit the purposes for which a certificate can be used. For example, the name constraints may indicate that all certificates from a particular company are "acceptable," but the policy constraints may limit the acceptable uses to e-mail (so that an arbitrary user certificate from that other company cannot be used to verify a signature on a legal contract).

Path length constraints (part of the *basic constraints* certificate extension) can be used to limit the number of cross-certificates that can appear in a valid certificate path. For example, CA_1 may explicitly decide that end-entity certificates issued by CA_2 are acceptable but prohibit certificates issued by any other CA with which CA_2 has cross-certified.

See "Internet X.509 Public Key Infrastructure: Certificate and CRL Profile" [RFC2459] for further discussion on name, policy, and path length constraints.

Entity Naming

A certificate is a signed data structure binding a key pair (explicitly the public key, but implicitly the private key as well) to an identity. But what is an *identity?* Ultimately, it must be something uniquely associated with a particular PKI entity, and it must be meaningful within a context of use. Otherwise, secure communication cannot be achieved: Alice uses a certificate for the purpose of encrypting data for Bob or for the purpose of verifying Bob's signature, but if the certificate is actually (unknown to Alice) associated with some other entity, security is effectively compromised.

Depending on the size of the domain, identity uniqueness may be simple, or very difficult, to achieve. In a small, closed environment, uniqueness may essentially come "for free;" even first names may be sufficient to distinguish between all entities. However, as environments get bigger, uniqueness gets harder to ensure; at the size of the Internet, some argue that globally unique names are a practical impossibility.

Considered in a theoretical light, global uniqueness of entity names is entirely achievable through the X.500 Distinguished Name mechanism (see Chapter 6 for a discussion of DNs). This is a hierarchical naming structure with a root at the top and a naming authority at every node (whose only purpose is to ensure the uniqueness of the nodes below it). The DN mechanism guarantees uniqueness if every entity that will be named in this way officially registers with the appropriate naming authority and accepts the name it is assigned, which is precisely what happens today with Internet Protocol (IP) addresses and RFC822 (e-mail) names; this is the basis for addressing and routing in modern electronic communications.

However, the DN mechanism has been less than entirely successful for at least two reasons:

- The utility of a Distinguished Name has never really struck a chord with the general public (due, at least in part, to the limited attraction of the X.500 Directory concept and the popularity and widespread use of the e-mail name as an alternative method to identify an entity).

- In many instances, a body that is authoritative for DNs does not exist: The naming authorities in the hierarchy are not a fundamental requirement for name assignment (that is, two entities can assign the same name to themselves entirely independent of any naming authority). Thus, global uniqueness is guaranteed only if everyone plays by the rules, but there is no way to ensure that such fair play will occur.

This situation has led some to seriously question the usefulness of entity names in certificates (see, for example, "SDSI—A Simple Distributed Security Infrastructure" [SDSI], The Simple Public Key Infrastructure charter [SPKI], and related work). In other contexts, the placeholder for a DN is retained in an X.509 certificate (because this is required by the standard syntax). However, provision is also made for "alternative" names of the subject, such as an IP address or an e-mail name (see the `subjectAltName` extension in the X.509 Recommendation [X.509] and in "Internet X.509 Public Key Infrastructure: Certificate and CRL Profile" [RFC2459]) to guarantee uniqueness of the total entity name and to provide a link to these other identity mechanisms.

Finally, it is worth noting that even if global uniqueness is difficult (perhaps impossible) to achieve, entity names almost always have local significance; that is, they are meaningful in a local environment. Therefore, it can be very useful for a certificate to bind a key pair to some form of name for a specific entity. In general, a useful practice is to rely on existing infrastructures where "identities" are already in place and authoritative naming registrars have already been established.

Certificate Path Processing

As alluded to in some of the trust model sections earlier, the purpose of certificate path processing is to find an unbroken path (or chain) of certificates between a given target certificate and a trusted key (a "trust anchor") and to check the validity of each certificate in this path. Ultimately, the final goal is for Alice to determine whether or not she can trust the public key in Bob's certificate (with respect to the purpose for which she would like to use it).

For more detail regarding path processing operations and algorithms, see the X.509 Recommendation [X.509] and "Internet X.509 Public Key Infrastructure: Certificate and CRL Profile" [RFC2459]; but in general, there are two phases to the processing:

- *Path construction* involves aggregating all the certificates necessary to form a complete path.

- *Path validation* involves examining each certificate in the path in turn, determining whether or not the key it contains can be trusted.

The target certificate (and, consequently, the contained public key) is trusted only if every certificate (and contained public key) in the path is found to be trustworthy.

Path Construction

Path construction can be a very complicated and time intensive operation, especially if a large number of cross-certificates are involved. This is because of the difficulties involved in locating the certificate of the entity that has signed a given certificate when that entity is outside the local environment. For example, assume that Alice is attempting to construct a path for Bob's certificate. Furthermore, assume that Bob was certified by CA_3, that CA_3 is cross-certified with CA_2 (among others), that CA_2 is cross-certified with CA_1 (among others), and that Alice holds a trusted copy of CA_1's public key. See Figure 9.6.

Figure 9.6   Path construction example.

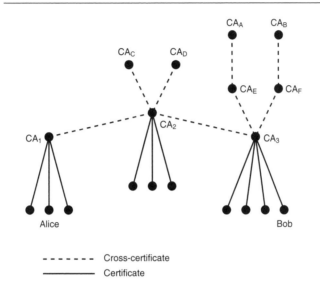

Because Alice holds Bob's certificate, she knows that CA_3 has certified Bob. Because CA_3 has cross-certified with several CAs (three in this example), Alice needs to determine which cross-certificate will add another link to her desired path. CA_1 has not signed any of CA_3's cross-certificates (that is, CA_E, CA_F, and CA_2 have signed them), so she needs to do some trial-and-error processing. She examines each of the cross-certificates associated with CA_E, CA_F, and CA_2 to see if CA_1 has signed any of these. In this example, CA_2 has a cross-certificate signed by CA_1, and so her path construction work is complete. Clearly, this task gets significantly more onerous if CA_3 and CA_2 have cross-certified with many other CAs and/or if the path between CA_1 and CA_3 involves many more intermediate CAs. In such cases, path construction may involve the use of graph-theoretic path-finding algorithms, including depth-first (not generally recommended, due to significant extra computation in the general case), breadth-first, or heuristic search techniques.

The underlying assumption in path construction is that Alice is able to retrieve (or other-wise acquire) all the certificates she needs in order to examine them and assemble the path. Chapter 11 covers certificate dissemination, storage, and retrieval.

Path Validation

Having constructed the certificate path, Alice now needs to determine if it is valid. As Chapter 6 has discussed, this involves doing the mathematical computation to see if each digital signature verifies. It also involves examining the validity period of each certificate (to ensure that the certificate has not expired); checking each revocation status (to ensure that the certificate has not been revoked); and looking at any applicable policies, key usage restrictions, name constraints, and so on.

Path validation is typically less onerous than path construction, but keeping track of name, policy, and path length constraints can get somewhat complicated, particularly if the path is relatively long.

Trust Anchor Considerations

It is worth noting that the trust model in use determines the choice of Alice's trust anchor. In particular, with the *strict hierarchy of CAs*, Alice's trust anchor is the CA that is logically furthest from her (the CA at the root of the hierarchy). With the *distributed trust architecture*, Alice's trust anchor is a CA that is logically closer to her (the root of the hierarchy covering her segment of the total PKI community, which may—for example, in the fully-peered architecture—even be the closest CA that actually certified her). In the *Web model*, Alice's trust anchor is really a set of anchors (the CA root keys that have come pre-installed in her browser). Finally, in the *user-centric trust model*, Alice's anchor is one or more CAs of her own choosing (which may be fine for her personal environment but less acceptable in a corporate environment).

The choice of trust model, therefore, plays an important role in determining the overall trust that can eventually be placed in the public key of the target certificate.

Summary

The trust model is an integral part of PKI architecture and operation. This chapter has given a brief introduction to four different trust models in use today, highlighting their similarities and differences.

Choosing the correct trust model (and its corresponding level of security) for the environment to be protected is of critical importance and is one of the early and fundamental decisions to be made when deploying a PKI.

Topics that form an important supplement to this material include the following:

- A good understanding of the environment under consideration for the PKI deployment; this discussion is presented in the chapters comprising Part III, "Deployment Considerations," of this book.

- A good understanding of the desired legal framework for PKI operation; see Chapter 13, "Legal Framework," for this discussion.

References

[Gar95]   Garfinkel, S. *PGP: Pretty Good Privacy*. Sebastopol, CA: O'Reilly and Associates, Inc., 1995.

[RFC1422]   Kent, S. "Privacy Enhancement for Internet Electronic Mail—Part II: Certificate-Based Key Management." Internet Request for Comments 1422. (February 1993).

[RFC1424]   Kaliski, B. "Privacy Enhancement for Internet Electronic Mail—Part IV: Key Certification and Related Services." Internet Request for Comments 1424. (February 1993).

[RFC2459]   Housley, R., W. Ford, W. Polk, and D. Solo. "Internet X.509 Public Key Infrastructure: Certificate and CRL Profile." Internet Request for Comments 2459. (January 1999).

[RFC2510]   Adams, C. and S. Farrell. "Internet X.509 Public Key Infrastructure: Certificate Management Protocols." Internet Request for Comments 2510. (March 1999).

[SDSI]   Rivest, R. and B. Lampson. "SDSI—A Simple Distributed Security Infrastructure"; see `http://theory.lcs.mit.edu/~cis/sdsi.html`.

[SPKI]   The Simple Public Key Infrastructure charter; see `http://www.ietf.org/html.charters/spki-charter.html`.

[X.509]   ITU-T Recommendation X.509. "Information Technology—Open Systems Interconnection—The Directory: Authentication Framework." June 1997 (equivalent to ISO/IEC 9594-8, 1997).

[Zim95]   Zimmermann, P. *The Official PGP User's Guide*. Cambridge, MA.: MIT Press, 1995 (second printing).

CHAPTER 10

Multiple Certificates per Entity

This chapter discusses the situation in which a single PKI entity holds multiple valid certificates, and gives a number of reasons that such a situation not only might be possible, but desirable. The concept of different uses for key pairs is presented; some attention is also given to the relationship between key pairs and certificates.

Multiple Key Pairs

As time goes on and PKI deployments grow in number and in function, it will typically be the case that a PKI entity will have a number of key pairs even if all key pairs, on the surface, appear to be used for the same purpose (such as signing data). This is because there can be a strong correspondence between a key pair and a "role"; that is, between a key pair and one of the many "hats" an entity might wear through the day, including both work and off-work hours. For example, an entity might use one key to sign a $100,000 purchase order for his/her department at work, but another key to electronically sign the rental form for a movie at the video store, and yet another key to sign personal e-mail to a friend.

Such a situation is not uncommon to many non-electronic circumstances of the present. As one simple example, it is not unusual for many business people to use one credit card while on company travel and another credit card for all other purposes. The business credit card may have been issued to the employee by the company rather than applied for privately, and may have certain privileges associated with it (such as high spending limits or accident insurance) that the personal credit card does not.

The same model holds for key pairs: One key might be generated and issued by the company instead of being generated locally at the PKI entity's workstation. Furthermore, it might be endowed with particular privileges or restrictions by the issuer (such as signing limits, or guarantees of compliance to certain government or corporate regulations regarding generation, storage, and backup procedures).

The concept of multiple key pairs per entity is perfectly reasonable for many environments, and such a practice should not seem surprising. By contrast, in many cases it would be surprising if a single key pair could meet all the varied needs of a PKI entity in all the roles that will be played throughout the day, week, month, and year.

Key Pair Uses

As discussed in the previous section, key pairs might be associated with different entity roles or actions (much as, in today's world, one card is used for gas purchases, another for bank transactions, and another for borrowing a book from the library). Aside from this, however, it is also the case that different key pairs can have intrinsically different uses. In particular, a key pair for the *Digital Signature Algorithm (DSA)* cannot be used for encryption and decryption when implemented according to the specifications. Similarly, a *Diffie-Hellman (DH)* key pair cannot be used for signing data and verifying the signatures. Furthermore, even a key pair for the *Rivest-Shamir-Adleman (RSA)* algorithm, though it can be *arithmetically* used for authentication, integrity, confidentiality, or key exchange, may be constrained by policy, decree, or implementation choice to only be used for a single purpose.

A key pair, then, may be available for only one use, either because this is determined by the cryptographic algorithm with which it is associated or because such a constraint has been externally imposed on it and the relevant key processing PKI implementation is built to honor this constraint.

However, the field of use of a key pair may be even narrower than this. Consider a digital signature key pair as one example. In many environments, it is important to be able to distinguish between a PKI entity signing some data for the purpose of entity authentication in an on-line challenge-response protocol on the one hand, and signing some data with the explicit intent of committing to the document contents on the other. Thus a key pair may be limited to *particular uses of its signature capability*, rather than all uses.

Even this may not be the finest granularity of use in some environments. For example, a key pair may be designated to authorize purchase transactions and nothing else (that is, it may be used to sign a purchase transaction but may not be used to sign any other type of document or data). However, it may be usable only for purchases up to a pre-determined limit (such as $100,000); purchase transactions of a higher value signed by this key will be rejected. Thus, a key pair may be associated with a specific policy that constrains it to

- A particular quality or quantity of use (for example, purchase transactions up to a given value), *within*

- A particular type of use (for example, authorizing purchase transactions), *within*

- A particular category of use (for example, data content commitment), *within*

- A particular service of use (for example, authentication)

Another kind of specificity might constrain key pair use to a particular application or protocol exchange, rather than to a particular granularity of its cryptographic capability. For example, a key pair might be usable for entity authentication within the Internet Protocol Security (IPsec) protocol, but not for entity authentication within the Secure Sockets Layer (SSL) protocol.

Just as the concept of multiple key pairs per entity is reasonable for some environments because of the different roles the entity may play, it appears also to be reasonable because of the narrow field of use to which a key pair might be constrained. To accomplish all the tasks that may be associated with even a single role (such as a purchasing agent for a corporation), a PKI entity may be required to hold multiple key pairs.

Relationship between Key Pairs and Certificates

If a PKI entity has multiple key pairs, it is likely to have multiple certificates, because the format of a certificate does not naturally allow it to hold more than a single public key (and the X.509 standard does not explicitly support the ability to put multiple keys into the SubjectPublicKeyInfo field). However, this does not preclude the possibility of a particular public key appearing in several certificates that are simultaneously valid. Thus, it is worth exploring briefly the relationship between key pairs and certificates.

By far, the most commonly cited benefit of a given public key appearing in multiple valid certificates is the perceived simplicity of *rollover* (referred to, in this case, as *certificate renewal*). If a key pair

- Has not been compromised (that is, if the private key has not been discovered by an unscrupulous party)

- Is still "cryptographically sound" (that is, if it is of sufficient length that it is not in imminent danger of cryptanalytic attack)

then simplicity arguments might suggest that as the certificate nears its expiration date, the public key might be placed in a new certificate with a new validity period. This "extends the life" of the key pair and does not force relying parties to update their knowledge of the subject's public key. Furthermore, the subject itself is not forced to change the key it uses and is thus freed from the burden of having to maintain a key history over time.

It turns out that the simplicity argument is relatively weak for many environments. In typical PKI implementations, relying parties do not hold "bare" public keys; rather, they retrieve a copy of the appropriate certificate when needed and use whatever public key is contained therein. Thus, the relying party will not notice whether the rolled-over certificate has the same old public key or a brand new public key.

Note

Although standard-track specifications exist that advocate the use of public-key technology without the use of certificates (for example, [X9.59]), it should be noted that such proposals are rather limited in their scope because they are targeted for a very specific class of applications which rely on centralized account authorities. As such, these proposals are not well suited for distributed applications such as secure e-mail between individual users.

Similarly, the certificate subject typically retrieves whatever private key is labeled as "current" in its local storage and uses that to sign, decrypt, or perform the appropriate cryptographic function. Again, whether this is the same private key as a week ago or it is a new private key will not be noticed by the subject. Finally, while it is true that maintaining a key history adds some complexity to local subject operation, it should be clear that a key history is required in any case because key compromise or cryptanalytic advances will mandate that a single key pair cannot live indefinitely.

There is a more compelling reason not to put a single public key in multiple certificates, however: It is too easy to "slip up" and not hold all other important aspects of these multiple certificates constant. For example, in one certificate, the key may be associated with a policy restricting use to authentication of e-mail; in another certificate, the policy may allow purchase transactions up to $100,000. In one certificate, the *key usage extension* (see Chapter 6, "Certificates and Certification") may specify digital signatures only; in another certificate, the extension may set the non-repudiation bit to TRUE. Such situations may allow an attacker (or even an underhanded certificate subject) to substitute one certificate for another so that what was once a merely signed piece of data now takes on an entirely new meaning. Mandating that different certificates always contain different public keys is a simple way to entirely preclude the risk of such substitution attacks.

Note

It is important to recognize the fact that a PKI entity has multiple certificates does not mean that the entity needs to remember multiple passwords/PINs to access these key pairs. In typical PKI implementations, a single password/PIN will unlock a file (or storage device, such as a smart card) that contains all the keys associated with that entity.

Real-World Difficulties

The price to pay for having multiple active certificates associated with different policies and key usages is that for any given activity, the "correct" private key must be selected. For example, signing a particular purchase order may necessitate the use of the "more than $100,000" key rather than the "up to $100,000" key. Cases will inevitably arise in which the user must be consulted. ("Do you agree to be contractually bound by the terms and conditions contained in this document?" If the answer is "Yes," the non-repudiation key is used.) However, for many situations, this key selection will occur automatically and transparently. (If an SSL session is being established, the client software may search the user's certificates for the one with a key usage extension appropriate for SSL and then use the corresponding private key for user authentication.) It is likely that as time goes on and PKI software becomes more sophisticated, the vast majority of key selections will be transparent.

Another difficulty that may arise is the limitations of current smart cards. In particular, the relatively small amount of available memory may preclude the storage of several private keys (especially if the corresponding certificates also need to be stored). Again, however, in the future this difficulty will diminish as smart cards get greater and greater capacity.

Independent Certificate Management

One other advantage to having distinct public keys in distinct certificates is the relative ease of independent certificate management in the case of certificate revocation (see Chapter 8, "Certificate Revocation," for a discussion of revocation). If a single public key is contained in multiple certificates and the private key is compromised (or any other circumstance occurs that requires revocation), it must be "remembered" (or discovered) which certificates contain this key so that they may *all* be revoked. Failure to revoke any of these certificates can constitute a serious security risk. By contrast, such a risk is greatly decreased if a public key appears in one and only one certificate because the administrative burden of finding and revoking that single certificate is relatively light.

Furthermore, distinct certificates associated with distinct key pairs are independent constructs: They may have independent validity periods, as well as independent policies, usage, and management procedures. One may expire or be revoked without affecting any of the others. Having the same public key in multiple certificates can complicate the administrative processes involved in certificate management.

Support for Non-Repudiation

If the PKI-enabled service of non-repudiation (see Chapter 5, "PKI-Enabled Services") is to be supported in an organization, the ability to maintain multiple key pairs—and, consequently, multiple certificates—per entity is a fundamental requirement. To have true support for non-repudiation, a necessary condition is that the private key involved in the intended non-repudiable action (such as signing a receipt for proof of delivery) must never be known to another party. Otherwise, the entity involved can simply claim that the other party may have performed the non-repudiable action. Regardless of whether such a claim can be proven (or even whether such a claim is plausible), the mere fact that another party has knowledge of the key may be sufficient to make repudiation a possibility in the opinion of an unbiased external judge. The service of non-repudiation may, therefore, be precluded.

Thus, the private key that corresponds to a certificate whose purpose is to support non-repudiation must never be exposed to another entity (including trusted entities, such as CAs). In some environments, such a key may be required to be generated on and to never leave a tamper-resistant hardware token. Keys not involved in non-repudiable actions may, by contrast, be required to be backed up by a trusted entity or may be permitted to be stored in software.

For example, in typical corporate environments, operational policy will dictate that private decryption keys must be backed up by a trusted entity. This is because the company simply cannot afford to lose access forever to all stored data encrypted for an employee if that employee happens to forget his/her password or becomes incapacitated in some way. Such data loss would be inconvenient for the company in most cases and may cripple continued operation in others. *Decryption keys must, therefore, be recoverable* if a corporation is to be expected to avoid potentially serious loss due to the inability to recover critical stored data. *Signing keys*, on the other hand (especially those that are to be used in non-repudiable actions), *must not be backed up*: They must be attributable—in as concrete a sense as possible—*only* to the entity named in the corresponding public-key certificate.

Such a conflicting pair of requirements necessitates at least two distinct key pairs (and associated certificates) per corporate PKI entity. This has been recognized in a number of prominent PKI requirements and profile documents, including "Public Key Infrastructure Roadmap for the Department of Defense" and RFC2459 [USDoD, RFC2459]. Some environments (Secured Electronic Information in Society [SEIS], for example) go further and mandate at least three distinct key pairs:

- One for decryption/encryption
- One for general-purpose signing/verification
- One for non-repudiable signing/verification

In any case, however, it appears that environments employing a single key pair per PKI entity will be much more the exception than the rule.

Summary

This chapter has discussed the concept of multiple key pairs and multiple certificates per PKI entity. Separate user "roles," separate key usage, independently managed certificates, and support for non-repudiation all lend weight to the claim that multiple keys/certificates per entity will be a common occurrence in real PKI deployments. The relationship between key pairs and certificates was also explored; that discussion suggested that putting a single public key in several certificates may lead to security risks and unnecessary administrative complexity.

To gain a fuller understanding of this topic, it may be useful to consider two related areas:

- Mechanisms for maintaining an identity across the multiple "roles" that an entity may play (perhaps using a `DistinguishedName` or a `SubjectAltName`—see Chapter 6)

- Mechanisms for automatically distinguishing between key types/uses (such as key usage extensions and policy OIDs—see Chapter 6)

References

[RFC2459] Housley, R., W. Ford, W. Polk, and D. Solo. "Internet X.509 Public Key Infrastructure: Certificate and CRL Profile." Internet Request for Comments 2459. (January 1999). (Page 61 of this specification includes the following statement: "The use of a single key for both encryption and signature purposes is not recommended, but is not forbidden.")

[SEIS] Secured Electronic Information in Society, a non-profit Swedish organization established to promote the development of a framework for IT security. The SEIS specifications have been standardized by the Swedish Standards Institute in documents SS 61 43 30, SS 61 43 31, and SS 61 43 32 (approved September 14, 1998). See http://www.seis.se for further information.

[USDoD] United States Department of Defense. "Public Key Infrastructure Roadmap for the Department of Defense." Version 2.0, Revision C. 21 April 1999. (Page 2 of this specification includes the following statement: "The DoD PKI will issue identity certificates and encryption certificates. The DoD PKI will support key recovery for private keys associated with encryption certificates to support data recovery.")

[X9.59] ANSI DSTU (Draft Standard for Trial Use) X9.59-199x. "Electronic Commerce for the Financial Services Industry: Account-Based Secure Payment Objects." draft. 19 August 1999.

PKI Information Dissemination: Repositories and Other Techniques

As Chapter 6, "Certificates and Certification," discussed, certificates provide a convenient (and typically necessary) structure for protecting the integrity of public keys. Ultimately, certificates need to be acquired by others to be useful (for example, so one end-entity can encrypt for, or verify signatures of, another end-entity). In addition, Chapter 8, "Certificate Revocation," discussed the need to disseminate certificate revocation information, including the use of *Certificate Revocation Lists (CRLs)* and/or CRL-based techniques.

The dissemination of certificate and certificate revocation information can occur in a number of ways. The purpose of this chapter is to discuss some of the methods for distributing this information.

Note

Given that most enterprise domains use repositories as the vehicles for posting and disseminating certificates and certificate revocation information (at least in an intradomain context), the primary focus within this chapter is on the use of repositories. However, this chapter also discusses and contrasts other methods.

Note

Although this chapter concentrates on the use of repositories to store and disseminate certificates and CRLs, it should be recognized that repositories can also be used to store and disseminate other PKI-related information, such as cross-certificates and policy-related information.

Private Dissemination

Perhaps the most basic of distribution mechanisms can be referred to as *private dissemination*. In this case, individual users convey certificates directly to one another. This can be accomplished via "out-of-band" mechanisms such as the following:

- "Hand delivery" via disk or some other storage medium

- An attachment to e-mail

In the private dissemination model, the exchange of revocation information is typically informal and unreliable. Revocation notifications can be conveyed via telephone or through the use of e-mail, but there is typically no guarantee that the revocation information will be conveyed reliably to all concerned individuals. Nor is there typically any software in place that can help the end-user determine the appropriate course of action when such revocation information is received.

Nonetheless, private dissemination can work reasonably well for small (and presumably friendly) user clusters, in which any two entities either know each other directly or have a relatively small set of mutual acquaintances.

An example of a protocol tailored after this model is *Pretty Good Privacy (PGP)* or, more recently, *OpenPGP*. Note, however, that although e-mail based on PGP enjoys widespread popularity, it is still useful only in relatively small user populations because the trust model is based on personal acquaintances.

Although some environments exist where the private dissemination model is viable, it is inappropriate for use in an enterprise domain for at least three critical reasons:

- Private dissemination of certificates does not scale (that is, only relatively small user communities can reliably be supported).

- Ad hoc dissemination of revocation information is inherently unreliable (for example, informal revocation notification is unlikely to reach all relying parties within a large user community—1,000 users or more—in a timely fashion).

- A user-centric trust model (refer to Chapter 9, "Trust Models") is inconsistent with the operational model of most enterprise domains in which centralized control over user actions is required.

Therefore, the enterprise must adopt other options, as the remainder of this chapter discusses.

Publication and Repositories

The most well known and most common method for the distribution of certificates and certificate revocation information is *publication*. The idea behind publication is that PKI information is posted in a widely known, publicly available, and easily accessible location. Publication is particularly attractive for large communities of users who, in general, are personally unknown to each other (that is, the PKI information does not have to be distributed directly to each individual).

The idea of publication in the context of public key cryptography was first introduced in "New Directions in Cryptography" [DH76]. This was the first publicly available paper on public key cryptography, and it postulated a model whereby public keys could be published and distributed in a form similar to a telephone book.

In today's enterprise, it is common practice to post (or publish) certificates and certificate revocation information (particularly revocation information based on CRLs) to a repository. A *repository* is a generic term used to denote any logically centralized database capable of storing information and disseminating that information when requested to do so.

In the enterprise context, repositories are typically remote servers based on the *Lightweight Directory Access Protocol (LDAP)* [RFC1777 or RFC2251], and/or on the X.500 Series of Recommendations [X.500]. However, the term *repository* can apply to a database or other form of information storage and distribution, such as an on-line revocation status responder. Refer to the discussion regarding the *Online Certificate Status Protocol (OCSP)* in Chapter 8. Some examples that fall under this definition of *repository* include the following:

- LDAP servers

- X.500 *Directory System Agents (DSAs)*

- OCSP Responders (although this is currently limited to revocation status information)

- *Domain Name System (DNS)* (with certificate and certificate revocation information supported in accordance with RFC2538)

- Web servers (that may contain certificates and certificate revocation information in accordance with RFC2585, which can be retrieved via the *Hypertext Transfer Protocol,* or *HTTP*)

- *File Transfer Protocol (FTP)*-based servers (that may contain certificates and certificate revocation information in accordance with RFC2585)

- Corporate databases (that may contain certificates and certificate revocation information, and that have well-defined management and access practices)

As you can see from this list, client systems can retrieve information from these repositories through a number of different access protocols (although LDAP is the most dominant repository access protocol in the enterprise PKI domain). Ideally, this will enable end-entities to retrieve certificates and certificate revocation information on demand, with little to no access control in place (recalling that certificates and CRLs are "self-protected" from an integrity perspective). In fact, it is common practice (although not always the case) that anonymous reads are used to retrieve certificates and CRLs within an enterprise domain. However, access control is a concern when it comes to the posting of certificates and CRLs to the repository because unauthorized access may introduce a security risk (for example, one CRL might be swapped for another CRL).

The location of a given repository (or set of repositories) can be communicated to the client in several ways. For example, a local client configuration file can be initialized with *Internet Protocol (IP)* addresses or DNS names of a primary and secondary LDAP server to be used by that client. In the case of revocation information, the client can determine the location of the target repository directly from the certificate, as in the case of CRL Distribution Points (refer to Chapter 8). Other methods, including out-of-band notifications and/or referrals, can also be used.

The judicious use of one or more repositories has several advantages. One advantage is that many organizations have already deployed an enterprise-wide repository system of some sort, and it is relatively simple to incorporate the additional PKI-related information within the existing enterprise repository infrastructure. And, unlike the private dissemination alternative discussed earlier, in which users exchange certificates with people they know, this method allows complete strangers to establish relationships for subsequent communication. It also provides a central location where this information can be retrieved. This can significantly reduce the number of certificates and CRLs that need to be stored locally when compared to the private dissemination alternative (as discussed previously). The caching of PKI information (to reduce network traffic between the client and the repository) may counterbalance the advantage, however. Finally, because the certificates and CRLs are "self-protected" (that is, the digital signature on these data structures guarantees integrity of the contents), the storage mechanism itself (that is, the repository) need not be secure from a data-integrity perspective—this lack of need for trusted repositories is viewed as a major advantage in the deployment of PKI. However, as stated earlier, actual publication of the information to the repository may require some form of access control to prevent unauthorized modification of data. Further, the repository can be protected from a confidentiality perspective whenever privacy concerns dictate.

Note

If the repository technology stores or supplies information that is not self-protected, the information must be protected through other means. For example, OCSP responses (which contain "raw" revocation information that is not self-protected) must be digitally signed to ensure the integrity of the response (including source and data integrity). Further, if the repository stores raw public keys and/or raw certificate revocation information, the information stored within the repository's database must be protected against unauthorized modification.

On the other hand, a publicly-accessible repository does have several disadvantages. For example, a certain amount of network overhead associated with the posting and subsequent retrieval of the certificates and CRLs is introduced. The deployment of on-line repositories capable of handling the performance demand associated with the community of interest it is meant to serve—which can be on the order of millions of users—is also required. Thus, the number of repositories required may be substantial. There may also be issues associated with the replication of information across multiple repositories (for example, impact on performance, propagation delay, and so on).

Note

The amount of this overhead in terms of network bandwidth and overall performance will naturally depend on the size of the user community, the frequency of updates and retrievals, the certificate sizes, the CRL sizes, and so on.

In any given deployment, certificate and certificate revocation information retrieval must not be the bottleneck in the PKI operation. Repository access and request processing times must be as short as possible to offer a timely level of service, and certificate and certificate revocation information sizes must be kept as small as possible to minimize the amount of network bandwidth consumed. As discussed in Chapter 8, CRL Distribution Points and Delta CRLs can help minimize the amount of bandwidth associated with the posting and retrieval of CRLs (when this is the revocation mechanism used). Certificate sizes may be harder to minimize, although certain things can be done to help in this regard. For example, the use of pointers to information rather than including the information within the certificate itself can make a substantial difference in the certificate size. Caching of recently used certificates and CRLs is a common practice to help enhance performance and decrease the impact on network overhead, but this must be tempered with the possibility of missing the "freshest" revocation information. (Refer to Chapter 8 for more information.)

Privacy Issues

Publicly-accessible repositories can also introduce privacy concerns, especially if sensitive information is contained within the certificates and/or CRLs (which is not recommended). Even if nothing is considered sensitive within each certificate per se, there may be fear that the aggregation of the certificates and CRLs associated with a given enterprise may be sensitive (for example, it may reveal some or all of the corporate structure of the organization).

Although privacy issues may not be of substantial concern in an intraorganizational context, they do tend to come to the forefront when it comes to information sharing in an interdomain context. Specifically, this problem arises when one enterprise domain wants to interoperate with another enterprise domain, either through the use of cross-certification or by virtue of the fact that the two enterprise domains are able to communicate under a common root Certification Authority (CA). Naturally, this implies that certificate and certificate revocation information from one domain will need to be conveyed to the other, and vice versa.

In the enterprise PKI, certificates and certificate revocation information is typically posted to a public repository (for example, an LDAP server), and the certificate revocation information is usually posted in the form of CRLs and/or CRL Distribution Points. The client software responsible for processing end-user certificates retrieves the certificates and CRLs on demand. In the interdomain context, the method used to convey this information and the frequency with which this information is conveyed are subject to agreement between the two cooperating domains.

There is increasing concern at the enterprise level that uncontrolled dissemination of certificates and certificate revocation information might introduce potential vulnerabilities. In this case, the concept of a publicly accessible database repository is at odds with certain corporate policies where the information within these repositories is deemed to be sensitive in nature and, therefore, is considered to be inappropriate for general public consumption. Sensitive information can include information regarding external clients, corporate infrastructure, employee names and related information such as telephone numbers, or it can simply be the aggregate of one or more of these information categories. This has led to a growing unwillingness among a number of organizations to share their corporate database information without the introduction of specific security control measures. Therefore, methods must be established that will allow the scalable dissemination of the requisite certificate and certificate revocation information without exposing the enterprise to these potential security concerns.

It is sometimes possible to avoid populating certificates and CRLs with sensitive information, and the corporate *Directory Information Tree (DIT)* can be organized in a relatively flat hierarchy to prevent the unwanted exposure of corporate infrastructure information that might otherwise be exposed.

In some cases, it is also possible to populate the *Distinguished Name (DN)* within a certificate with a (locally) unique identifier that has significance only to some central authority (which, in essence, is the single relying party). In this case, the DN is meaningless to anyone who might intercept the certificate. In practice, this alternative has been used when the relying party is essentially a central entity (for example, in the case where a bank—and only the bank—validates the certificates of its customers, the DN can be assigned in a manner that has meaning only to that bank). Specifically, the DN might simply be a (locally) unique integer that maps into a specific bank customer account known only to the bank. Such certificates are sometimes referred to as *anonymous certificates* (although this is just one example of what might be considered to be an anonymous certificate). Although this may be suitable under certain scenarios, note that the use of this particular mechanism is limited. (For example, it is impractical for e-mail that is sent and received between individuals.)

As might be expected, it is not always possible to implement these particular safeguards. Other methods must be established to allow the scalable dissemination of the requisite certificate and certificate revocation information, and these methods must eliminate the potential security concerns to the maximum extent possible.

Interdomain Repository Deployment Options

Figure 11.1 illustrates a number of possible configurations associated with the deployment of repositories in the interdomain scenario. Option A depicts the use of direct access from external entities to the corporate repository (that is, the corporate repository is accessed through the corporate firewall boundary). Option B illustrates two possible scenarios. The first is the partial replication of the data stored within the corporate repository to a point outside the corporate firewall boundary. The repository that houses the partially replicated information is often referred to as a *border repository*. The second scenario under Option B is that the border repository becomes an *intermediate repository*, or *proxy*, and incoming requests are chained to the target repository without any further end-user involvement. Note that Options A and B can be used together in some environments. The two derivatives under Option B can also be used in concert with one another.

Figure 11.1 Interdomain repository deployment options.

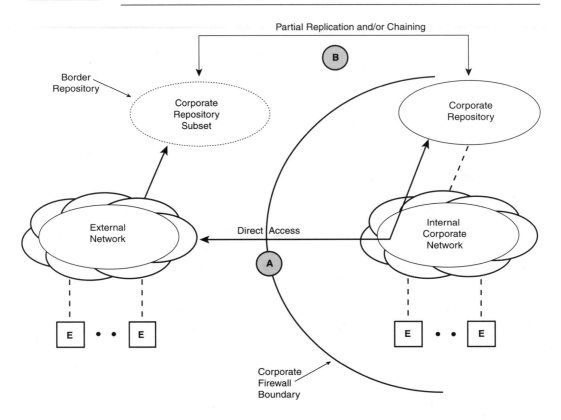

The following subsections discuss these and other deployment options. Note that these alternatives are not necessarily mutually exclusive; one or more of these options can be deployed as needs dictate.

Direct Access

The *direct access* alternative enables the end-user client software in one domain to directly access the repository in the other domain, and vice versa; or it enables an external repository to chain directly to the internal corporate repository. This may be appropriate when the trust relationship between the two domains is reciprocal and/or when the repository itself is secure and protected against unauthorized access. This orientation is one embodiment of Option A in Figure 11.1.

In addition to access control, a confidentiality mechanism may be required to prevent unauthorized disclosure of the information as it is transmitted from one enterprise domain to another. This can be accomplished in a number of ways (for example, through the use of security protocols such as *Transport Layer Security*, or *TLS*; the Encapsulating Security Payload from IPsec; or the use of certain application-layer protocols such as the X.500 *Directory Access Protocol*, or *DAP*).

Shared Repository

A *shared repository* permits each PKI domain to post its applicable certificate and certificate revocation information to a common repository so that the other PKI domain can retrieve this information when required. The shared repository can be co-owned and co-operated by two (or more) domains, or a third-party service provider can support the shared repository. The posting and retrieval mechanisms that each domain uses might be different—as long as the structure and frequency of the updates are maintained as mutually agreed-upon, and as long as the shared repository is capable of supporting multiple protocols for this purpose. Access control to the shared repository can be implemented to prevent unauthorized access to the information stored within the repository, and underlying confidentiality services (for example, TLS) can be used to prevent unauthorized disclosure while the information is in transit.

Interdomain Replication

Interdomain replication involves copying the applicable certificate and certificate revocation information directly from one domain to the other, and vice versa. However, the capability to automate this process depends on the protocols used. For example, if both domains support Directory Services based on X.500, this can be achieved through existing protocol mechanisms (that is, through the *Directory Information Shadowing Protocol*, or *DISP*). On the other hand, if the only common protocol between the two domains is LDAP, an industry-accepted protocol to achieve replication is not yet available. The *LDAP Duplication/Replication/Update Protocol (LDUP)* Working Group within the *Internet Engineering Task Force (IETF)* is currently working on this issue, and so you may see the introduction of an LDAP-based replication protocol into future products within a year or two. In any case, the underlying session used to copy the information from one enterprise domain to another should be protected. The use of the *LDAP Data Interchange Format (LDIF)*-based file transfer may offer another short-term alternative.

LDAPv2 and LDAPv3

Although LDAPv2 [RFC1777] has been the mainstay of the early enterprise PKI deployments, it is generally considered to be deficient in the following areas:

- The mandatory-to-implement authentication mechanism between a client and the repository is based on a userid and password transmitted in the clear.

- No standard access control scheme exists.

- No standard mechanism for data replication between LDAP data repositories exists (in fact, no support for any server-to-server communications exists).

- Existing LDAP search filters are considered to be inadequate.

- No agreed confidentiality mechanism is in place to protect stored data or data in transit.

- No agreed signed operations capability exists.

The shortcomings of LDAPv2 are widely recognized, and a number of new features are being introduced with the advent of LDAPv3 [RFC2251] to correct these deficiencies. In particular, the IETF LDAPext Working Group is working on a number of enhancements, including (but not limited to) the following:

- Stronger authentication mechanisms

- Standard access control model

- Support for referrals

- Support for session confidentiality

- Support for digitally signed operations

You can retrieve the latest Internet Drafts and RFCs produced by the IETF LDAPext Working Group from `http://www.ietf.org/html.charters/ldapext-charter.html`.

Related work also is underway under the auspices of the IETF LDAP Duplication/Replication/Update Protocols (LDUP) Working Group. Specifically, the LDUP Working Group is addressing support for replication between LDAP servers. You can retrieve the latest Internet Drafts and RFCs produced by the LDUP Working Group from `http://www.ietf.org/html.charters/ldup-charter.html`.

Border Repository

Perhaps one of the more popular deployment alternatives is the use of a *border repository*, in which a separate repository is maintained outside the corporate firewall boundary of any of the participating organizations. The applicable certificates and certificate revocation information is posted to the border repository as determined (and controlled) by each enterprise, or the information can be retrieved by the border repository from the internal repository via chaining. Note that the use of chaining would require the use of the X.500 Directory System Protocol (DSP), or a proprietary mechanism would be required. Currently, the LDAP specifications do not explicitly support chaining.

External access to the border repository may or may not be controlled, depending on the requirements and sensitivity of the information provided. In any case, remote clients would be able to access the necessary certificates and certificate revocation information without traversing the corporate firewall and, consequently, without directly accessing the potentially sensitive corporate database. Option B in Figure 11.1 shows this alternative.

Guard

This alternative involves the deployment of a *guard* mechanism that would accept external requests and, after some sort of reasonable access-control checks, could retrieve the requested information from internal repositories and return the response back to the external end-entity. Although similar to a typical corporate firewall, this differs in the sense that the guard does not allow the original requests to traverse the internal corporate network and directly access the target repository. This can be considered to be a *proxy* mechanism; the external requests are intercepted, and the appropriate information is retrieved only by the guard when permitted. The results (which may also be filtered by the guard) are then passed back to the requestor.

In-Band Protocol Exchange

Private dissemination and publication are not the only methods that can be used to convey certificates and certificate revocation information. *In-band protocol exchange* of certificates and CRLs can also be supported as part of the communications protocol exchange. For example, this could be achieved with *Secure/Multipurpose Internet Mail Extensions (S/MIME)* Version 3-based e-mail. Other protocols capable of certificate and CRL exchange include TLS and IPsec (specifically, the *Internet Key Exchange*, or *IKE*, protocol). See Chapter 16, "Major Standards Activities," for the full set of references for these protocols.

In some environments, in-band protocol exchange of PKI information may be the only way to convey this information to the intended recipients. For example, the Internet relies on this mechanism because no ubiquitous repository system exists that can be used to support the dissemination of certificates and CRLs. However, we are likely to see a shift toward the use of on-line certificate status checking within the Internet for some applications in the near future. Whether a ubiquitous repository system (perhaps based on the

Domain Name System, or *DNS*) will ever materialize for the Internet remains to be seen.

Note that the use of an in-band protocol exchange of certificate information may supplement the use of a repository rather than completely replace it. For example, the verification certificate (as defined in Chapter 7, "Key and Certificate Management") of the originator can be sent along with a digitally signed e-mail. This allows the recipient to verify the originator's digital signature without the need to retrieve the verification certificate from a repository. However, the encryption certificate for the intended recipient may be retrieved from a repository on message origination, and the revocation information associated with the originator's certificate may also be retrieved from a repository as part of the digital signature-verification process. This orientation is commonly found in implementation practice today.

Summary

This chapter discussed the various methods used to disseminate certificates and certificate revocation information, with primary focus on the enterprise PKI domain and the use of repositories. This chapter also reviewed a number of deployment alternatives when it comes to sharing public-key related information between two or more cooperating PKI domains. It also reviewed privacy concerns.

As PKI-supported environments scale to tens of thousands, hundreds of thousands, or even millions of users, the timely and robust dissemination of PKI information will be critical. This is one of the most fundamental requirements for the successful deployment of any large-scale PKI. To more fully appreciate the content of this chapter, you should review the following:

- Certificate revocation techniques, as discussed in Chapter 8

- Client-side software necessary to acquire certificates when needed, as discussed in Chapter 12, "PKI Operational Considerations"

- Requirements associated with the on-line operation of repositories, as discussed in Chapter 12

References

[DH76]   Diffie, W. and M. Hellman. "New Directions in Cryptography." *IEEE Transactions on Information Theory* 22 (1976): 644–654.

[RFC1777]   Yeong, W., T. Howes, and S. Kille. "Lightweight Directory Access Protocol." Internet Request for Comments 1777. (March 1995).

[RFC2251]   Wahl, M., T. Howes, and S. Kille. "Lightweight Directory Access Protocol (v3)." Internet Request for Comments 2251. (December 1997).

[X.500]   ITU-T X.500 Series of Recommendations. X.500 through X.530. International Telecommunication Union. Geneva, Switzerland. 1997 (equivalent to ISO/IEC 9594-9 through 9594-10).

CHAPTER **12**

PKI Operational Considerations

To operate a PKI successfully, you must take into consideration a number of requirements, characteristics, and options. This chapter defines *PKI operational considerations* as those practices, components, or facilities necessary for the PKI to function (these do not include, for example, explicit PKI operations themselves). In general, such operational considerations are sufficiently fundamental to the overall architecture that concrete decisions must be made and explicit actions must be taken in advance of PKI deployment.

This chapter discusses a number of these operational considerations, including client-side software, on-line requirements, physical security, hardware components, user key compromise, and disaster preparation and recovery.

Client-Side Software

As discussed in Chapter 3, "The Concept of an Infrastructure," a PKI is, above all, an infrastructure. By definition, an *infrastructure* is an ubiquitous, "substrate" architecture that is engineered to solve a particular problem and offer a set of services to a wide range of "applications" that may make use of these services. The infrastructure offers consistency and uniformity with respect to these services, across the full range of potential "applications." For the PKI, these "applications" are the client applications, protocol engines, libraries, operating systems, and so on, that require security services such as authentication, integrity, confidentiality, notarization, and non-repudiation (see Chapter 4, "Core PKI Services: Authentication, Integrity, and Confidentiality," and Chapter 5, "PKI-Enabled Services"). This security infrastructure, therefore, must necessarily exist outside (that is, be distinct from) all these "applications."

A client-side PKI component is essential today due to limitations in current software applications (for example, with respect to revocation checking, key life cycle management, or Certificate Policy enforcement during validation). However, don't conclude from this that there will be a decreased need for client-side PKI software over time as off-the-shelf applications (for example, Web browsers) incorporate greater security awareness and functionality. Such reasoning ignores the fact that regardless of how powerful or how important a client application (such as a Web browser) may be, it is still only one of many applications that Alice will access or run on her platform. For consistent, uniform security *across applications*, the security functionality must be located outside (but callable from) any single application. This is the scalable, manageable architecture that is the true reflection of the definition of a PKI. Note that embedding this security functionality in the operating system is still not sufficiently general because this can hinder multi-platform security uniformity. The client-side PKI component must be an independent library (module, toolkit, applet, or whatever form it takes), callable even by the operating system itself.

Note

Unless every operating system (OS) and software application uses the same client-side PKI component, multi-platform uniformity will not be achieved. Furthermore, some may argue that PKI support functions in user/application space are more vulnerable to attack and modification than functions embedded in the OS (accessible through standardized interfaces such as CDSA [CDSA] and CAPI [CAPI]).

However, it is not certain that the OS is always less vulnerable (it depends on the characteristics of the operating system and the client-side component). Also, different OSs will yield different levels of assurance and different PKI functionality for the foreseeable future. Uniformity through a client-side component seems more likely to be achievable, at least in the short term.

In some circumstances, it can be desirable to push particularly complex, computationally expensive, or memory-intensive functionality off the local client. Devices such as *Personal Digital Assistants (PDAs)*, cellular telephones, pagers, and so on, may not have the capacity or processing power to incorporate such functionality locally. PKI operations may be one good example of this. The users of these devices may want to enjoy the benefits of authentication, integrity, and confidentiality in their communications, but the devices themselves may be physically unable to implement complete PKI operations (for example, full certificate path validation and key life cycle management). One possible solution (other than to wait until these devices become sufficiently powerful) is to off-load functionality. The device, instead of doing certificate path processing itself, for example, sends the certificate to some trusted server and says, "You do the path construction and validation for me, and then let me know if it's okay to trust this certificate."

Note

It is not universally agreed that off-loading PKI functionality is a good architectural decision. Some argue that security and performance implications can render such a model unattractive for some environments. However, we mention it here simply because this model is being considered in some circles as a way of bringing PKI services within reach of the very constrained devices.

Such architecture appears to argue in favor of no client-side PKI component because a central server can perform all PKI operations, whereas the local platform simply makes requests for these operations and waits for the responses. However, it can still be argued that some form of client-side module is fundamentally the right architecture, even for these devices. This architecture protects the devices (their operating systems, local applications, and so on) from the need to understand and process security (specifically, the security associated with the request/response protocol with the PKI server) correctly. Furthermore, this architecture can ease administration. For example, if a security flaw is found in the request/response protocol itself, it may be much easier to update one client-side module than to modify the (potentially numerous) client applications that have implemented this protocol directly.

Client-side PKI software is an operational consideration. Administrators need to be aware of, and take into account, this architectural model when planning a PKI deployment across an organization's potentially wide range of platforms and devices.

Off-Line Operations

An architectural decision that must be made with respect to PKI deployment concerns the on-line/off-line requirements of PKI operation: Must users of the PKI be on-line to function, or is off-line operation permissible? This decision is important because it must be recognized that at least some members of the user population will be disconnected from the network on occasion (for example, while traveling). Are these users then simulta-neously disconnected from all PKI services, or is some (perhaps limited) functionality still available to them?

Note that this is largely a function of the applications being employed in the environment. Some applications require real-time connectivity (and so users must be on-line); others are designed to operate off-line or in a staged delivery fashion (so that off-line PKI support will also be required).

One example of desirable off-line operation is e-mail composition on a laptop computer. If off-line PKI operation is possible, composed e-mail may be digitally signed and also encrypted for its intended recipients by using certificates, revocation information, and other relevant data that is cached on the local machine. On the other hand, if off-line operation is prohibited (for example, by disallowing local caching of PKI-relevant data), e-mail can be composed, but cannot be encrypted for the intended recipients. This means that it must be stored in the clear on the local machine until the user is able to reconnect to the network, encrypt the message, and transmit it.

With respect to off-line operation, certain security implications must be taken into consideration. For example, although revocation information (such as a CRL—see Chapter 8, "Certificate Revocation") can be cached locally, such information can be slightly "stale" by the time that the off-line user is ready to consult it. That is, the off-line user, by virtue of being disconnected from the network, may not have access to the most current revocation information (for example, if this has become available subsequent to the time at which the user was last connected to the network). The user, therefore, may accept a certificate that has recently been revoked as valid (that is, declared invalid). Relying on this certificate is a security risk. In particular, for cases in which the revocation reason is "key compromise," accepting the certificate may cause the user to be the unwitting victim of an impersonation attack.

As well, the possibility of off-line operation necessarily implies that some on-line-only PKI-enabled services will be inaccessible. A time stamp server, for example, will be unavailable to the off-line user, as will any form of notarization or non-repudiation service. Furthermore, access to certificates and revocation information that has not been cached locally will be unavailable, along with any key life cycle management functionality (such as key rollover or key recovery). Depending on the policies of the environment, the inability to access such services may have security implications and may limit the PKI-relevant work that the user is trying to accomplish.

Enabling or disabling off-line operation is an operational consideration: Enterprise policy will need to explicitly dictate whether off-line PKI operation would be of value to the user population in a specific environment. This decision may depend to a great extent on the types of applications employed by the users, and whether these applications require PKI support for on-line connectivity or off-line operation. In typical environments, many PKI users will require both on-line and off-line operation at different points in time.

Physical Security

The most sensitive PKI components should be physically protected in high-security environments to make unintended access, modification, or destruction of these components substantially more difficult. Physical security includes one or more of the following:

- Restricting or eliminating network access

- Locating components in a locked, reinforced room

- Installing proper access control devices (perhaps including biometric devices) to restrict room entry

- Using proper safeguards on tape or CD backups

Furthermore, any data transfer between the network and the physically secured component should use "clean" (for example, demonstrably virus-free) tapes, floppies, or CDs.

It must be recognized, however, that there is always a trade-off between system security and system ease-of-use. For example, stringent physical security is likely to introduce manual intervention, operational complexity, and performance delays that may not occur in a system with more relaxed physical security.

The amount of physical security to be incorporated in a given PKI installation is an operational consideration that must be decided prior to deployment. This decision will be based on the system security requirements, a full risk assessment of the intended environment of operation, and due consideration of the ease-of-use degradation that can be tolerated. In many environments, the "off-line CA" (that is, the Certification Authority removed from the network and located in a locked, windowless room with adequate access control procedures) with an on-line Registration Authority may be a reasonable and attractive architectural model.

Hardware Components

A software-only PKI installation (particularly for end-entity operation) is likely to be perfectly suitable for some environments. However, application software (as well as the operating system it runs on) can be vulnerable to penetration from hackers, Trojan horses, viruses, and so on. Even well-intentioned users can cause security breaches by modifying or crashing system software inadvertently.

To help protect against the risks associated with software-only implementations of PKI, selected hardware components can be employed. For example, additional security may be gained through the use of some combination of the following:

- Hardware devices to perform the cryptographic operations

- Smart cards, PCMCIA cards (typically referred to as "PC cards"), or other hardware tokens to store private keys and other sensitive information

- Biometric devices to enable multi-factor user identification (and to unlock/enable the client-side PKI functionality)

As with physical security, there is an inevitable trade-off between system security and ease-of-use. However, the trade-off here has greater implications than the trade-off for physical security (and consequently must be weighed more carefully). With the addition of hardware components, the degradation in ease-of-use is likely to affect a substantial segment of the PKI user population. The physical security of locked rooms with controlled access, on the other hand, will affect only a relatively small number of people (such as CA and RA administrators).

The addition of hardware components is a significant operational consideration because such add-ons can have quite adverse effects on performance (especially smart cards and similar devices due to I/O, memory, or processing limitations), on user appeal or acceptance, and on total PKI deployment costs.

User Key Compromise

The topic of *key compromise* (that is, disclosure of a private key to an unauthorized or unintended party) can be considered in two contexts:

- Compromise of an end-entity private key

- Compromise of a CA private key

Because disclosure of a CA private key is considerably more disastrous than disclosure of an end-entity key, that aspect of key compromise is discussed in the following section, "Disaster Preparation and Recovery;" this section will focus on end-entity (or user) key compromise.

Knowing or Suspecting Key Compromise

How does Alice come to know or suspect that her key has been compromised? Unfortunately, there are few simple, concrete answers. The difficulty, of course, is that this is not equivalent to Eve breaking into Alice's house and stealing the money from her purse. Rather, it is similar to Eve breaking into Alice's house and memorizing the number and expiration date on her credit card, but leaving the card in Alice's purse. That is, it may not be immediately obvious to Alice that anything is amiss, but Eve now has the ability to order goods and services over the phone, for example, using Alice's credit card information.

PKI end-entities must be trained to watch for anything suspicious in their environments, such as files that have been moved or deleted, directories that have been modified, or objects that have appeared without reason. Just as Alice may check her door locks and windows regularly to see if her house has been broken into, PKI end-entities need to be watchful for unsuspected changes in their local environments. Anything unusual should cause a PKI end-entity to worry about key compromise and to consider replacing the relevant key pairs. Note that this includes the situation in which the platform itself—a laptop, for example—is lost or stolen.

Of course, Alice may be more certain of key compromise if there is strong evidence that someone else knows her private key. For example, Alice's signature may appear on a document that she is certain she did not sign, or Bob may demonstrate knowledge of the contents of a document that was encrypted only for Alice. In such situations, revocation of the compromised key pair—and generation of a replacement key pair—should be done without delay.

As soon as Alice discovers (or suspects) that her private key has been compromised, she must do the following:

- Send a revocation request to the appropriate authority so that some kind of notice can be issued to inform all relevant relying parties that they must discontinue use of the corresponding public key.

- Take steps, if desired, to generate and certify a new key pair so that secure communications with her may continue.

The first action listed in the preceding list is critically important and must be performed with utmost urgency because delay creates a larger window of opportunity for the entity who now (illegitimately) holds a copy of Alice's key to successfully impersonate Alice. In fact, in an effort to allow Alice to minimize the size of this window, some of the standards specifying techniques for revocation (such as X.509 [X.509] and PKIX-CMP [RFC2510]) include the concept of an estimated compromise date in both the revocation request and the resulting CRL. Therefore, Alice may say, in effect, "I discovered this compromise today, but I am just back from a one-week vacation, so the compromise may have occurred any time in the past week. Please revoke this certificate immediately and inform users that my estimated date of compromise is one week ago." This is a very useful mechanism for dealing with uncertainty of the exact date of compromise and for allowing Alice to minimize her resulting risk.

However, this mechanism is also subject to misuse, particularly with respect to the PKI-enabled service of non-repudiation (see Chapter 5 for a discussion on non-repudiation). Alice, who wants to repudiate her signature on a contract three days ago, simply needs to send a message to the appropriate authority and claim a suspected compromise four days ago, a week ago, or whatever day suits her purpose. The certificate is revoked, the notification reflects the offered date, and Alice is no longer bound to the contract. Note that there is no way to protect against this sort of misuse by legitimate but dishonest PKI entities. "Estimated compromise date" can, therefore, be good or bad and should be implemented with caution in a PKI. In particular, if non-repudiation support is to be offered by the PKI, "estimated compromise date" should not be generally available to PKI entities.

The second action listed earlier (certifying a new key pair) is theoretically optional, but it is typically done in practice so that entities enjoy continued PKI operation. This process of "recertification" may be automated, or may require almost as much manual intervention and out-of-band communication as the original initialization process itself. The determining factor is whether the user still has a (non-compromised) signing key and corresponding verification certificate. If so (depending on the flexibility of the protocol in use), a certification request message for the new key pair may be signed with the non-compromised signing key, and the validity of the verification certificate attests to the authenticity of the request. On the other hand, a valid signing key may not be available any longer (for example, if the entity had only one signing key and this is the key that was compromised). The process of certification of a new key pair could then require an out-of-band exchange with the CA or RA, possibly including a physical meeting or telephone call, to establish the requisite authenticity.

The specific consequences of a key compromise to an end-entity, Alice, depend on the key type to a great extent. For example, if a signing key is compromised, Alice must revoke the corresponding certificate immediately but (in an environment that makes proper use of digital time stamping; see Chapter 5) may need to take no further action with respect to previously signed documents. The revocation prevents the perpetrator, Charlie, from impersonating Alice with the (now known) signing key. Time stamps prevent him from signing a new document with a date of three weeks before and claiming that Alice signed it before the compromise. Note, however, that if time stamps are not used, all documents signed by Alice with this key become suspect because it cannot be proven conclusively which ones were legitimately signed by Alice prior to compromise. Also, even if time stamps are used properly, security concerns may not disappear entirely. For example, Charlie may use his knowledge of Alice's public key and his new-found knowledge of Alice's private key to request a verification certificate for himself, binding that key pair to his name. He may then be able to substitute his certificate for Alice's in the "signer information" of a signed message and successfully impersonate Alice as the signer. This attack will not work if the data originally signed includes a copy of the certificate to be used to verify the signature (a recommended practice whenever possible, by the way), but few enveloping protocols currently include a standardized facility for doing this.

If the compromised key is a decryption or key exchange private key, not only must Alice revoke the corresponding certificate immediately, but she also must find all important documents that are encrypted with a symmetric key that was protected with this compromised key pair. These documents must then be reprotected (otherwise, Charlie may read their contents). Again, however, no solution is perfect. Copies of Alice's sensitive documents may exist elsewhere without Alice's knowledge. (Charlie may even be in possession of such documents.) Because they were encrypted, Alice may naturally not have been careful about where she stored or backed up these protected documents.

The preceding discussion indicates that key compromise can lead to significant inconvenience and non-trivial security concerns. End-entities should be trained to do everything in their power to avoid it at all costs. User key compromise is an operational consideration because an end-entity must take explicit action (initiate a revocation request or take steps to acquire a new certificate) in order to keep the PKI operational from his/her point of view.

Disaster Preparation and Recovery

As noted in the previous section, key compromise may involve an end-entity private key or an authority (for example, CA or RA) private key. Compromise (as well as destruction or any other event resulting in total loss of use) of an authority private key can be disastrous on quite a significant scale. This is because of the trust that a (potentially large) group of PKI entities places in that authority and because of the power it has to enable security in the environment.

In general, authority key compromise is a greater problem than loss of use of a key: Both events require the establishment of trust in a new key, but key compromise also destroys entity trust in existing signed statements from that authority (such as certificates). If Charlie is able to gain knowledge of the CA's private certificate-signing key, Charlie effectively becomes the CA and can issue whatever certificates (with whatever validity periods) he likes within the domain of that CA. He can also create cross-certificates that may cause PKI entities within the domain of the compromised CA to extend trust to an otherwise untrustworthy CA. The security implications of this event are extreme, which is why this topic is typically discussed in the context of PKI disaster scenarios.

Relying Party Notification

One of the reasons that CA key compromise does not have a well-defined and universally agreed-upon series of steps for recovery is that, for some environments, simply notifying the relying party community that a disaster has occurred is an unsolved—and unsolvable—problem. For example, in the Web model (see Chapter 9, "Trust Models," for a discussion of this trust model), a CA whose public key is embedded in one or more of the popular browsers cannot know precisely who its relying parties are. Browsers have been downloaded or otherwise acquired by tens of millions of Internet users; it is impossible to determine which users have which browsers, and who among those users is relying on any particular embedded key. Thus, if the private key of "CA Company, Inc." is compromised, there is no reliable way to inform the relevant PKI entities that this has occurred and to warn them not to accept certificates signed with this key.

For some environments, the problem of relying party notification can be partially addressed by placing the self-signed certificate corresponding to the compromised CA private key on an *Authority Revocation List*, or *ARL* (see Chapter 8 for a discussion of CRL and ARL technology). Although somewhat counterintuitive (it is not immediately obvious why a revocation list signed by a key that it claims was compromised would be trusted by anyone), there is value in doing this. If Charlie has discovered a CA private key, precisely the last thing he wants to do is immediately nullify his new-found power by revoking its corresponding certificate. Even if Charlie wants to do one or two "bad" things and then revoke the certificate to try to cover his tracks in some way, an ARL claiming that the CA's private key was compromised should be taken seriously by the affected PKI entities. Thus, reliance on the corresponding public key should be discontinued.

An alternative mechanism for enabling ARL notification is the one employed in the *Secure Electronic Transaction (SET)* specification [SET]. In this mechanism, an ARL containing the compromised key is issued, signed by the new (that is, replacement) CA private key. Relying parties are able to validate this signature by retrieving the new CA public key, computing the hash of this key, and comparing the result with the hash value embedded in the old CA certificate. This method works well, but it requires that the CA generate its next (replacement) key pair at the time of certification of its current key pair (so that it can include the hash of the next public key in the current certificate). Thus, the current and next key pairs exist simultaneously, increasing the probability that compromise of one may lead to compromise of the other (for example, if they are stored in the same location).

In any case, inclusion in an ARL is only a partial solution, as noted earlier, for at least two reasons. First, a CA public key is not always packaged as a self-signed certificate in the local environment of a given relying party (it may be stored as a "bare" key). In such cases, there is no way to point to this key in an ARL, as currently defined, because ARL syntax points to certificates using issuer name and certificate serial numbers. Second, and perhaps more important, relying party software may be capable of checking a CRL for an entity certificate, but may not be general enough to also check an ARL (because such revocation lists are typically used only in environments that support cross-certification).

Thus, out-of-band notification of CA key compromise is always useful and always recommended. This may take the form of direct, targeted messaging (whenever members of the relying party community are known to the CA), it may employ mass-market advertising (something a CA may, in some cases, be reluctant to do), or it may use some other means.

Preparation

Obviously, the best way to prepare for any catastrophe is to try to ensure that the catastrophe never occurs. Therefore, each CA must take every step imaginable to protect its private key(s) so that any form of compromise or loss of use would be highly unlikely. One example of this is the use of high-quality cryptographic hardware for CA private key protection (for example, FIPS 140-1 Level 3 or 4 devices [FIPS]).

In the unfortunate event of an actual key compromise, however, a CA can do one or more of the following to help minimize the resultant damage:

- Try, in whatever way possible, to get detailed knowledge of precisely who the relying party community is, so that notifications may be sent to (only) this set of entities if a compromise occurs. This is difficult or impossible in the Web model as currently defined, but it can be achieved in some of the other PKI trust models. Targeted notifications can help to minimize the embarrassment of a mass-market advertisement.

- Store the trusted public key as a certificate in the local domain of the relying parties, support the publication of a periodic ARL, and encourage relying party (PKI-relevant) software to do ARL checking. This can help to minimize damage because trust in the compromised key can be canceled in an automated way, without end-entity intervention. This mechanism is most suited to environments that check certificate status via revocation lists, but may also be appropriate for environments in which status is checked via other authorized servers (using, for example, OCSP [RFC2560] or similar protocols; see Chapter 8).

- Have a validity period on the signing key pair that is of reasonable duration. A key that is compromised after 10 years of use typically results in much more damage to the relying party community than a key that is compromised after one year of use; shorter validity periods, therefore, can help minimize damage. There is, however, a trade-off between trying to reduce the damage that would be caused by key compromise and trying to reduce the disruption that can occur from frequent CA key update.

- Implement a controlled and automated CA key rollover mechanism. Such a mechanism (for example, see the one described in PKIX-CMP [RFC2510]) can help to minimize the damage associated with CA key compromise in two ways. First, the fact that this can be completely automated and transparent to the relying party in some environments means that shorter validity periods for self-signed CA certificates can be acceptable (see preceding bullet point). Second, this approach allows a phased rollover of the relying party community to the next CA key, so that at any given time the number of entities affected by a CA key compromise will be smaller than the entire relying party community.

It is recommended that CA administrators spend time (prior to PKI deployment!) understanding and preparing for compromise of a CA private key.

Recovery

If a CA's private key has been compromised, there is no shortcut to the recovery process. Nothing ever signed by that key can be trusted, including certificates, CRLs, and ARLs (except, as noted earlier, the statement in an ARL that its own signing key has been revoked may be taken as valid). If that signing key has also been used for other purposes, such as authenticating protocol messages, or policy or practice statements (which is not generally recommended usage), these also can no longer be trusted.

Note

The fact that everything ever signed by the compromised key is now suspect highlights the desirability of using *key usage* bits (see Chapter 6, "Certificates and Certification") to distribute distinct signing functions among multiple CA keys. Each of these keys may then be used in a restricted context (for example, certificate signing, CRL signing, OCSP response signing, CP/CPS signing, and so on), and compromise of one key does not invalidate any of the other signatures.

The only road to recovery in the case of a compromised CA private key is the long one: The PKI must be reinitialized, essentially from scratch, for the entire affected relying party community. That is, a new CA signing key pair must be generated, and some trusted, out-of-band process must be used to install a copy of the public key in the local environment of every relevant PKI entity. No other mechanism involving the use of the old (compromised) key can be trusted to shorten, simplify, or circumvent this process. The PKI must be rebuilt as if it had never existed before for this set of entities.

Additional Observations

The compromise of a CA private key brings with it serious security consequences. To those who directly hold a copy of the corresponding public key as a trust anchor, it is an operational disaster. To those who have indirectly been made members of the relying party community through cross-certification, the damage is, at some level, less extensive. This is because the revocation of the cross-certificate by the directly trusted CA immediately and automatically cancels all further trust in the compromised CA and, by extension, in the certificates of its subject community. For both sets of entities (that is, the direct and the indirect relying party communities), everything signed by the compromised key is immediately invalid unless extensive use has been made of secure time stamps. In that case, it must be proven to an objective third party precisely which signatures were created prior to the time of compromise. The rarity of this practice, combined with the upheaval for entities when it is not done, underscores the importance of careful disaster preparation by CA administrators prior to PKI deployment.

Summary

This chapter looked at the significance of operational considerations with respect to the deployment of a PKI. It discussed the importance of designing or choosing the appropriate architectural model for the environment to be protected. It also gave a brief overview of a number of topics, including client-side software, on-line requirements, physical security, hardware components, end-entity key compromise, and disaster preparation and recovery.

Supplementary material that can lead to a deeper understanding of this area includes the following topics:

- A good understanding of the legal framework for PKI operation (This subject, although itself a PKI operational consideration as defined at the beginning of this chapter, is discussed separately in Chapter 13, "Legal Framework.")

- A good understanding of the environment under consideration for PKI deployment (This is the focus of the chapters in Part III, "Deployment Considerations.")

References

[CAPI]   Microsoft Corporation. "Cryptographic Application Program Interface (Crypto API)"; see `http://www.microsoft.com/security/default.asp` (in the "Technologies" section) for pointers to documentation and introductory material on this topic.

[CDSA]   Intel Corporation. "Common Data Security Architecture"; see `http://developer.intel.com/ial/security` for pointers to documentation, presentations, white papers, articles, and books on this topic.

[FIPS]   FIPS 140-1. "Security Requirements for Cryptographic Modules." Federal Information Processing Standards Publication 140-1. U.S. Department of Commerce/NIST, National Technical Information Service. Springfield, Virginia, January 1994.

[RFC2510] Adams, C. and S. Farrell. "Internet X.509 Public Key Infrastructure: Certificate Management Protocols." Internet Request for Comments 2510. (March 1999).

[RFC2560]   Myers, M., R. Ankney, A. Malpani, S. Galperin, and C. Adams. "X.509 Internet Public Key Infrastructure: Online Certificate Status Protocol—OCSP." Internet Request for Comments 2560. (June 1999).

[SET]   MasterCard/VISA. Secure Electronic Transaction; see `http://www.setco.org/`.

[X.509]   ITU-T Recommendation X.509. "Information Technology—Open Systems Interconnection—The Directory: Authentication Framework." June 1997 (equivalent to ISO/IEC 9594-8, 1997).

Legal Framework

Before proceeding with this chapter, it is important to note that we are not attorneys, and we are in no way attempting to offer legal advice in this chapter. However, we do attempt to highlight many of the legal issues that can have an impact on any organization that plans to offer services based on PKI technology.

Also note that this chapter is not trying to portray "doom and gloom" for electronic commerce. Although there are a number of problems that require resolution, this field is still young, and we expect to see improvements in these areas in the fullness of time.

Note

There are several sources of information regarding U.S. and international legislation, including the following:

- "The Limits of Trust: Cryptography, Governments and Electronic Commerce" by Stewart Baker and Paul Hurst [LOT]

- "Moving with Change: Electronic Signature Legislation as a Vehicle for Advancing E-Commerce" by Thomas Smedinghoff and Ruth Hill Bro [MWC]

In addition, *the Information Technology and Electronic Commerce (ITEC)* Law Department of the Chicago law firm McBride Baker & Coles provides a Web site (see `http://www.mbc.com/ds_sum.html`) that contains summaries of U.S. state, U.S. federal, and international legislation and/or initiatives.

These are excellent sources of information if you are interested in a more detailed overview of this topic.

Legal Status of Digital Signatures

There are a significant number of legislative efforts designed (at least in part) to attach a legal significance to digital signatures in the same vein as handwritten signatures. Since the original conception of the Utah Digital Signature Act and the American Bar Association (ABA) Digital Signature Guidelines [ABA], it is interesting to note that every U.S. state has either adopted or is ready to adopt some form of "electronic signature" or "digital signature" legislation. (See `http://www.mbc.com/ds_sum.html` for a summary of existing and planned legislation.) There are also more than 20 countries that have developed (or are developing) legislation or guidelines in this area (see `http://www.mbc.com/ds_sum.html` for a summary).

On the surface, this would appear to be good news. After all, won't the adoption of "digital signature" legislation promote and expedite global electronic commerce? Unfortunately, the answer to this question may actually be *no*. This is due to the fact that the various legislation and guidelines related to digital signatures are inconsistent (and sometimes contradictory). For example, as discussed in "Moving with Change: Electronic Signature Legislation as a Vehicle for Advancing E-Commerce" [MWC, pp. 15–18] and "The Limits of Trust: Cryptography, Governments and Electronic Commerce" [LOT, pp. 261–265], U.S. state legislation appears to fall into one of four categories:

- All forms of "electronic signature" have legal significance (that is, the legislation is completely technology-neutral). It does not levy any restrictions on what constitutes a legal or binding signature, other than it must be *something* that represents an intent to authenticate on the part of the signer [MWC, p. 16].

- Only forms of "electronic signature" that possess certain security properties have legal significance. That is, the legislation is technology-neutral, but the signature must be unique and under the sole possession of the person using it, it must be verifiable by others, and it must be bound to the data so that the signature is rendered invalid if the data has been modified in any way.

- Only digital signatures based on public-key cryptography have legal significance (that is, the legislation is strictly technology-dependent).

- Nothing is said about what constitutes a legal signature (presumably, this would be left to the court's discretion [LOT, p. 264]).

As a result of these inconsistencies, Smedinghoff and Hill Bro [MWC, p. 18] warn:

> These inconsistent approaches create a certain level of uncertainty for businesses trying to do e-commerce in multiple jurisdictions, especially if such businesses do not use electronic signatures that comply with requirements in all jurisdictions.

Also, some of the legislation is much more focused (or expressed another way, more limiting) than others [MWC, pp. 19–20 and LOT, pp. 259–261]. For example, some legislation identifies the types of electronic transactions that apply and/or the specific parties to which they apply. Other legislation does not address this at all.

Smedinghoff and Hill Bro [MWC, p. 20] succinctly summarize the dilemma that all of this brings, as follows:

> The bottom line is that in trying to remove barriers, we may have created more uncertainty. While there may be disagreement on the proper definition of an electronic signature, or on exactly which types of transactions are not appropriately conducted by electronic means, the lack of uniformity between the states may be creating a more significant barrier to e-commerce.

Electronic Signatures and Digital Signatures—What's In a Name?

Remember our discussion regarding terminology difficulties surrounding the use of "certificate," "digital certificate," and "public-key certificate" from Chapter 6? The issues surrounding the use of an "electronic signature" and a "digital signature" suffer a similar problem.

The problem here is that there is no universal agreement on what these terms mean or how they should be applied within a given context. Arguably, the correct definition for an electronic signature is any signature that can be represented electronically. This could be anything from a digitized handwritten signature to a *digital signature* based on public-key cryptography (as discussed in Chapter 2, "Public-Key Cryptography," and defined within the X.509 Recommendation [X.509]). Thus, a *digital signature* is a subset of a class of signatures referred to as *electronic signatures*.

Although these definitions are consistent with a number of sources such as the X.509 Recommendation [X.509, Section 3, Clause 9, pp. 13–14], and Smedinghoff and Hill Bro [MWC, Section II, pp. 7–8], these are not always the definitions encountered in some of the so-called "digital signature" legislation that has been produced. For example, some U.S. states use the term *digital signature* synonymously with the broader definition of *electronic signature* as defined earlier. Others closely follow the definition provided in the X.509 Recommendation [X.509].

In any case, it is clear that there is a lack of a uniform interpretation for these two terms. In the absence of universally agreed-upon terminology, it would be prudent to clearly articulate terminology to avoid unnecessary doubt and confusion. Specifically, when one is referring to public-key-based digital signatures, it may be prudent (or even necessary) to fully qualify the context as "digital signatures based on public-key cryptography." And, in many cases, the various legislation is more appropriately referred to as "electronic signature legislation." The exception to this is when the legislation is focused specifically on digital signatures based on public-key cryptography (for example, the Utah Digital Signature Act).

Similarly, there are significant differences between the digital signature legislation and guidelines in the international arena. A survey of these legislative efforts on a country-by-country basis is provided in "The Limits of Trust: Cryptography, Governments and Electronic Commerce" [LOT, pp. 291–317]. Summaries can also be found at `http://www.mbc.com/ds_sum.html`.

In response to the diverse and contradictory national legislation, Baker and Hurst [LOT, p. 283] warn:

> Unfortunately, the proliferation of digital signature laws, which is a solvable problem inside the United States, threatens to be nearly unsolvable on an international scale.

However, there are also efforts to bring some semblance of uniformity across international boundaries. These initiatives include the following (see [LOT, pp. 285–290] and [MWC, pp. 4–5] for further discussion):

- The European Commission Proposal for European Parliament and Council Directive on a Common Framework for Electronic Signatures (see `http://www.ispo.cec.be/ief/policy/com98297.html`)

- The Organization for Economic Co-operation and Development (see `http://www.oecd.org/`)

- The United Nations Commission on International Trade Law (UNCITRAL) Model Law on Electronic Commerce (see `http://www.uncitral.org/english/texts/electcom/ml-ec.htm`)

- The European Telecommunications Standards Institute (ETSI) draft report Telecommunications Security: Electronic Signature Standardization Report (see `http://www.etsi.org/sec/ESRep042.pdf`)

- The ongoing efforts of the Working Group on Electronic Commerce of UNCITRAL (see `http://www.uncitral.org/`)

However, it remains to be seen how much influence these efforts (and others) will have in ultimately breaking down the barriers to international electronic commerce that the otherwise disjointed and contradictory national legislation may introduce.

Legal Framework for PKIs

The purpose of this section is to discuss some of the legal issues and considerations associated with CA licensing requirements, and the roles and responsibilities associated with

CAs, subscribers, and relying parties. A brief discussion on the way these issues might apply in the context of a private enterprise PKI is also provided.

CA Licensing Requirements and Liability

In addition to the legal issues associated with electronic signatures, some of the technology-dependent legislation (both state and international) also discusses Certification Authority (CA) licensing requirements.

According to Baker and Hurst [LOT, pp. 268–270], most of the U.S. technology-dependent state legislation requires a CA to

- Demonstrate proficiency in encryption technology

- Prove possession of sufficient working capital

- Maintain an office or agent in-state

- Be available for routine independent audit

- Be a subscriber to a centrally approved (certification) authority for verification

- Not employ people convicted of fraud-related felonies

- File a guaranty with the state

- Use a trustworthy system

- Follow other requirements to be specified later, in regulations

Granted, this list is not exactly unambiguous (for example, what constitutes a "trustworthy system?"), but it does clearly levy certain restrictions on anyone operating a CA that falls under the jurisdiction of the applicable legislation. Note that some states are somewhat less restrictive, and some states are even more restrictive [LOT, p. 269]. Also, note that many states do not address CA licensing requirements because their legislation is, by intention, technology independent.

Some of the technology-dependent legislation also addresses the issue of CA liability. According to Baker and Hurst [LOT, p. 270], most of the U.S. technology-dependent state legislation exempts a licensed CA from

- Punitive or exemplary damages

- Damages due to pain and suffering

- Damages due to lost profits, savings, and opportunity

However, as in the case of licensing requirements, there are individual state variations on these exemptions [LOT, pp. 270–271].

Similar discussion with an international focus is provided in "The Limits of Trust: Cryptography, Governments and Electronic Commerce" [LOT, pp. 283–290].

Although the licensing requirements listed here may be optional for a CA within a given state, it is likely that the exemptions from liability will be a strong motivator for an organization that wants to offer PKI services within one of these states. Further, given the requirement that some states levy specific requirements in terms of audits, it is not surprising that many third-party organizations appear to be positioning themselves to offer independent audit capabilities.

Note

It is interesting to note that most of the existing legislation appears to be silent (or unclear) in other areas that may be critical to the overall long-term success of a PKI in support of electronic commerce (or other services). For example, the requirements associated with time stamping and/or notarization services that are likely be required in support of non-repudiation services are unclear. As another example, the requirements associated with archival services for the secure, long-term storage of certificates, certificate revocation information, and so on, that might be required for dispute resolution years in the future are also not well-defined.

Roles and Responsibilities

As discussed throughout this chapter, the various components of a PKI, and even the consumers of a PKI, have certain responsibilities that must be honored if the services facilitated by the PKI are to be maintained at an acceptably secure level. Not surprisingly, the technology-dependent legislation addresses the responsibilities associated with subscribers as well as CAs. The responsibilities of a relying party must also be addressed (although this appears to be a bit more nebulous when compared to subscribers and CAs). Figure 13.1 illustrates the three primary roles typically encountered in an electronic commerce scenario based on PKI technology. The responsibilities associated with each of these entities are described further in the subsections that follow.

Subscriber Responsibilities

As discussed in "Moving with Change: Electronic Signature Legislation as a Vehicle for Advancing E-Commerce" [MWC, p. 30], an end-user that acquires a certificate for subsequent use (often called the *subscriber*) is obligated to

- Make truthful representations in applying for a certificate

- Review and accept a certificate before using it

- Make certain representations upon acceptance of the certificate

- Control and keep confidential the corresponding private key

- Promptly revoke the certificate upon compromise of the corresponding private key

Figure 13.1   Roles—The usual suspects.

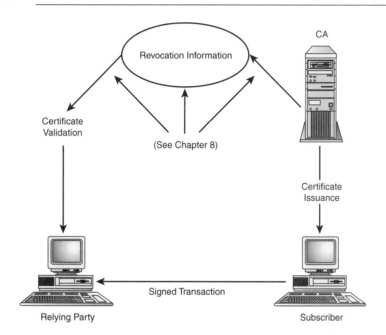

Note that the last two obligations require a substantial amount of understanding on the part of the subscriber. For example, the subscriber needs to be educated on how to "keep his/her private key private." In certain cases, this responsibility may be assisted by technology-specific means (for example, through the use of a smart card or hardware token). In any event, certain guidelines need to be conveyed to the subscriber that will, in certain cases, be technology-dependent. (For example, is the private key stored on a smart card versus a software token or some other storage medium?)

The obligations surrounding "suspected key compromise" are even harder to convey to the individual subscribers. For example, what constitutes compromise? Under which circumstances should a subscriber suspect (or know) that his/her private key has been compromised? The events that might constitute a serious breach of security must be conveyed to the subscriber so that the subscriber more fully understands his/her obligations in this regard. Even the reporting procedures and amount of delay between suspecting a compromise and reporting the suspicion (which might vary from state to state and country to country) have to be understood by the subscriber.

CA Responsibilities

As discussed in "Moving with Change: Electronic Signature Legislation as a Vehicle for Advancing E-Commerce" [MWC, p. 30], a CA is obligated to

- Use a trustworthy system

- Disclose its practices and procedures

- Properly identify a prospective applicant for a certificate

- Publish issued certificates in a repository

- Suspend and/or revoke certificates

- Make warranties to the certificate applicant upon issuance of the certificate

- Make warranties to persons using the certificate to verify digitally signed messages

To summarize in PKI-vernacular, the CA is obligated to implement adequate end-entity registration procedures, and to develop a *Certification Practice Statement*, or *CPS* (see Chapter 6, "Certificates and Certification") or equivalent in support of the disclosure requirement (and also in support of independent audits). There is also the obligation to generate and post certificates and certificate revocation information, and to make express warranties to both the subscribers and the relying parties using the certificates issued by that CA.

Relying Party Responsibilities

The responsibilities of a relying party appear to be a bit more obscure than those specified for the subscriber and the CA, at least from a legislative perspective. However, the relying party is likely to be responsible for at least four things:

- Verification of digital signatures from originating subscribers (including certificate path validation, as discussed in Chapter 9)

- Knowledge of the rules associated with digital signature acceptance (for example, is a relying party obligated to accept a legitimate digital signature, or is there a choice?)

- Record-keeping to help resolve any disputes that may arise in the future

- Understanding what to do when things go wrong, and/or when something occurs that requires the intervention or action of the relying party

Of course, no one expects the relying party to use a calculator to verify the digital signature. It is tacitly assumed that the relying party will be aided with software that is designed to verify digital signatures (including certification path validation, as discussed in Chapter 9).

The same can be said for record-keeping; either there should be software local to the relying party that helps to record relevant transactions, or a trusted third party should be available to support this service. At a minimum, important transactions should be stored in their digitally-signed form. There are likely to be time stamping and/or notarization requirements associated with this service in the future as well.

The last bullet in the preceding list deals with things that might require the direct intervention of the relying party. For example, what happens when the necessary revocation information is unavailable? What is the relying party allowed/expected to do or not do in this case? What happens when the relying party receives an indication that a certificate has been suspended? Assistance may be supplied to the relying party; for example, the relying party may be instructed to telephone an authority that can supply additional instructions to the relying party (see Section 5.3.2 of "Internet X.509 Public Key Infrastructure Certificate and CRL Profile" [RFC2459]). However, this may not always be the case.

As in the case of the subscriber, it really comes down to properly educating the individuals involved in these transactions so that they can more fully understand and execute their specific responsibilities.

Private Enterprise PKIs

So, what does all of this mean in the context of a private enterprise PKI? It is unclear if, how, and when some of this legislation might or might not apply in the context of an enterprise PKI, in which confidentiality and/or digital signature services are offered solely to the employees of that organization (that is, the enterprise does not offer services to external sources). One could argue that this is something that should be subject to normal terms and agreements between the organization and the individual employees. However, this may not always be the case.

To illustrate the problem, consider the following scenario. An employee's personnel file is exposed due to negligence on the part of the company. For example, key sizes mandated by the company were known to be inadequate within the industry, or someone deceived the key recovery center into releasing the decryption private key of someone in the personnel department, and thereby gained access to the employee's confidential records. What recourse is available to an individual whose sensitive employee records have been compromised? Alternatively, if that same individual carelessly gave away his/her credentials that are then used to unlock highly sensitive corporate data, what recourse does the organization have? Compliance with applicable PKI legislation may be an appropriate course of action for the private enterprise because this may allow legal recourse in some situations.

Along with any legal recourse motivations, if the private enterprise happens to be a state or national government agency, it is reasonable to assume that the government agency will ask that the PKI vendor comply with the applicable legislation. Even in the case of a private sector enterprise, compliance with certain legislation might be required, either because it is actually mandated within the jurisdiction that applies to the private sector enterprise, or because the legislation is viewed to be a sensible criterion for vendor selection—much the same as an organization looks at other selection criteria to determine which vendor offers the best possible solution in response to their requirements (see Chapter 22, "Deployment Issues and Decisions").

While the debate over the specificity of legislation continues, it seems prudent to perform the necessary due diligence, even in a private enterprise context. Legislation might help an organization to better understand the level of due diligence required. However, given the inconsistencies between various state and national legislation, note that broad-brush statements such as "The CA/PKI vendor must comply with all applicable legislation and guidelines" may be more harmful than good, especially if there are multiple jurisdictions involved.

Other Contractual-Based Frameworks

As discussed in Chapter 9, a number of frameworks can be used to establish contractual relationships between two or more PKI domains. For example, bilateral cross-certification agreements can be used to establish trust relationships between organizations based on certificate policies, CPSs, or both. The "bridge CA" concept may also be used to establish certification relationships between multiple organizations based on certain policies and rules of conduct such that each individual organization does not have to analyze the Certificate Policy and/or CPS of another organization. It is unclear how some of the legislation discussed within this chapter applies under these circumstances.

What about Confidentiality?

Although the focus of this chapter has concentrated on legislation and guidelines surrounding the use of electronic signatures and, in particular, digital signatures, it should be noted that a number of legal issues surround confidentiality as well.

Baker and Hurst [LOT, pp. 1–39] provide an interesting overview of the political landscape surrounding the cryptographic issues associated with confidentiality services, including export, import, and the domestic use of cryptography. They also include a summary of international initiatives related to cryptography [LOT, pp. 41–78] and a country-by-country guide related to encryption regulations [LOT, pp. 79–241].

Summary

The primary focus of this chapter has been on electronic signature legislation or, in some cases, the digital signature legislation based specifically on public-key technology. It summarized various requirement, highlighted the roles and responsibilities of the various entities involved (CA, subscriber, and relying party), and provided pointers to more specific documentation.

This chapter also discussed the dilemma associated with the proliferation of inconsistent legislation that has been passed within the U.S. and on an international basis. Given that almost every U.S. state and more than twenty nations have passed one form of legislation or another, it is important that an enterprise review its situation carefully, especially if it happens to fall under multiple jurisdictions.

Ultimately, the important thing for any enterprise is to mitigate risk to the maximum extent possible. And although the CA licensing requirements in most states might be optional, there are legitimate reasons for an organization to insist that the CA or PKI technology vendor adhere to those requirements, quite possibly demanding that conformance be evaluated by a third-party auditor.

On the other hand, the lack of uniformity across domestic and international borders can create serious consequences for the service provider, and it can also wreak havoc with the technology vendors. Specifically, how is a given technology vendor going to offer a set of products that can conform to every variation that might be encountered? Unless there is significant overlap among all these rules, regulations, and evaluation/audit criteria, this is problematic at best. One can argue, therefore, that conflicting legislation will do nothing but undermine the very success of global electronic commerce. Fortunately, a number of efforts are underway, which may help to rectify this undesirable situation.

To better understand the significance of legal framework for PKI operation, a good understanding of PKI concepts is required (see Chapters 6–12). In addition, the various deployment issues and alternatives should be reviewed (see Part III, "Deployment Considerations").

References

[ABA]   American Bar Association (ABA). "Digital Signature Guidelines: Legal Infrastructure for Certification Authorities and Electronic Commerce." 1995.

[LOT]   Baker, Stewart A. and Paul R. Hurst. "The Limits of Trust: Cryptography, Governments and Electronic Commerce." Kluwer Law International, 1998.

[MWC]   Smedinghoff, Thomas J. and Ruth Hill Bro. "Moving with Change: Electronic Signature Legislation as a Vehicle for Advancing E-Commerce." Originally published in *The John Marshall Journal of Computer and Information Law*, Vol. XVII, No. 3 (Spring 1999); available on-line at http://www.mbc.com/.

[RFC2459]   Housley, R., W. Ford, W. Polk, and D. Solo. "Internet X.509 Public Key Infrastructure Certificate and CRL Profile." Internet Request for Comments 2459 (January 1999).

[X.509]   ITU-T Recommendation X.509. "Information Technology—Open Systems Interconnection—The Directory: Authentication Framework." June 1977 (equivalent to ISO/IEC 9594-8, 1997).

CHAPTER 14

Conclusions and Further Reading

Part I of this book has considered the many aspects of PKI. The treatment has been intentionally generic, in the sense that every attempt has been made to avoid references to specific vendor interpretations or product implementations of any particular topic. Instead, the focus of the discussion has been to introduce concepts, explain terminology, highlight issues, and discuss the benefits of this technology, all as an aid to understanding this subject area.

Conclusions

PKI is a rich and complex topic, encompassing all the facets required to turn public-key cryptography into an infrastructural platform for security services. Put simply,

$$PKI = (PK)^I$$

(*PKI* is *public key* raised to the power of an *infrastructure*). Thinking of PKI first and foremost as an infrastructure puts many of its concepts into perspective and helps to clarify why things such as user transparency and cross-application/cross-platform consistency are intrinsic to the definition of PKI. This results in concepts such as automated key and certificate life cycle management, and application-independent client software, being fundamental to a proper PKI implementation (otherwise, the implementation is providing public-key technology and services, but not an infrastructural solution).

The PKI, as described by the extended definition in Chapter 3, "The Concept of an Infrastructure," encompasses functionality to meet a wide range of security needs. A particular PKI implementation for a particular operating environment may not require this full functionality; some subset of the described functionality may be sufficient. However, the extended definition is useful because a PKI that meets this description should be able to meet the needs of any environment today, as well as the growing needs of that environment as time moves on.

Further Reading

One of the primary reasons for writing this book was the relative scarcity of good introductory material on this topic. PKI is beginning to get a lot of attention in the trade journals, but very little of this literature aims to explain concepts and terminology to any significant breadth or depth. Moreover, it is difficult to find a *single* source that explains a broad range of PKI topics in sufficient detail so that a beginner may quickly become familiar with this area.

If you're interested in further reading in the areas of public-key cryptography and PKI, you may want to consult the following references.

Feghhi, J., J. Feghhi, and P. Williams. *Digital Certificates: Applied Internet Security.* Reading, MA: Addison Wesley, 1999.

Ford, W. and M. Baum. *Secure Electronic Commerce: Building the Infrastructure for Digital Signatures and Encryption.* Englewood Cliffs, NJ: Prentice Hall, 1997.

Lewis, J. "Public Key Infrastructure Architecture." *The Burton Group Network Strategy Report* 1 (9 July 1997).

Menezes, A., P. van Oorschot, and S. Vanstone. *Handbook of Applied Cryptography.* Boca Raton, FL: CRC Press, 1997.

Schneier, B. *Applied Cryptography: Protocols, Algorithms, and Source Code in C, Second Edition.* New York: John Wiley & Sons, 1996.

PART

II

Standards

CHAPTER **15**

Introduction

Part II of this book takes a brief look at the standards and non-standards activities most relevant to PKI technology. This part is deliberately small due to the recognition that such activities are volatile and fluid at best, defying prediction and challenging the wisdom of static preservation in a book. Nevertheless, it is of value to highlight the major groups working in this area, to provide some background in terms of their history and purpose, and to give pointers to the specifications that are stable enough to warrant implementation efforts.

Chapter 16, "Major Standards Activities," discusses some of the most prominent activities taking place within formal standards bodies. As you will notice, a good number of these activities are currently occurring within the Internet Engineering Task Force (IETF) of the Internet Society.

Chapter 17, "Standardization Status and Road Map," provides the current and projected near-term standardization status of some of the most significant specifications, and includes references to where these documents may be found and where their progress may be tracked.

Chapter 18, "Standards: Necessary but Not Sufficient," considers the fact that the existence of a "standard," whether it is the product of a formal standards body or not, is necessary but not sufficient to guarantee that the products of different vendors will interoperate with each other. Some of the reasons for this are given, along with a discussion of the usefulness of profiling activities and interoperability pilots.

Finally, Chapter 19, "Conclusions and Further Reading," contains concluding remarks and some suggestions for further reading on the topic presented in this part of the book.

Major Standards Activities

This chapter discusses a number of the high-visibility standards activities relevant to PKI concepts or techniques. It is not meant to be exhaustive, but it does include many of the groups that have captured significant attention in recent times as awareness of security (and especially PKI) has grown.

The groups listed here are interrelated to various degrees. Those defining certificate formats include X.509, SPKI, OpenPGP, and EDIFACT; these, to a large extent, are independent efforts. Those profiling certificates (primarily X.509v3 certificates) for specific environments and uses include PKIX, TC68, S/MIME, IPsec, and TLS; these efforts overlap to a much greater degree. Certificate and CRL repository issues (primarily, again, for X.509 formats) are the topic of the X.500 and LDAP efforts.

X.509

The *X.509* [X.509] portion of the ISO and CCITT/ITU-T X.500 suite of standards is in many ways the single most important factor in the transition of PKI concepts from small, closed-network, trial environments to large, open deployments. As noted in Chapter 6, "Certificates and Certification," the concept of a certificate makes public-key technology feasible when the entities are, for the most part, unknown to each other. Therefore, to bring PKI to large multi-national corporations or to millions of Internet users, a useful certificate format was necessary. To allow interoperability among multiple tools and applications, a certificate format needed to be standardized and widely adopted. It is precisely this role that X.509 has played: This specification defined and standardized a general, flexible certificate format. Its widespread adoption is perhaps testimony (in equal measure) to its technical suitability for many environments and its availability as an international standard just at the time when a number of vendors were ready to begin implementing products.

The real utility of X.509 comes from the powerful extension mechanism it has defined for its Version 3 certificates and Version 2 CRLs. This mechanism is perfectly general in that any extension whatsoever may be defined and placed into a certificate or CRL; furthermore, a criticality flag indicates whether or not a verifier must understand and examine this extension as part of its verification process. Thus, certificate and CRL contents can readily be tailored to specific environments with or without restricting their usability in other environments, as desired.

Although it is an international standard, X.509 has continued to evolve in some ways. Any problems found through operational experience have been (and will continue to be) addressed in the standard through a formal defect reporting and resolution process. Amendments to the standard can also be incorporated in some cases to clarify text or to provide additional detail; one example of this is the amendment addressing the definition and use of attribute certificates for general privilege management (see Chapter 5, "PKI-Enabled Services," for a discussion on privilege management).

PKIX

The Internet Engineering Task Force (IETF) is the body primarily responsible for creating, standardizing, and promoting the protocols/functions that make the Internet useful and interesting (examples include TCP/IP, SMTP, FTP, Telnet, and HTTP). This work is carried out by a number of working groups; these are organized into various areas of common interest.

One of the working groups in the IETF Security Area is *Public-Key Infrastructure, X.509*, commonly referred to as *PKIX*. The PKIX Working Group was formed at the end of 1995 with the explicit intention of tailoring the certificate and CRL work done in the X.509 standard [X.509] to the Internet environment to specify an Internet PKI (IPKI).

As the vision of the working group was being formalized in the IETF, it was recognized that there is more to defining an Internet PKI than profiling the X.509 certificate and CRL work. Thus the PKIX charter was written to encompass four specific areas of activity [PKIX]:

- The certificate and CRL profile

- Certificate management protocols

- Operational protocols

- Certificate Policy (CP) and Certification Practice Statement (CPS) framework

The first item was the original motivating task—the profile of the X.509 syntax, including detailed specification of the mandatory, optional, critical, and non-critical extensions (see Chapters 6 and 8 for a discussion of extensions) in a "PKIX-compliant" certificate or CRL.

The second item was to specify the protocols for all the management operations required in the IPKI, including initialization/certification of entities and their key pairs, certificate revocation, key backup and recovery, CA key rollover, cross-certification, and so on.

The third item, operational protocols, was to specify the protocols for day-to-day IPKI operation, such as certificate/CRL retrieval from a public repository and on-line checking of the revocation status of a certificate.

Finally, the fourth item was to provide guidelines to writers of CP and CPS documents, suggesting topics and formats that may be useful for inclusion in particular environments, and so on.

These four PKIX work items became the subjects of separate documents so that the work could move ahead independently under independent authors and no one part would have its progression impeded by unforeseen delays in any of the other parts. In due course, the certificate management protocol and operational protocol work items were also split into multiple documents to accommodate the needs and desires of different PKI environments. The specifications that have stabilized within the PKIX Working Group include RFC2459, RFC2510, RFC2511, RFC2527, RFC2559, RFC2560, RFC2585 and RFC2587.

PKIX has played an essential and significant role in bringing the concept of a PKI to the Internet. The protocols and functions it has defined make a PKI possible, even in the diverse enclaves of the Internet, because their flexibility and generality can satisfy the requirements of greatly differing environments. The work continues to evolve as well: The PKIX Charter was expanded in 1999 to include new work items on time stamping protocols, data certification services, and attribute certificates.

X.500

The ISO/ITU-T suite of standards for the directory, commonly known as the *X.500* series of specifications [X.500], is the framework within which the X.509 document was originally created. The X.500 Directory is a highly sophisticated repository of arbitrary information and includes such features as client-to-directory access protocols, server-to-server communication protocols, full and partial replication of directory data, chaining of servers to respond to a query, complex search filtering capabilities, and so on. Recognition of the need for access control to the directory, including the requirement for strong authentication in some environments, led to the specification of certificate and CRL formats and other PKI concepts in the X.509 standard.

Of particular importance to PKI, X.500 has defined a *schema*, a standardized method to store certificate and CRL data structures in an entity's directory entry. Thus, regardless of which vendor has supplied the X.500-compliant directory in an environment, the PKI implementation will be able to retrieve the certificates and CRLs it needs to operate correctly. Although the directory has achieved nothing like the worldwide deployment its originators hoped, the standardized schema alone has made it an important part of many PKI deployments. Furthermore, the technical feasibility of linking directory servers together makes it possible for these independently deployed PKIs to be joined together when necessary to permit secure communications between and among separate communities.

LDAP

The *Lightweight Directory Access Protocol (LDAP)* [HS97] was originally conceived as a simple-to-describe, simple-to-implement subset of the capability of the *X.500 Directory Access Protocol (DAP)*. Over time, this "subset" of useful functions and features has expanded to incorporate the needs of the many different environments that have chosen to use LDAP as the access protocol for their repository (X.500-compliant directory or otherwise). This has led some to question whether the "L" in LDAP still applies, just as the "S" in some of the IETF "Simple" protocols occasionally raises eyebrows.

Nevertheless, many vendors worldwide deploy LDAP Version 2 [RFC1777], and LDAPv3 [RFC2251], with its useful extension mechanism for incorporating new capabilities over time in a standardized way, will likely see even greater deployment. The IETF Working Group LDAPext [LDAPext] has been formed to define and standardize particular useful extensions for LDAPv3, such as an access control mechanism.

As with X.500, a schema [RFC2587] has been specified for LDAP-compliant repositories to provide a standardized method and location for certificate and CRL information storage for PKI entities. This greatly enhances the possibility of interoperability between PKI products from different vendors in an LDAP environment.

ISO TC68

Working Group 8 of Sub-Committee 2 of Technical Committee 68 in ISO (*ISO TC68/SC2/WG8*, referred to here simply as *TC68*) is concerned with standardizing aspects of public-key technology, primarily for the use and purposes of the financial industry [TC68]. This working group, like PKIX, has profiled the X.509 certificate and CRL structures for the particular needs of its focus environment. To that end, it has specified the optional or mandatory, critical or non-critical status of the X.509-defined extensions (see Chapters 6 and 8 for further details on the certificate and CRL extension mechanism). It has also defined new extensions required to meet the unique needs of the financial sector.

ANSI X9F

The *American National Standards Institute (ANSI)* committee X9 (Financial Services) develops and publishes standards for the Financial Services Industry in order to facilitate delivery of financial products and services. Subcommittee *X9F* is responsible for standards related to data and information security and includes working groups focused on cryptographic tools (X9F1), protocols (X9F3), and digital signature and certificate policy (X9F5), among others. X9F has published a significant number of standards (see, for example, the online catalog at `http://www.x9.org`) and is active in submitting some of its more mature draft documents as new work items to the related ISO group TC68.

S/MIME

In 1995, a consortium of industry vendors led by RSA Data Security, Inc. took the *Multipart Internet Mail Extensions (MIME)* specifications in the IETF and decided on the particular mechanisms required to add security—specifically in the form of encryption and digital signatures—to MIME-compliant messages. The *Secure MIME (S/MIME)* specifications, though not the product of any formal standards body, achieved some measure of recognition and consensus in the Internet messaging community. To build on and expand this success, the S/MIME documents (then at Version 2) were brought into the IETF process [RFC2311, RFC2312], and all enhancements to this work were to be carried out within an IETF S/MIME Working Group created for this purpose.

The initial and primary focus of the S/MIME Working Group was to incorporate a number of new security features into the specification while maintaining compatibility (to the greatest extent possible) with products implemented according to the previous version of the specifications. In particular, the standards-track S/MIMEv3 specifications [RFC2630-RFC2634] include the ability to label messages securely (for example, "secret," "top secret," or "company confidential") and the ability to request and receive a *signed receipt* (that is, proof that the intended recipient had actually received a prior message). Also included is the ability to use key management techniques other than RSA (for example, Diffie-Hellman—see Chapter 2 for a discussion of the RSA and D-H algorithms).

The S/MIMEv3 specifications include discussion of PKI concepts such as certificate format, certificate processing, and CRLs. These specifications give a profile for X.509 certificates that is compliant with PKIX [RFC2459] but that specifies the extensions relevant to S/MIME. Furthermore, provision is made in the message envelope to carry arbitrary numbers of certificates and CRLs to assist the recipient with the task of path construction and certificate validation.

IPsec

The upgrade of the Internet Protocol Version 6 (IPv6) included a set of new features and functions, one of which was due consideration, within the standards-track specifications, of the security architecture for this protocol [RFC2401]. A new IETF working group was created for the purpose of designing and standardizing the IP Security (IPsec) set of concepts and protocols. An important component of this architecture is a protocol for key exchange between IP nodes for the purpose of authenticity, integrity, and confidentiality. This work is embodied in the *Internet Key Exchange (IKE) protocol* [RFC2409], a combination of a general framework for key management in this environment (Internet Security Association and Key Management Protocol, ISAKMP [RFC2408]) and a specific protocol for accomplishing key exchange within this framework (Oakley [RFC2412]).

IKE provides for strong, certificate-based authentication at the IP layer and, to this end, specifies a profile of X.509 certificates suitable for its purposes. This profile is compatible with the PKIX profile [RFC2459] but concentrates on the extensions relevant to the IP layer. Currently, the only extension specified is the IPsec key usage flag.

TLS

The *Transport Layer Security (TLS)* specification is the IETF standards-track version of the Secure Sockets Layer Version 3.0 (SSLv3.0) protocol found in millions of client browsers and Web servers around the world. TLS creates a secure channel between source and destination entities at the transport layer, providing certificate-based authentication, information integrity, and data confidentiality.

Like S/MIME and IPsec, the TLS specification includes discussion of a profile for X.509 certificates that aims for compatibility with the PKIX profile [RFC2459]. While total compatibility is not always possible due to the conflicting requirements of these different user groups, such efforts help to illustrate the respect for, and influence of, the PKIX specifications within the IETF community as a whole. The efforts undergone in the PKIX Working Group to define a PKI for the Internet appear to be meeting the goals of these various groups and serving the IETF community well. The fact that other (that is, non-IETF) standards groups and industry sectors also take PKIX compatibility into consideration when finalizing their specifications highlights the fact that the PKIX work is general enough to encompass the needs of communities other than IETF.

SPKI

The *Simple Public Key Infrastructure (SPKI)* IETF Working Group was created in 1996 as an alternative to the PKIX effort. One of the fundamental premises of this group was that

X.509 is a complicated and bulky certificate format that, by explicitly binding a key pair to an *identity*, rests upon an inherently flawed foundation. The proponents of SPKI argue that the concept of a globally unique identity (that is, an X.500 `DistinguishedName`, as adopted by X.509) will never be realized. Instead, they advocate the idea of the public key as the identity of relevance. Where necessary and meaningful, a name or other identifying information may be associated with the key (building on the work in "SDSI—A Simple Distributed Security Infrastructure" [SDSI]), but this is optional and, in any case, only intended to have local significance.

The SPKI specifications [RFC2692, RFC2693] discuss the concepts and philosophy behind this approach to an Internet PKI and provide the detailed certificate format and processing rules required for implementation (see also [SPKI]). Unlike the initial focus of both X.509 and PKIX, SPKI explicitly encompasses authorization as well as authentication: The sophisticated certificate format makes it possible to express, in a general way, what a key is *allowed to do*. Such capability unfortunately (and perhaps not surprisingly) has done much to diminish the originally intended simplicity of the *Simple* Public Key Infrastructure. This has perhaps cost it some credibility and lost it some enthusiasts in specific environments. Nevertheless, the SPKI specifications have reached a level of maturity and stability within the working group, and its proponents have begun to concentrate their efforts on implementation and interoperability testing.

Although SPKI embodies a number of interesting ideas and research contributions, it has not gained the widespread support of the corporate and governmental environments that X.509 has enjoyed. It remains to be seen, therefore, how many vendors will include SPKI certificates in their products and whether the SPKI definition of an Internet PKI will ever occupy more than a niche market.

OpenPGP

Like S/MIME, SSL, and X.509, the popular *Pretty Good Privacy (PGP)* security framework was brought under the auspices of the IETF to formalize the specification within a recognized standards body and to make it more relevant to the wider Internet community. This resulted in the *OpenPGP* Working Group and associated specification [RFC2440].

OpenPGP defines the PGP certificate format (an alternative to both X.509 and SPKI) and specifies the processing rules required to validate such a certificate, predicated on the familiar PGP "Web-of-trust" model (see Chapter 9). It also specifies the enveloping protocols required to construct and process PGP-protected e-mail messages.

Despite a large and loyal installed base, OpenPGP has not captured a significant portion of the corporate or government security infrastructures. This may be due to the fact that the inherently user-centric trust model cannot easily be controlled centrally on an organization-wide basis (to ensure, for example, that each individual user will conform to a predefined corporate policy regarding the appropriate trust anchor(s) for certificate path verification); or this may be due to the fact that its key management can become quite complex over time for inexperienced users. However, it seems likely that OpenPGP will continue to be popular with individual Internet users. In an effort to ensure this popularity and to enhance interoperability with other applications and environments, the OpenPGP specification also includes discussion regarding interworking with alternative certificate formats such as X.509.

EDIFACT

The X.400 Electronic Data Interchange standards effort has produced a certificate format known as *EDIFACT* [EDIFACT]. Although used in selected business environments, this format does not appear to have the momentum behind it that X.509 has and, furthermore, does not seem to have been widely adopted in any non-corporate environments (such as governmental, academic, or individual Internet user environments).

Other Activities

There are a number of activities within various communities that are not formal standards activities but whose output will specify (or dictate) product implementation at some level of detail for a variety of vendors. Such specifications have the strength of a formal standards document within a particular community of interest. The importance of such activities should not be understated. Although there are numerous examples of formal standards that fell into oblivion because they were never widely adopted, the presence and energy of the activities discussed here indicates that PKI will not suffer the same fate. A growing number of communities, both large and small, are actively planning or building PKIs to satisfy their own requirements.

This chapter discusses a few of the many such activities. The examples included are meant to be representative, not comprehensive. Furthermore, similar activities will arise from time to time to address the needs of other particular environments or industry sectors.

U.S. FPKI

The *United States Federal Public-Key Infrastructure (FPKI)* [FPKI] is an initiative by the U.S. government to define a PKI suitable for its own use. One of its focuses is the production of an acceptable profile for X.509 certificates and CRLs (see earlier in this chapter as well as Chapter 17, "Standardization Status and Road Map," for a discussion of X.509), but the ultimate goal is a full PKI specification. This specification is to encompass all relevant PKI entities (including end-entities [EEs], CAs, RAs, so-called "Bridge CAs"—to link CAs from different domains—and so on) in terms of their functionality and primary implementation characteristics. It also includes the security-relevant communications protocols between these entities, and the operational policies and procedures required for the PKI to be useful.

The final U.S. FPKI set of specifications will impose compliance requirements on vendors wanting to sell PKI products to the U.S. government. However, the hope is that the FPKI will be sufficiently similar to PKIs for other environments that compliance will not unduly restrict vendors from selling their products, unmodified, to these other communities.

MISPC

The *Minimum Interoperability Specifications for PKI Components (MISPC)* [MISPC] may be seen as one component of the full U.S. FPKI vision, though in some respects it is largely independent of that effort. The goal in MISPC, as implied by its title, is to understand and to specify the minimum functionality required of PKI entities that will still enable them to interoperate usefully with other PKI entities. Thus, for example, the certificate and CRL profile portion of MISPC identifies which of the many optional fields in the X.509 and PKIX specifications really must be implemented for these data structures to be processable by other entities in the PKI.

Interestingly, MISPC is more than a detailed specification; a CD containing a complete reference implementation compliant with the specification is also available. Thus, vendors have a straightforward way of testing whether or not their products are MISPC compliant.

GOC PKI

The *Government of Canada Public-Key Infrastructure (GOCPKI)* [GOCPKI], the first large-scale governmental PKI initiative in the world, has a goal slightly broader than the U.S. FPKI initiative: It defines a PKI suitable for Canadian federal government use, but eventually for nationwide use as well (that is, for all citizens of Canada). It is a full PKI specification, including certificate and CRL profiles, entity functionality and characteristics, communications protocols, and operational policies and procedures.

The GOCPKI will impose compliance requirements on vendors, but it is hoped that this will not preclude these *"Commercial Off-the-Shelf"* (COTS) products from being suitable for other environments as well.

SET

The *Secure Electronic Transaction (SET) specification* [SET] defines protocols for certificate issuance and processing rules in the context of credit card payment over the Internet.

Initiated in February 1996 by MasterCard and VISA and completed in May 1997 (SET v1.0), this specification was intended to be the backbone for electronic commerce (e-commerce) over the World Wide Web.

SET was created to meet the following business requirements:

- To provide confidentiality of payment information and to enable confidentiality of order information transmitted along with the payment information

- To ensure the integrity of all transmitted data

- To provide authentication that a cardholder is a legitimate user of a branded payment card account

- To provide authentication that a merchant can accept branded payment card transactions through its relationship with an acquiring financial institution

Interoperability testing between SET components implemented by different vendors is an on-going activity. The SETCo Web site documents and maintains the results [SET].

SEMPER

Secure Electronic MarketPlace, EuRope (SEMPER) [SEMPER] is a project designed to facilitate e-commerce, primarily in the European countries but ultimately on a worldwide scale. It specifies the functionality and operational characteristics of the principle entities involved in e-commerce transactions (the purchaser, the purchaser's bank, the merchant, and the merchant's bank), as well as the required secure communications protocols between them.

An aspect of SEMPER that currently seems to be more developed than similar projects elsewhere is the approach to risk management and the legal implications of entity actions. For example, which party or parties incur the cost of various kinds of failure modes in the defined electronic transactions? A detailed and fairly comprehensive risk model within the SEMPER project addresses these and similar questions. Comparable initiatives in other countries might do well to look at the progress made within SEMPER on this important topic.

ECOM

The *Electronic Commerce (ECOM)* project of the Electronic Commerce Promotion Council of Japan [ECOM] has been in existence since January 1996. Phase II of this project, covering the period 1998–1999, is focused on encouraging a further global expansion of e-commerce.

ECOM encompasses a number of working groups that concentrate on a variety of topics including consumer issues, authentication/notary, electronic settlements, risk/insurance, and international transaction/trade procedures. Several specifications have been produced, including technical guideline documents on the following topics:

- Certification Authorities (CAs)

- Cross-certification

- Transactions between virtual merchants and consumers

- Protection of personal data in e-commerce in the private sector

- Selling transactions by shops

The ECOM project is interested in enabling e-commerce on a global scale. To this end, it is actively pursuing more complex topics such as establishing a trustworthy environment, creating new business opportunities for EC, and solving cross-border EC issues.

Summary

This chapter has looked briefly at a number of standards activities that have particular relevance to PKI for one of the following reasons:

- They define and formalize PKI concepts.

- They specify certificate formats and processing rules.

- They make particular use of certificates to accomplish security functions (such as authenticity, integrity, and confidentiality).

Much of this activity is taking place within the various working groups of the IETF, highlighting its importance in the area of security and PKI.

The list of activities provided within this chapter is not meant to be exhaustive, but it does attempt to highlight some of the most important and most visible activities. These activities differ in terms of their approach (that is, how are the problems being solved?), their focus (that is, which aspect(s) of PKI are being addressed?), and their scope (that is, for which user community is this being tailored?). However, what they have in common is that within the community of interest, the activity puts constraints upon vendor implementations in the same way that a formally approved standard specification might.

The primary benefits of these activities typically include decreased time to completion of the specification and increased participation of the members of the eventual user community. This ultimately results in PKI products that are relevant and readily available for use to the communities for which they are targeted.

The following chapter will examine the standardization status of some of the more important specifications in this area.

References

[ECOM]   Electronic Commerce Promotion Council of Japan; see http://www.ecom.or.jp/ecom_e/.

[EDIFACT] ISO 9735. EDIFACT specification.

[FPKI]   United States Federal Public-Key Infrastructure; see http://csrc.nist.gov/pki/

[GOCPKI]   Government of Canada Public-Key Infrastructure; see http://www.cse-cst.gc.ca/

[HS97]   Howes, T. and M. Smith. *LDAP: Programming Directory-Enabled Applications with Lightweight Directory Access Protocol.* Indianapolis, IN: Macmillan Technical Publishing, 1997.

[LDAPext] The LDAP Extension Working Group charter; see http://www.ietf.org/html.charters/ldapext-charter.html.

[MISPC]   Minimum Interoperability Specifications for PKI Components, NIST Special Publication 800-15; see http://csrc.nist.gov/pki/mispc/welcome.html.

[PKIX]   The PKIX Working Group Charter; see http://www.ietf.org/html.charters/pkix-charter.html.

[RFC1777] Yeong, W., T. Howes, and S. Kille. "Lightweight Directory Access Protocol." Internet Request for Comments 1777. (March 1995).

[RFC2251] Wahl, M., T. Howes, and S. Kille. "Lightweight Directory Access Protocol (v3)." Internet Request for Comments 2251. (December 1997).

[RFC2311] Dusse, S., P. Hoffman, B. Ramsdell, L. Lundblade, and L. Repka. "S/MIME Version 2 Message Specification." Internet Request for Comments 2311. (March 1998).

[RFC2312] Dusse, S., P. Hoffman, B. Ramsdell, and J. Weinstein. "S/MIME Version 2 Certificate Handling." Internet Request for Comments 2312. (March 1998).

[RFC2401] Kent, S. and R. Atkinson. "Security Architecture for the Internet Protocol." Internet Request for Comments 2401. (November 1998).

[RFC2408]   Maughan, D., M. Schertler, M. Schneider, and J. Turner. "Internet Security Association and Key Management Protocol (ISAKMP)." Internet Request for Comments 2408. (November 1998).

[RFC2409]   Harkins, D. and D. Carrel. "The Internet Key Exchange (IKE)." Internet Request for Comments 2409. (November 1998).

[RFC2412]   Orman, H. "The OAKLEY Key Determination Protocol." Internet Request for Comments 2412. (November 1998).

[RFC2440]   Callas, J., L. Donnerhacke, H. Finney, and R. Thayer. "OpenPGP Message Format." Internet Request for Comments 2440. (November 1998).

[RFC2459]   Housley, R., W. Ford, W. Polk, and D. Solo. "Internet X.509 Public Key Infrastructure Certificate and CRL Profile." Internet Request for Comments 2459. (January 1999).

[RFC2510]   Adams, C. and S. Farrell. "Internet X.509 Public Key Infrastructure Certificate Management Protocols." Internet Request for Comments 2510. (March 1999).

[RFC2511]   Myers, M., C. Adams, D. Solo, and D. Kemp. "Internet X.509 Public Key Infrastructure Certificate Request Message Format." Internet Request for Comments 2511. (March 1999).

[RFC2527]   Chokhani, S. and W. Ford. "Internet X.509 Public Key Infrastructure Certificate Policy and Certification Practices Framework." Internet Request for Comments 2527. (March 1999).

[RFC2559]   Boeyen, S., T. Howes, and P. Richard. "Internet X.509 Public Key Infrastructure Operational Protocols—LDAPv2." Internet Request for Comments 2559. (April 1999).

[RFC2587]   Boeyen, S., T. Howes, and P. Richard. "Internet X.509 Public Key Infrastructure LDAPv2 Schema." Internet Request for Comments 2587. (June 1999).

[RFC2630]   Housley, R. "Cryptographic Message Syntax." Internet Requests for Comments 2630. (June 1999).

[RFC2631]   Rescorla, E. "Diffie-Hellman Key Agreement Method." Internet Requests for Comments 2631. (June 1999).

[RFC2632]   Ramsdell, B. "S/MIME Version 3 Certificate Handling." Internet Requests for Comments 2632. (June 1999).

[RFC2633]   ———. "S/MIME Version 3 Message Specification." Internet Requests for Comments 2633. (June 1999).

[RFC2634]   Hoffman, P. "Enhanced Security Services for S/MIME." Internet Requests for Comments 2634. (June 1999).

[RFC2692]   Ellison, C. "SPKI Requirements." Internet Request for Comments 2692. (September 1999).

[RFC2693]   Ellison, C., B. Frantz, B. Lampson, R. Rivest, B. Thomas, and T. Ylonen. "SPKI Certificate Theory." Internet Request for Comments 2693. (September 1999).

[SDSI]   Rivest, R. and B. Lampson. "SDSI—A Simple Distributed Security Infrastructure;" see `http://theory.lcs.mit.edu/~cis/sdsi.html`.

[SEMPER]   Secure Electronic MarketPlace, Europe; see `http://semper.zurich.ibm.com`.

[SET]   MasterCard/VISA, Secure Electronic Transaction; see `http://www.setco.org/`.

[SPKI]   The Simple Public Key Infrastructure Charter; see `http://www.ietf.org/html.charters/spki-charter.html`.

[TC68]   ISO/TC68/SC2. "Banking—Certificate Management Part 1: Public Key Certificates." ISO/CD-15782-1 (20 August 1998), and "Banking—Certificate Management Part 3: Certificate Extensions." ISO/WD-15782-3 (25 February 1998).

[X.500]   ITU-T Recommendation X.500. "The Directory—Overview of Concepts and Models." International Telecommunication Union. Geneva, Switzerland. 1997 (equivalent to ISO/IEC 9594-1; see also related parts 9594-2 through 9594-10).

[X.509]   ITU-T Recommendation X.509 "Information Technology—Open Systems Interconnection—The Directory: Authentication Framework." June 1997 (equivalent to ISO/IEC 9594-8, 1997).

Standardization Status and Road Map

This chapter presents a snapshot of the current status (at the time of this writing) of PKI and PKI-related standardization efforts. The reason for including such a snapshot in this book is to demonstrate that this field has reached at least the first plateau of stability in the various standards arenas. Not every problem has been solved; not every protocol has been defined; not every service has been specified; not every possible piece of syntax has been nailed down. But significant progress has been made, and a solid foundation for PKI implementation, deployment, and interoperation has been laid.

Also included in this chapter is a brief look at the "next wave" of standardization work that is currently on-going in various groups.

Current Standardization Status

This section discusses the documents that have reached some level of stability and standardization within PKI-relevant standards groups.

X.509

X.509 is an International Standard [X.509]. It has reached the highest level of standardization within ISO/ITU-T and, therefore, is considered to be a stable document. However, there is a formal defect reporting system whereby errors, editorial corrections, or clarifications can be incorporated into the standard through an amendment process. Such an amendment is currently underway, but this includes primarily clarifying material and minor editorial modifications to the base text on certificates and CRLs. (See the section "On-Going Standardization Work" later in this chapter for new work being done within the context of this amendment.)

PKIX

The full set of core PKIX documents is at Proposed Standards status. Although this is only the first level of standardization within the IETF (standard-track documents in IETF may progress from *Proposed Standard* to *Draft Standard* and finally to *Standard*), many vendors consider Proposed Standards to be sufficiently stable and suitable for implementation. This set of documents includes

- Certificate and CRL Profile [RFC2459]
- LDAPv2 Profile [RFC2559]
- LDAPv2 Schema [RFC2587]
- FTP/HTTP Operational Protocols [RFC2585]
- Online Certificate Status Protocol, OCSP [RFC2560]
- Certificate Management Protocol, CMP [RFC2510]
- Certificate Request Message Format, CRMF [RFC2511]

It, therefore, covers all the core functionality needed for PKI initialization and operation.

X.500

X.500 is an International Standard [X.500]. The client-to-server Directory Access Protocol (DAP) and the server-to-server Directory Service Protocol (DSP) are considered to be stable.

LDAP

LDAPv2 and LDAPv3 are Proposed Standards. Version 2 of the Lightweight Directory Access Protocol [RFC1777] is widely deployed and is considered to be quite stable. Version 3 of LDAP [RFC2251] has seen less deployment to date but appears to be relatively stable as well.

S/MIME

The full set of core S/MIME documents is at Proposed Standards status. This set includes

- S/MIMEv2 Message Specification [RFC2311]
- S/MIMEv2 Certificate Handling [RFC2312]
- S/MIMEv3 Message Specification [RFC2633]

- S/MIMEv3 Certificate Handling [RFC2632]

- Cryptographic Message Syntax [RFC2630]

- Enhanced Security Services for S/MIME [RFC2634]

- Diffie-Hellman Key Agreement Method [RFC2631]

Therefore, it covers the core functionality needed for an e-mail system whose security rests on the existence of public-key certificates.

IPsec

The full set of core IPsec documents is at Proposed Standards status. This set includes

- Security Architecture for the Internet Protocol [RFC2401]

- IP Authentication Header [RFC2402]

- IP Encapsulating Security Payload [RFC2406]

- The Internet Key Exchange [RFC2409]

- The ESP DES-CBC Transform [RFC1829]

- The Use of HMAC-MD5-96 Within ESP and AH [RFC2403]

- The Use of HMAC-SHA-1-96 Within ESP and AH [RFC2404]

- The NULL Encryption Algorithm and Its Use with IPsec [RFC2410]

It also includes a number of other specifications; see the IP Security Document Roadmap [RFC2411] for a complete list. Therefore, it covers the core functionality needed for an Internet Protocol communications layer whose security rests on the existence of public-key certificates.

TLS

The Transport Layer Security (TLS) version 1.0 protocol is a Proposed Standard [RFC2246]. It covers the functionality needed for unilateral or mutual authentication between a client and server in a Web environment whose security rests on the existence of public-key certificates. Also provided in TLS is message confidentiality and sequenced integrity. Note that TLS version 1.0 is the IETF standards-track variant of the *Secure Sockets Layer (SSL)* version 3.0 protocol found in many Web browsers.

Toolkit Requirements (APIs and Mechanisms)

The specifications needed for toolkit-based session security are Proposed Standards. The Generic Security Service Application Program Interface, GSS-API [RFC2078], and the underlying Simple Public-Key GSS-API Mechanism, SPKM [RFC2025], together enable a toolkit to be implemented that calling applications or protocol engines can plug into for security services. These services enable peer-to-peer *session* security (including unilateral or mutual authentication, key establishment, secure algorithm negotiation, integrity, and confidentiality) that relies on the existence of public-key certificates. A companion API for *store-and-forward* security services, the Independent Data Unit Protection specification, IDUP-GSS-API [RFC2479] (although an Informational, rather than a standards-track, specification) is also a stable document. IDUP, with suitable underlying mechanisms (such as ones based on S/MIME or OpenPGP), enables toolkit-based store-and-forward security.

Others

A variety of other PKI-related documents are also on the standards-track within IETF, including OpenPGP [RFC2440] and Domain Name System Security [RFC2538, RFC2539]. Also, a number of public-key-related specifications exist (for example, public key encoding formats or key agreement protocols) in other standards groups that have reached stability, including IEEE P1363 (formats and protocols for RSA, DSA, ECDSA, and key agreement), ANSI X9.31 (RSA Signatures) and X9.62 (Elliptic Curve DSA), and ISO 11770-3 (Key Agreement) and 13888-3 (Non-Repudiation).

It is clear that there is now a significant foundation for PKI implementation within the body of standardized specifications.

On-Going Standardization Work

Along with all the specifications that are relatively stable, many of the standards groups have other PKI-related work that is on-going. The following examples from IETF are representative of the scope of standardization work that is currently underway:

- *Privilege Management Infrastructure (PMI) (specifically in the area of Attribute Certificates)*—This is being looked at primarily in X.509 (through the formal amendment process) and IETF PKIX, although a number of other groups are following this work closely and will likely adopt it or profile it in their own contexts.

- *Secure time stamping protocols*—This is being looked at primarily in PKIX, although one or two other groups (Secure Network Time Protocol [STIME], for example) are following this work closely.

- *Data certification server protocols*—This is being looked at primarily in PKIX. (This work is sometimes referred to as *protocols for digital notary services*, although this latter terminology is inappropriate because the word *notary* means different things in different countries of the world.)

- *Certificate Policy and Certification Practices framework*—This is currently an Informational (rather than a standards-track) specification [RFC2527] but is undergoing a major revision to reflect operational feedback from environments that have used it to write their CP and CPS documents.

- *Protocols to off-load PKI-related processing (for example, certificate path construction and validation) from a constrained client platform to a trusted server*—This is being looked at in PKIX, although other groups (such as *Wireless Access Protocol,* or *WAP*) are interested in this topic as well.

- *Extensions to provide additional functionality to the basic LDAP protocol*—This is being looked at in LDAPext and includes such things as strong authentication for requests and responses (including using the *Simple Authentication and Security Layer (SASL)* mechanism [RFC2222]) and access control to LDAP information.

- *Security policy languages, protocols, and processing procedures*—This is being looked at in IPSEC, although many other groups are interested in this topic.

- *A mechanism to associate digital signatures with (all or parts of) an XML document*—This is being looked at in XMLdsig, a joint working group of the IETF and the World Wide Web Consortium (W3C).

It is expected that within the two to three year time frame, much of this and other work will be relatively stable and available in the portfolios of a number of PKI product vendors or service providers. This work will enhance the functionality of PKI product or service offerings and significantly add to the richness and usefulness of a PKI.

Summary

This chapter has provided a brief overview of where the standards are now and the directions in which they are currently going. With respect to PKI and PKI-related standards, an impressive list of work products has already achieved consensus and stability within the formal organizations, and all indications are that many of these will also enjoy widespread adoption across the industry (largely because so many of the major PKI-related companies have had active participation in the creation of these specifications).

To make full use of the standards status given in this chapter, the following topics will be beneficial:

- A good understanding of what each of the standards bodies (and corresponding specifications) covers; this is the subject of Chapter 16, "Major Standards Activities."

- A good understanding of the environment under consideration for deployment (so that those in charge of deployment can make the necessary decisions and mandate compliance to the appropriate standards for the environment); this is the subject of Part III, "Deployment Considerations."

References

[RFC1777] Yeong, W., T. Howes, and S. Kille. "Lightweight Directory Access Protocol." Internet Request for Comments 1777. (March 1995).

[RFC1829] Karn, P., P. Metzger, and W. Simpson. "The ESP DES-CBC Transform." Internet Request for Comments 1829. (August 1995).

[RFC2025] Adams, C. "The Simple Public-Key GSS-API Mechanism (SPKM)." Internet Request for Comments 2025. (October 1996).

[RFC2078] Linn, J. "Generic Security Service Application Program Interface, Version 2." Internet Request for Comments 2078. (January 1997).

[RFC2222] Myers, J. "Simple Authentication and Security Layer (SASL)." Internet Request for Comments 2222. (October 1997).

[RFC2246] Dierks, T. and C. Allen. "The TLS Protocol, Version 1.0." Internet Request for Comments 2246. (January 1999).

[RFC2251] Wahl, M., T. Howes, and S. Kille. "Lightweight Directory Access Protocol (v3)." Internet Request for Comments 2251. (December 1997).

[RFC2311] Dusse, S., P. Hoffman, B. Ramsdell, L. Lundblade, and L. Repka. "S/MIME Version 2 Message Specification." Internet Request for Comments 2311. (March 1998).

[RFC2312] Dusse, S., P. Hoffman, B. Ramsdell, and J. Weinstein. "S/MIME Version 2 Certificate Handling." Internet Request for Comments 2312. (March 1998).

[RFC2401] Kent, S. and R. Atkinson. "Security Architecture for the Internet Protocol." Internet Request for Comments 2401. (November 1998).

[RFC2402] Kent, S. and R. Atkinson. "IP Authentication Header." Internet Request for Comments 2402. (November 1998).

[RFC2403]   Madson, C. and R. Glenn. "The Use of HMAC-MD5-96 Within ESP and AH." Internet Request for Comments 2403. (November 1998).

[RFC2404]   Madson, C. and R. Glenn. "The Use of HMAC-SHA-1-96 Within ESP and AH." Internet Request for Comments 2404. (November 1998).

[RFC2406]   Kent, S. and R. Atkinson. "IP Encapsulating Security Payload (ESP)." Internet Request for Comments 2406. (November 1998).

[RFC2409]   Harkins, D. and D. Carrel. "The Internet Key Exchange (IKE)." Internet Request for Comments 2409. (November 1998).

[RFC2410]   Glenn, R. and S. Kent. "The NULL Encryption Algorithm and Its Use with Ipsec." Internet Request for Comments 2410. (November 1998).

[RFC2411]   Thayer, R., N. Doraswamy, and R. Glenn. "IP Security Document Roadmap." Internet Request for Comments 2411. (November 1998).

[RFC2440]   Callas, J., L. Donnerhacke, H. Finney, and R. Thayer. "OpenPGP Message Format." Internet Request for Comments 2440. (November 1998).

[RFC2459]   Housley, R., W. Ford, W. Polk, and D. Solo. "Internet X.509 Public Key Infrastructure: Certificate and CRL Profile." Internet Request for Comments 2459. (January 1999).

[RFC2479]   Adams, C. "Independent Data Unit Protection Generic Security Service Application Program Interface (IDUP-GSS-API)." Internet Request for Comments 2479. (December 1998).

[RFC2510]   Adams, C. and S. Farrell. "Internet X.509 Public Key Infrastructure: Certificate Management Protocols." Internet Request for Comments 2510. (March 1999).

[RFC2511]   Myers, M., C. Adams, D. Solo, and D. Kemp. "Internet X.509 Certificate Request Message Format." Internet Request for Comments 2511. (March 1999).

[RFC2527]   Chokhani, S. and W. Ford. "Internet X.509 Public Key Infrastructure: Certificate Policy and Certification Practices Framework." Internet Request for Comments 2527. (March 1999).

[RFC2538]   Eastlake, D. and O. Gudmundsson. "Storing Certificates in the Domain Name System (DNS)." Internet Request for Comments 2538. (March 1999).

[RFC2539]   Eastlake, D. "Storage of Diffie-Hellman Keys in the Domain Name System (DNS)." Internet Request for Comments 2539. (March 1999).

[RFC2559] Boeyen, S., T. Howes, and P. Richard. "Internet X.509 Public Key Infrastructure: Operational Protocols—LDAPv2." Internet Request for Comments 2559. (April 1999).

[RFC2560] Myers, M., R. Ankney, A. Malpani, S. Galperin, and C. Adams. "Internet X.509 Public Key Infrastructure: Online Certificate Status Protocol—OCSP." Internet Request for Comments 2560. (June 1999).

[RFC2585] Housley, R. and P. Hoffman. "Internet X.509 Public Key Infrastructure Operational Protocols: FTP and HTTP." Internet Request for Comments 2585. (May 1999).

[RFC2587] Boeyen, S., T. Howes, and P. Richard. "Internet X.509 Public Key Infrastructure: LDAPv2 Schema." Internet Request for Comments 2587. (June 1999).

[RFC2630] Housley, R. "Cryptographic Message Syntax." Internet Request for Comments 2630. (June 1999).

[RFC2631] Rescorla, E. "Diffie-Hellman Key Agreement Method." Internet Request for Comments 2631. (June 1999).

[RFC2632] Ramsdell, B. "S/MIME Version 3 Certificate Handling." Internet Request for Comments 2632. (June 1999).

[RFC2633] Ramsdell, B. "S/MIME Version 3 Message Specification." Internet Request for Comments 2633. (June 1999).

[RFC2634] Hoffman, P. "Enhanced Security Services for S/MIME." Internet Request for Comments 2634. (June 1999).

[STIME] The Secure Network Time Protocol Charter; see
http://www.ietf.org/html-charters/stime-charter.html

[X.500] ITU-T Recommendation X.500. "The Directory—Overview of Concepts, Models." International Telecommunication Union. Geneva, Switzerland, 1997 (equivalent to ISO/IEC 9594-1; see also related parts 9594-2 through 9594-10).

[X.509] ITU-T Recommendation X.509. "Information Technology—Open Systems Interconnection—The Directory: Authentication Framework." June 1997 (equivalent to ISO/IEC 9594-8, 1997).

CHAPTER 18

Standards: Necessary, but Not Sufficient

Although standards are instrumental in promoting interoperability, many standards do not guarantee it in a multi-vendor environment. The purpose of this chapter is to explain the role of standards, and to discuss the importance of additional activities such as profiling of standards and multi-vendor interoperability testing. This is followed by specific examples of industry- and government-sponsored interoperability initiatives.

The Role of Standards, Profiles, and Interoperability Testing

It has been said that a camel is actually a horse designed by committee. Although this may seem a bit disparaging to some, we invoke this anecdote to illustrate the difficulties typically encountered when attempting to reach agreement on the numerous technical (and sometimes political) issues that arise during the standards process. It should be noted that we are not trying to "bash" standards. In fact, standards play a critical role. We are simply trying to make it clear that standards alone are not *always* sufficient to guarantee multi-vendor interoperability.

Standards come in a variety of forms, and there are numerous standards bodies that engage in the development of these standards. In general, the purpose of a standard is to provide a common specification of syntax and semantics that can be used as a foundation for implementation—although sometimes some of the semantics are missing or incompletely defined, which can lead to interoperability difficulties.

Note

From a PKI perspective, one of the most important standards is the X.509 Recommendation [X.509] as discussed in Chapter 16, "Major Standards Activities."

A number of issues can have an influence on the success or failure of a given standard, and on whether or not a given standard is sufficiently detailed and error free to lead to multi-vendor interoperability. Some of these issues include the following:

- Participation in the various standards organizations is typically voluntary in nature; there is really no such thing as a "professional standards guru" (although arguably there are a few individuals who might be deserving of such a title).

- Usually more than one agenda or set of requirements is involved, which often leads to compromise through the specification of options, or through the practice of leaving certain issues general enough to accommodate more than one point of view.

- Sometimes there is very little implementation experience, or worse, there is conflicting implementation experience that might be inappropriately reflected in the standard.

- Not all standards committees or subcommittees are "created equal"; the quality of the various standards can vary dramatically, depending on the participants and on the rules of participation established by the governing standards body.

- Very seldom is a given solution perfect in every way, which tends to promote the specification of multiple solutions that address the same problem. For example, a solution that works well in one environment may not address the specific needs of another environment. Sometimes specifying multiple solutions is essential to meet the needs of multiple target domains.

- Sometimes aspects of a standard are simply misinterpreted, and/or the standard is simply implemented improperly.

- No matter how good a particular solution may be, it is common practice to include extensibility mechanisms within the standards to support new capabilities when and as required.

Thus, it is reasonable to conclude that standards alone may not suffice to realize multi-vendor interoperability.

Profiles and Interoperability Testing

There are at least two things that need to be done beyond the development of a standard to help reach the desired level of multi-vendor interoperability.

The first is to profile the standards that apply to a particular environment. The purpose of a *profile* is to clearly identify which features of the more generic standard are mandatory, optional, or prohibited for a given environment. Specific usage rules and implementation guidelines are also typically included. In the specific case of a PKI, it is necessary to profile the PKI protocols used, the schema and protocols associated with the ancillary repository components, and the certificates and CRLs themselves. In particular, both certificates and CRLs include extensions that must be profiled to eliminate ambiguities and adequately specify particular uses for those extensions within a given target environment.

X.509 Recommendation Certificate and CRL Profile

Let's look at some specific examples to illustrate the necessity of a certificate and CRL profile for the X.509 recommendation [X.509]. Note that the PKIX certificate and CRL profile [RFC2459] defines such a profile for the Internet environment.

Consider the certificate extension *Subject Directory Attributes*. According to the X.509 standard [X.509], the *Subject Directory Attributes* extension may be used to " . . . convey any desired Directory attribute values for the subject of the certificate . . . " Clearly, this is an extremely broad statement, and there is no guarantee that the implementation of this extension in one domain will have any meaning whatsoever in another. Allowed values and the context of their presence needs to be defined before one can expect interoperability between two different implementations.

It is interesting to note that one common use of this extension is to indicate access control information associated with the subject of the certificate. In particular, it can be used to convey security clearance information (among other things). Both the U.S. Department of Defense and the Canadian Department of National Defence have used the *Subject Directory Attributes* extension in this manner.

As another example, consider the *Authority Key Identifier* extension that can be used to uniquely identify the key used by a CA to sign a given certificate or CRL. This allows a convenient method to distinguish between multiple keys that might be associated with a given CA. The key used to sign the certificate or CRL can be identified by several methods. Specifically, the key can be identified by a unique octet string (such as a hash of the public component), or it can be identified through a combination of the distinguished name of the certificate issuer plus a unique serial number of that key (in relation to the issuer), or both methods may be used.

Given that one implementor may choose to use one method and another implementor may choose another, it makes sense to agree on the specific use of this extension. As an example, a given profile may dictate that only the unique key identifier is to be used, and that the value of the unique identifier will be the 160-bit SHA-1 hash of the public key. Note that in this example, not only does the profile dictate the method used to calculate the unique identifier value, it goes so far as to say that the alternative method of using the identifier of the certificate issuer combined with the unique serial number is not to be used. Note also that this level of specificity is still in compliance with the X.509 standard [X.509].

The second thing that is required to help realize the goal of multi-vendor interoperability is to establish interoperability test scenarios and to conduct interoperability testing.

One possibility to accommodate this requirement is to establish vendor neutral interoperability test centers that would offer reference implementations that can be used to assess the compliance of a given product against a specific set of criteria (which typically includes a set of established profiles).

An alternative (or perhaps complimentary) approach that seems to be rather prevalent in the PKI industry is to participate in industry and/or government sponsored interoperability initiatives. Examples of some of these interoperability activities are provided in the following section.

Interoperability Initiatives

The purpose of this section is to briefly highlight of some of the industry- and/or government-sponsored interoperability initiatives and to provide pointers to additional information where appropriate.

Automotive Network eXchange

The *Automotive Network eXchange (ANX)* is a TCP/IP-based network that uses Virtual Private Network (VPN) technology based on the IPSec and PKIX standards. The ANX is designed to provide a common infrastructure that will facilitate secure communications among automotive manufacturers.

The ANX activity has produced a certificate and CRL profile that is included as an annex to the ANX certificate policy document entitled *Automotive Network eXchange (ANX) Certificate Policy* [ANX]. Additional information regarding ANX can be found at `http://www.anxo.com`.

Bridge CA Demonstration

Initiated in January 1999, the *Bridge CA demonstration* is a U.S. government sponsored initiative designed to demonstrate interoperability between two (or more) PKI domains based on different trust models (trust models are discussed further in Chapter 9, "Trust Models"). Specifically, this demonstration is designed to prove that a single CA can act as a bridge between multiple PKI domains through the use of cross-certification. The driving application for this particular demonstration will be based on Secure/Multi-purpose Internet Mail Extensions Version 3 [SMIMEv3].

Profiling activities are expected to include a minimum certificate and CRL profile, a directory schema and interoperability profile, and a S/MIMEv3 interoperability profile. Certificate path discovery and validation processes will also be established.

Federal Public Key Infrastructure

The U.S. federal government initiated the Public Key Infrastructure Technical Working Group (PKI-TWG) in October 1994 to address implementation issues associated with the (U.S.) Federal Public Key Infrastructure (FPKI). The PKI-TWG is chaired by the National Institute of Standards and Technology (NIST) and is comprised of participants from U.S. federal government agencies and industry.

This working group has developed a fairly comprehensive profile entitled *Federal Public Key Infrastructure Certificate and CRL Extensions Profile* [FPKI]. This document, as well as a number of other useful references, can be retrieved from `http://csrc.nist.gov/pki/twg/welcome.html`. Additional discussion with respect to the FPKI activity is provided in Chapter 16, "Major Standards Activities."

Minimum Interoperability Specification

Formally initiated in June 1996, the NIST launched an initiative to develop a minimum interoperability specification in cooperation with a number of leading industry technology vendors, including

- AT&T

- BBN (now GTE CyberTrust)

- Certicom

- Cylink

- DynCorp

- IRE

- Motorola

- Northern Telecom (Entrust)

- Spyrus

- VeriSign

The initial specification entitled *Minimum Interoperability Specification for PKI Components, Version 1* [MISPCv1] was published in June 1997. The MISPC initiative also includes a reference implementation that can be used to test conformance against the minimum interoperability profile. This enables the PKI and CA vendor community to demonstrate MISPC compliance.

The MISPC work continues to evolve to take advantage of emerging standards related to PKI technology. The second version of the MISPC document is entitled *Minimum Interoperability Specification for PKI Components, Version 2—Second Draft* [MISPCv2], published in November 1998. This version of the document adds support for confidentiality services and incorporates some of the Internet Engineering Task Force (IETF) Public Key Infrastructure X.509 (PKIX) work that was formally published in late 1998 and early 1999 (in particular, *Internet X.509 Public Key Infrastructure Certificate and CRL Profile* [RFC2459], *Internet X.509 Public Key Infrastructure Certificate Management Protocols* [RFC2510], and *Internet X.509 Certificate Request Message Format* [RFC2511]).

National Automated Clearing House Association

The National Automated Clearing House Association (NACHA) sponsored a successful interoperability pilot referred to as the *CA Interoperability Pilot (Phase I)*, completed in October 1998. Participating vendors included

- CertCo

- Digital Signature Trust (DST)

- Entrust Technologies

- GTE CyberTrust

- IBM

- VeriSign

As illustrated in Figure 18.1, this pilot activity was based on a four-corner model consisting of a consumer, the consumer's bank, a merchant, and the merchant's bank. The pilot essentially emulated the "Web shopping experience" where a consumer would engage in purchasing activities with the merchants using digital signatures to authorize the transactions. The fundamental operating assumption for this pilot was that each of the participating banks would act as its own CA, and all trust decisions relative to the transactions would emanate from the banks.

From a technology perspective, one of the primary objectives of this pilot activity was to demonstrate that multiple vendor technologies could be used to support the four-corner model. To that end, the participating banks used different CA products supplied by the participating technology vendors. Further, the participating vendors collaborated to define a certificate and CRL profile, and the interoperability testing was performed against that profile.

Figure 18.1   Four-corner model.

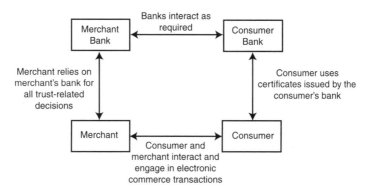

The NACHA CA Interoperability Pilot activity was a good example of multi-vendor (and multi-bank) cooperation, and a number of valuable lessons were learned from this experience. The lessons learned from this activity have been published in a document entitled "Certification Authority Interoperability: From Concept to Reality—Results of the NACHA Internet Council CA Interoperability Pilot" [NACHA]. NACHA continues to sponsor activities in this area, and it is expected that the Phase I pilot activity will lead to the definition and roll-out of subsequent initiatives (perhaps including alternative payment models and additional functions supported by the underlying PKI technologies).

Additional information regarding the NACHA pilot activities can be found at `http://internetcouncil.nacha.org/`.

Public Key Infrastructure X.509

The IETF PKIX working group (which is described further in Chapter 16) is devoted to defining PKI protocols and X.509 certificate and CRL profiles for Internet use. The certificate and CRL profile once known as PKIX Part 1 became a proposed standard RFC in January 1999 [RFC2459].

The publication of RFC2459 is viewed by many to be a landmark occurrence, and many of the other profiling activities described within this chapter attempt to align with RFC2459 to the maximum extent possible. Although technically this profile was designed for use within the Internet, there is a significant amount of information that can be used to the advantage of the enterprise as well.

Note

To help illustrate the importance of RFC2459, the Federal PKI Certificate and CRL Extensions Profile [FPKI] contains an annex that summarizes the degree of compliance with the PKIX specified profile. Both the NACHA and SIRCA profiles also took the PKIX profile into consideration.

Securities Industry Root CA Proof of Concept

The *Securities Industry Root CA (SIRCA) proof of concept* was designed to demonstrate the feasibility of an industry root CA in a two-level hierarchy. Somewhat analogous to the bridge CA concept (as discussed in Chapter 9), the purpose of the SIRCA root CA was to facilitate the introduction of trust between two or more PKI domains that would otherwise be required to enter bilateral agreements with every other PKI domain with which they need to conduct business. This significantly reduces the overhead associated with bilateral cross-certification agreements from the order of N^2 to N, where N is the number of distinct PKI domains.

The SIRCA proof of concept used a relatively simple certificate profile (which can be found at `http://www.sia.com/sirca/html/profile.html`). The driving application for this proof of concept was S/MIMEv2-based e-mail [SMIMEv2]. The S/MIME application was profiled in the sense that it was required that the complete certification path be included with each signed message. Note that CRLs were not profiled because they were not included as part of this activity.

The results of the SIRCA proof of concept were encouraging and will likely lead to further activity in this area.

Summary

This chapter has discussed the role of standards as well as the importance of complementary interoperability profiles and interoperability testing to fully realize the benefits of a given set of standards.

There are a number of interoperability initiatives that will help to establish useful and interoperable products from multiple PKI and CA vendors, including ANX, Bridge CA demonstration, MISPC, NACHA, PKIX, and SIRCA.

Pilot activities such as these are instrumental in demonstrating that many of the PKI vendors are collaborating to offer better levels of service that will respond to the market demand, and that these vendors will be able to provide interoperable products in complex and heterogeneous environments.

See the following chapters for additional information regarding standards and other related activities:

- Chapter 16, "Major Standards Activities," summarizes numerous standards activities related to PKI.

- Chapter 17, "Standardization Status and Road Map," provides a summary of the PKI-related standards, including their status (at the time of this writing) as well as pointers to additional information.

References

[ANX]   Automotive Industry Action Group. *Automotive Network eXchange (ANX) Certificate Policy*. Southfield, Michigan, undated.

[FPKI]   Booz-Allen and Hamilton Inc. *Federal Public Key Infrastructure (PKI) X.509 Certificate and CRL Extensions Profile*. 4 January 1999.

[MISPCv1]   Burr, William, Donna Dodson, Noel Nazario, and W. Timothy Polk. *Minimum Interoperability Specification for PKI Components, Version 1*. National Institute of Standards and Technology. 5 June 1997.

[MISPCv2]   National Institute of Standards and Technology (NIST) Project Team. *Minimum Interoperability Specification for PKI Components, Version 2—Second Draft*. 2 November 1998.

[NACHA]   Prince, N. and J. Foster. "Certification Authority Interoperability: From Concept to Reality—Results of the NACHA Internet Council CA Interoperability Pilot." The National Automated Clearing House Association. (1999).

[RFC2459]   Housley, R., W. Ford, W. Polk, and D. Solo. "Internet X.509 Public Key Infrastructure Certificate and CRL Profile." Internet Request for Comments 2459. (January 1999).

[RFC2510]   Adams C. and S. Farrell. "Internet X.509 Public Key Infrastructure Certificate Management Protocols." Internet Request for Comments 2510. (March 1999).

[RFC2511]   Myers, M., C. Adams, D. Solo, and D. Kemp. "Internet X.509 Certificate Request Message Format." Internet Request for Comments 2511. (March 1999).

[SMIMEv2]   Dusse, S., P. Hoffman, B. Ramsdell, L. Lundblade, and L. Repka. *Request for Comments 2311, S/MIME Version 2 Message Specification*. (March 1998).

[SMIMEv3] B. Ramsdell. *S/MIME Version 3 Message Specification*, Internet Draft (work in progress). see `http://www.ietf.org/html.charters/smime-charter.html` for current status.

[X.509]   ITU-T Recommendations X.509. "Information Technology—Open Systems Interconnection—The Directory: Authentication Framework." June 1977 (equivalent to ISO/IEC 9594-8, 1997).

CHAPTER 19

Conclusions and Further Reading

The purpose of this chapter is to provide a summary of the significant issues discussed in Part II, "Standards," and to supply suggestions for further reading.

Summary

Part II of this book has concentrated on some of the more significant standards activities related to *public-key infrastructure (PKI)* protocols, services, and information. Part II has explored the role of these standards and has supplied a snapshot of the current state of these standards.

Part II has noted that not all standards are created equal; by design, some standards (for example, X.509) require profiling. This part also has emphasized the need for interoperability testing to ensure multi-vendor interoperability and has introduced a number of industry initiatives related to multi-vendor interoperability trials. Because this is becoming such an important area, the authors expect that vendor-neutral, third party interoperability testing centers will grow in number and significance in the near future.

Suggestions for Further Reading

A number of sources of information are relevant with respect to PKI standards and/or interoperability. These are listed in the following subsections.

Certificate/CRL Syntax and Life Cycle Management Protocols

Specifications related to certificate and CRL syntax and comprehensive life cycle management include

- *Directory Authentication Framework.* Joint Recommendation|Standard ITU-T X.509 and ISO/IEC 9594-8, 1997.

- Adams, C. and S. Farrell. "Internet X.509 Public Key Infrastructure Certificate Management Protocols." Internet Request for Comments 2510. (March 1999).

- Myers, M., C. Adams, D. Solo, and D. Kemp. "Internet X.509 Certificate Request Message Format." Internet Request for Comments 2511. (March 1999).

As discussed throughout this book, the X.509 Recommendation provides the syntax (and semantics) for the Version 3 public-key certificate and the Version 2 *Certificate Revocation List (CRL)*. It also includes the syntax (and some semantics) for Attribute Certificates. RFC2510 and 2511 combine to provide comprehensive key/certificate life cycle management protocol and message exchange formats.

Two other important specifications related to PKI protocol and message formats are

- *PKCS#7: Cryptographic Message Standard*. Version 1.5. RSA Laboratories.

- *PKCS#10: Certification Request Syntax Standard*. Version 1.5. RSA Laboratories.

While it is recognized that these public-key cryptographic standards (PKCS) provide the foundation for more than simple PKI-related message exchanges, they are included here because they are commonly used as the basis for certificate request and retrieval over the Internet. They can also be used to facilitate off-line cross-certification (Chapter 9, "Trust Models," discusses cross-certification).

In the future, we may see more sophisticated certificate management services over the Internet based on PKCS#7 and PKCS#10. This may come to fruition through some of the work currently underway in the *Internet Engineering Task Force (IETF) Public-Key Infrastructure X.509 (PKIX)* Working Group.

Certificate/CRL Storage and Retrieval

Specifications related to the storage and/or exchange of certificate and certificate revocation information between a client and a server include

- Boeyen, S., T. Howes, and P. Richard. "Internet X.509 Public Key Infrastructure Operational Protocols—LDAPv2." Internet Request for Comments 2559. (April 1999).

- Boeyen, S., T. Howes, and P. Richard. "Internet X.509 Public Key Infrastructure LDAPv2 Schema." Internet Request for Comments 2587. (June 1999).

- Housley, R. and P. Hoffman. "Internet X.509 Public Key Infrastructure Operational Protocols: FTP and HTTP." Internet Request for Comments 2585. (May 1999).

All three of these RFCs were developed under the auspices of the IETF PKIX Working Group. RFC2559 specifies the requirements for retrieving certificates and CRLs via

Version 2 of the *Lightweight Directory Access Protocol (LDAP)*. RFC2587 is the LDAP Version 2 schema. Work on Version 3 of LDAP is expected to follow. RFC2585 defines the syntax and semantics associated with the retrieval of certificates and CRLs via the *File Transfer Protocol (FTP)* and the *Hypertext Transfer Protocol (HTTP)*.

Specifications related to the on-line retrieval of revocation information include

- Adams, C. and R. Zuccherato. *Internet X.509 Public Key Infrastructure Data Certification Server Protocols*. Internet Draft, <draft-ietf-pkix-dcs-00.txt> (subject to update; see www.ietf.org for latest status).

- Malpani, A. and P. Hoffman. *Simple Certificate Validation Protocol*. Internet Draft, <draft-ietf-pkix-scvp-00.txt> (subject to update; see www.ietf.org for latest status).

- Meyers, M., R. Ankney, A. Malpani, S. Galperin, and C. Adams. "Internet X.509 Public Key Infrastructure Online Certificate Status Protocol—OCSP." Internet Request for Comments 2560. (June 1999).

As Chapter 8, "Certificate Revocation," discussed, the *On-line Certificate Status Protocol (OCSP)* defines a method for returning the revocation status of one or more certificates. The *Simple Certificate Validation Protocol (SCVP)* is an Internet Draft that provides a method for on-line validation of certificates and certification paths. The *Data Certification Server Protocols (DCSP)* is also an Internet Draft that essentially replaced the original notion of a "notarization" protocol. Because all three of these protocols overlap one another in terms of the functionality they support, the final fate of OCSP, SCVP, and DCSP has yet to be determined.

Note

Note that all Internet Drafts are subject to change without notice, and they generally expire six months after issue (although a new issue may replace them). You should always consult the IETF Web site (www.ietf.org) for the latest status regarding any Internet Draft.

Note that there are also some PKI-enabled protocols that enable the direct exchange of certificates and, in some cases, certificate revocation information. Examples include the *Secure Sockets Layer (SSL)/Transport Layer Security (TLS)* protocols, *Secure/Multipurpose Internet Mail Extensions (S/MIME)*, and *Internet Protocol Security (IPsec)*.

Interoperability Initiatives

Documents related to PKI interoperability include

- Automotive Industry Action Group. *Automotive Network eXchange (ANX) Certificate Policy*. Southfield, Michigan, undated; see http://www.aiag.org/anx/anxpol.html.

- National Institute of Standards and Technology (NIST) Project Team. *Minimum Interoperability Specification for PKI Components, Version 2—Second Draft.* 2 November 1998 (work in progress).

- Booz-Allen and Hamilton Inc. *Federal Public Key Infrastructure (PKI) X.509 Certificate and CRL Extensions Profile.* 4 January 1999; see `http://csrc.nist.gov/pki/twg/welcome.html`.

- Burr, William, Donna Dodson, Noel Nazario, and W. Timothy Polk. *Minimum Interoperability Specification for PKI Components, Version 1.* National Institute of Standards and Technology. 3 September 1997; see `http://csrc.nist.gov/pki/mispc/welcome.html`.

- Housley, R., W. Ford, W. Polk, and D. Solo. "Internet X.509 Public Key Infrastructure Certificate and CRL Profile." Internet Request for Comments 2459 (January 1999).

- Prince, N. and J. Foster. "Certification Authority Interoperability: From Concept to Reality—Results of the NACHA Internet Council CA Interoperability Pilot." The National Automated Clearing House Association. (1999).

The ANX, Federal PKI, and RFC2459 each define a certificate and CRL profile targeted for use in a specific environment. Both versions of *The Minimum Interoperability Specification for PKI Components* (also referred to as *MISPC*) are designed to provide vendors with a minimum set of implementation criteria.

Standards Bodies Web Sites

Most of the standards bodies (or other related organizations) provide at least some information on-line. Sometimes you can retrieve the standards (or drafts of the standards) directly via the Internet. Other sites simply provide information on the standards process associated with that particular standards body along with information on how to order the standards under their control. The pointers to some of these Web sites are

- International Electrotechnical Commission (IEC); see `www.iec.ch`

- International Standards Organization (ISO); see `www.iso.ch`

- International Telecommunications Union (ITU); see `www.itu.int`

- Internet Engineering Task Force (IETF); see `www.ietf.org`

Books

Several books also contain useful material related to standards, including the following:

- Ford, Warwick. *Computer Communications Security: Principles, Standard Protocols and Techniques.* Upper Saddle River, NJ: PTR Prentice Hall, 1994.

- Menezes, Alfred J., Paul C. van Oorschot, and Scott A. Vanstone. *Handbook of Applied Cryptography.* Boca Raton: CRC Press (1997): 645–661.

- Schneier, Bruce. *Applied Cryptography: Protocols, Algorithms, and Source Code in C, Second Edition.* New York: John Wiley & Sons, 1996: 561–595.

- Stallings, William. *Cryptography and Network Security: Principles and Practice.* Upper Saddle River, NJ: Prentice Hall, 1995, 1999: 323–473.

PART

Deployment Considerations

CHAPTER 20

Introduction

The purpose of Part III is to introduce the concepts and issues associated with the deployment of large-scale PKIs. Note that this part of the book is not intended to be a step-by-step deployment handbook. Part III is deliberately small; more specific deployment details could easily be the topic of an entire book. The idea is to familiarize the reader with the basic issues likely to be encountered when deploying a large-scale PKI in the enterprise domain. (Although the focus of this material is directed toward the enterprise, many of these issues also apply to the Internet domain.)

Chapter 21, "Benefits (and Costs) of a PKI," discusses the benefits realized through the deployment of a PKI. Cost considerations are also discussed. This chapter identifies sound business reasons for deploying a PKI in the enterprise environment.

Chapter 22, "Deployment Issues and Decisions," discusses a number of issues that should be resolved before initial deployment occurs. Essentially, this chapter provides a basic foundation for product selection.

Chapter 23, "Barriers to Deployment," addresses some of the more common hurdles to deployment. These are issues one must consider in terms of long-term strategy.

Chapter 24, "Typical Business Models," explains some of the more common business models one may want to implement. This chapter also provides a brief discussion of some of the global trust initiatives.

Chapter 25, "Conclusions and Further Reading," concludes Part III and offers suggestions for further reading.

Benefits (and Costs) of a PKI

The purpose of this chapter is to consider some of the benefits realized through the deployment of a PKI. It also briefly discusses cost considerations (from a generic perspective).

Ultimately, it should be recognized that a sound and justifiable business case must drive the deployment of any technology. This applies equally to PKI technology. The key is to focus on business drivers, not technology.

While it is not the intent of this chapter to provide a boilerplate for the development of a business case, it does identify many of the factors that should be taken into consideration when developing such a business case.

Business Case Considerations

As discussed in Chapter 3, "The Concept of an Infrastructure," a PKI is a comprehensive security infrastructure, not myriad point solutions. A PKI offers a single security infrastructure that can be used across multiple applications in the most heterogeneous of environments. Specifically, a PKI can be used to enable confidentiality, integrity, authentication, and non-repudiation services in numerous contexts, including one or more of the following:

- Secure e-mail

- Secure Electronic Data Interchange (EDI)

- Secure electronic forms

- Secure desktop (for example, encryption of sensitive information on a laptop or PC)

- Secure intranets

- Secure extranets

- End-entity access control

- Secure remote access (for example, in support of mobile users or work-at-home)

- Secure Web applications

- Object signing

- Reduced logon

The benefits realized from offering these services are extensive, albeit in many cases hard to quantify. Some of the benefits that can be realized through the judicious deployment of a PKI are

- *Improvements in work-flow efficiency*—Significant time savings can be realized (for example, letters, memos, and contracts can be handled electronically rather than through physical correspondence).

- *Work-force optimization*—End-users can spend more time on the job at hand rather than spending time dealing with details associated with the security infrastructure itself.

- *Work-force reduction*—The deployment and operation of a single, unifying architecture rather than multiple point solutions requires fewer administrative resources.

- *Paper reduction*—Savings can be realized in a number of ways, including lower material costs, less storage space, waste reduction, and less environmental intrusion.

- *Less administrative overhead*—End-users are less likely to require as much on-going administrative assistance (for example, help desk support).

- *Reduced losses due to electronic theft*—Corporate data is protected, which significantly decreases the risk of unauthorized disclosure.

- *Telecommunications cost savings*—The ability to create a Virtual Private Network (VPN) over a public network such as the Internet can result in significant cost savings over leasing private lines.

- *Revenue generation*—Not only can a PKI be used to save money, in some cases a PKI can be also used as the basis for offering "for-fee" services (for example, a financial institution may offer transaction validation services based on digital signatures and public key certificates).

It is also becoming clear that electronic theft and fraud are on the rise, and we can only assume that this trend will continue. A good source of information that helps to illustrate this trend can be found in *Issues and Trends: 1999 CSI/FBI Computer Crime and Security Survey* [CSI].

Although statistics of this nature are difficult to verify, few would argue that the threat is not real, and the very fact that it is perceived to be a problem makes it something that must be addressed. And it is important to recognize that these threats originate from both external and internal sources. Therefore, any comprehensive security solution must be able to secure both internal and external communications and corporate resources.

To help put things into perspective, consider what would happen if the CEO of your company had his/her laptop stolen. Is the sensitive information on that laptop encrypted? If not, try to imagine how much damage would be done if that sensitive corporate data fell into the wrong hands. Recall from Chapter 4, "Core PKI Services: Authentication, Integrity, and Confidentiality,"and Chapter 5, "PKI-Enabled Services," that a PKI offers the foundation for providing confidentiality services that can be used to protect against threats like this.

Although it is recognized that the CEO's laptop in the preceding example could have been secured without the use of a PKI, these solutions do not offer the comprehensive set of services a PKI can offer. To illustrate this point, consider the case where the laptop was not stolen, but that the CEO was rendered incapacitated for some reason. How would the encrypted corporate data on that laptop be recovered? Arguably, the value of a PKI that helps to protect and recover mission-critical data is almost impossible to measure.

Cost Considerations

Unfortunately, there is no single formula that can be applied to all organizations to determine the cost of deploying a PKI. Many organizations are able to leverage their existing IT investments to help offset the cost of deploying the PKI. This applies both to personnel and to facilities. For example, Certification Authorities (CAs) need to be housed in protected facilities so that access by unauthorized personnel can be prevented and accountability can be maintained. Some organizations, especially large organizations, may have these types of facilities already available. Further, existing IT personnel can be utilized to help deploy and operate the components that comprise the PKI. Clearly, the degree of this leverage will tend to vary with each organization.

As discussed in Chapter 3 and Chapter 11, "PKI Information Dissemination: Repositories and Other Techniques," a ubiquitous repository service is also an important part of a large-scale enterprise PKI. Exploiting existing directory services is also possible in many organizations. This allows the PKI to consume directory services that are already part of the existing corporate IT infrastructure, thereby reducing procurement costs and distributing operational costs across multiple directory uses.

In any case, a number of considerations must be evaluated to help determine the *Total Cost of Ownership (TCO)* within a given organization, including the following:

- How many hardware components (that is, Registration Authorities [RAs], CAs, directory servers, and so on) are required to meet the demands of the target community? The number of components may depend on a variety of factors including the scale of the target community, geographic considerations, and the amount of autonomy afforded to the various departments or communities of interest.

- What is the cost of the necessary software and support tools? Both initial software procurement and on-going software maintenance costs should be considered.

- How much of the existing corporate IT infrastructure can be exploited to support the target community? For example, is a separate directory product required, or can an existing corporate directory service be utilized?

- What are the resource requirements associated with the planning, deployment, operation, and ongoing maintenance of the infrastructure?

- What are the resource requirements associated with defining the policies and procedures necessary to support external users and/or external organizations?

- Are the necessary facilities available to house the infrastructure components; if not, what is required, and how much will it cost?

- What are the component availability requirements; is full redundancy of any of the components (for example, the CAs) necessary?

- What are the training costs? This applies to administrators/operational personnel as well as end-users.

- What level of administrative support is required (for example, help desk support, end-entity registration procedures, and so on)?

- Will the deployed PKI interoperate with other PKIs that may be based on technology provided by different vendors? Adopting standards-based technology is essential.

- What is required in terms of legal/policy related doctrine? Liability protection is essential in many cases, especially when interoperability is required with external users or other PKI domains.

Ultimately, the key to success is to plan ahead; understanding as many of the issues as possible will help lead to the development of a solid business strategy.

Deployment: Now or Later?

A number of trade journal articles and conference presentations suggest that PKI is still "in its infancy" and that caution should be exercised when making a deployment decision. Some of the criticism stems from the fear that the technology is still fairly new and that the necessary standards and interoperability testing facilities necessary to guarantee multi-vendor interoperability are only beginning to mature. However, these very same articles indicate that PKI is inevitably a "must-have" technology. We also see numerous statistics that imply electronic commerce will burgeon to hundreds of billions of dollars (in USD) worldwide by the year 2002. Many suggest that PKI will be an instrumental technology in realizing these numbers.

Given the short-term uncertainty coupled with the promise that PKI is the technology of the future, many organizations are entering into the PKI fray with small-scale pilot programs. These pilots typically focus on a single application (for example, secure e-mail), and they limit the size of the end-user community (typically no more than a few hundred end-users). The main purpose of these pilots is to

- Educate administrators and operations personnel through controlled, hands-on experience

- Establish a small core of educated end-users—including key players within the organization—to help promote corporate-level acceptance

- Allow a graceful roll-out of new services over time

- Protect the initial PKI investment as new services are offered

- Demonstrate that the PKI technology is viable and that it will offer significant cost savings

- Allow additional time to achieve corporate-level "buy-in." Occasionally, even the most skeptical can be swayed through actual demonstration.

The industry has witnessed a dramatic rise in these pilot programs in recent years, and there is every indication that this trend will continue.

Summary

This chapter has focused on the benefits of a PKI, and it has briefly discussed some of the cost considerations that should be evaluated as part of the business case development process. It is clear that the promise of ubiquitous security is seldom a sufficient business driver in itself. Ultimately, it is the business drivers and associated cost justification that should dictate whether or not a given technology is appropriate.

In addition to understanding the benefits and associated costs of a PKI, it is also important to realize that corporate-level "buy-in" is instrumental in achieving a successful deployment. Approval from all major departments will greatly increase the chances that the deployment of the PKI will be both graceful and successful. Further, if a given security solution is too intrusive and/or too expensive, it is usually dismissed as non-practical.

For many environments, a properly deployed PKI offers a non-obtrusive, cost-effective solution that can be used to secure multiple applications across multiple domains.

See Chapter 22, "Deployment Issues and Decisions," and Chapter 23, "Barriers to Deployment," for additional information related to PKI deployment.

Reference

[CSI]   Computer Security Institute. *Issues and Trends: 1999 CSI/FBI Computer Crime and Security Survey.* 1999.

CHAPTER 22

Deployment Issues and Decisions

The purpose of this chapter is to briefly discuss many of the issues an organization needs to consider before launching a PKI deployment. Most of these issues will also help an organization determine the best technology vendor (or service organization) available to meet its needs. As with most of Part III, "Deployment Considerations," the primary focus is on the enterprise PKI. Some of the enterprise issues to consider include

- Trust models

- In-source versus out-source

- Build versus buy

- Closed environment versus open environment

- X.509 versus alternative certificate formats

- Targeted applications versus comprehensive solution

- Standard versus proprietary solutions

- Interoperability considerations

- On-line versus off-line operation

- Peripheral support

- Facility requirements

- Personnel requirements

- Certificate revocation requirements

- End-entity roaming requirements

- Key recovery requirements

- Repository requirements

- Disaster planning and recovery

- Security Assurance

- Risk mitigation

The following subsections discuss these issues further.

Trust Models: Hierarchical Versus Distributed

Two fundamental trust models apply in the enterprise context. The first is a strict hierarchy based on superior/subordinate relationships. The second is a distributed mesh based on cross-certification. Although typically not required in an intra-organizational environment, it is also possible to implement a hybrid of the two. Most vendors offer support for one or the other, although a few vendors do support both.

In the enterprise context, it can be argued that the distributed model is more flexible because it allows CAs to come and go with minimal disruption to the other interconnected CA domains. This is true in both an intra- and inter-organizational context. In the case of a strict hierarchy, the disruption caused by the failure (for example, due to a compromise of the CA's signing private key) of a particular CA depends on the location (in terms of level) within the hierarchy. The closer to the top of the hierarchy the CA is, the more disruptive the failure of that CA will be to the enterprise as a whole. Of course, it is reasonable to expect that additional safeguards should be implemented for the higher levels—especially at the root level. The additional safeguards might include a longer key size (for example, a 2048-bit RSA signing key rather than a 1024-bit RSA signing key), and/or it may include a hardware module where the private keying material can be stored more securely.

The hierarchical model is currently the rule in the Web environment, and some enterprise domains are also adopting it. Selection of this model in an enterprise domain is largely a function of the technology supported by the chosen vendor. Circumstances may also exist where a hierarchical model is perceived to be a good mechanism for maintaining policy-related controls on subordinate CAs. However, this is mainly a perception issue, because similar controls can be levied on cross-certified CAs as well.

Note

Chapter 9 discusses trust models further. We recommend that each organization examine the pros and cons of these trust models in light of their specific requirements.

In-Source Versus Out-Source

In-sourcing is when an enterprise decides to deploy its own internal PKI—utilizing its own resources (including personnel, hardware, and so on) and/or hiring external resources to help with any or all of the PKI's internal operation. The key here is that the PKI is under the control of the enterprise. *Out-sourcing* is when an organization allows an external party to supply and operate some aspects—perhaps even all aspects—of its PKI. In this case, at least some—perhaps all—of the PKI operation is not under the direct control of the enterprise.

Sometimes the decision of whether to in-source or out-source is based purely on economic considerations. However, it is usually much more complicated than that. Not all organizations perceive things the same way, and many factors can impact this decision. For example, some organizations insist on maintaining total control over all aspects of the enterprise, especially anything to do with security and the source of trust associated with offering a particular service. These organizations are usually unwilling to be dependent on a third-party service provider. On the other hand, some organizations do not consider these factors to be as important with respect to their particular needs. Further, smaller organizations are much more likely to opt for an out-sourcing arrangement due to economic and resource constraints.

Note

There are various degrees of in-sourcing and out-sourcing. For example, an organization may decide to outsource the services of a *Certification Authority (CA)* from a third party, but the *Registration Authority (RA)* function would be retained in house. As another example, an organization may want total control of the PKI, but it requires external resources to help deploy and operate the PKI. This is sometimes done as a transitional step that enables the organization's internal resources to develop, with the goal that the organization will take over complete operation of the PKI at some later point in time.

Hype and marketing propaganda, rather than the organization's real requirements, can sometimes impact the question of in-source versus out-source. To ensure that it makes the right choice, the organization should exercise caution when making this decision. In the end, the basis of this decision should be a cost/benefit trade-off analysis that takes into consideration as many relevant factors as possible. These factors include the following:

- Total cost of in-sourcing versus out-sourcing (including all related software, hardware, maintenance, personnel, facilities, training, legal fees, and so on)

- Degree of control that the organization feels must be maintained over the operation of the PKI

- The perceived source of trust that will be translated to the consumers of the PKI services (although simply ensuring that the issued certificates are appropriately branded may control this)

- Response time (for example, for end-entity and CA certificate requests, revocation information dissemination, and so on)

- Level and availability of help desk support

- Flexibility and scalability considerations

- Ability (and willingness) of the vendor to evolve to meet the future needs of the organization

- Disaster planning and recovery

Build Versus Buy

A *build* option implies that an organization is willing to invest in the development of PKI technology (for example, in CA and/or RA technology). A *buy* option simply means that an organization will purchase PKI products or services, either through in-sourcing or out-sourcing.

While there is little evidence that organizations are willing to pursue a build option, we do leave room for the possibility that an organization may want to actually build their own PKI components under certain (albeit extreme) circumstances.

However, a number of barriers should be considered before contemplating such an option:

- First, PKI technology is relatively complex to implement. Most vendors that offer PKI software have invested substantially in the technology, and a return on investment can be realized only through sales to multiple organizations. It is difficult to see how costs would be recovered in an organization that elected to build its own PKI.

- Second, given the complexity of the software, it is unlikely that most organizations would have sufficient (and proper) resources in place to even begin such a venture.

- Finally, technology patents exist that might impact the development of such a product. Either royalties would have to be paid, or workarounds to the patents (which are not always possible) would be required. A number of patents exist in the areas of revocation technology, time stamping (which is necessary to help support non-repudiation), and in privilege management, to name a few. Additional patents related to PKI technology are likely to be introduced in the future.

Given these difficulties, it is fair to say that most organizations do not even consider the option of building their own PKI.

Closed Versus Open Environment

For the purposes of this book, a *closed environment* is an environment where only intra-domain communications are of concern. The domain can be a single enterprise, or it can be a collection of enterprises all operating under identical technical and operational procedures and constraints. An *open environment* is an environment where inter-domain communications will be required and supported. In this case, multiple technical and operating procedures are likely to be encountered.

Although multi-vendor interoperability may seem to be a relatively minor concern in a closed environment, multiple sources could conceivably supply technology in such an environment. Therefore, it is important to be careful so that proprietary solutions do not hinder potential interoperability—especially as the needs of the closed community grow over time.

Multi-vendor interoperability is clearly a concern in the case of the open environment. The technology selected should be based on industry accepted standards, and the technology vendor should demonstrate a commitment to multi-vendor interoperability.

X.509 Versus Alternative Certificate Formats

As discussed in Chapter 6, "Certificates and Certification," alternative certificate formats to the X.509 Version 3 public key certificate exist. Not surprisingly, there are proponents of each format. For example, proponents of the *Simple Public Key Infrastructure (SPKI)*—as discussed in Chapter 6—would suggest that the SPKI certificates are attractive because they focus on the notion of roles and authorizations, rather than identity. Further, a *Pretty Good Privacy (PGP)* or OpenPGP advocate might claim that PGP certificates are more flexible than X.509 Version 3 public-key certificates and that they are more suitable for establishing trust relationships among individuals.

Although some of these alternative points of view may have merit in certain contexts, much of this debate is moot when it comes to meeting the needs of an enterprise. To date, corporate demand has overwhelmingly been in favor of X.509 Version 3 public-key certificates. If the market evolves in such a way that these environments require support for alternative certificate formats, these requirements will filter back to the technology vendors, and the products will evolve accordingly. At the moment, however, the vast majority PKI vendors support only X.509-based certificates.

Targeted Applications Versus Comprehensive Solution

It is possible to implement many of the security services discussed within this book (in particular, Chapters 4 and 5) without the benefit of a PKI. These are typically point solutions, and the specific security features are usually embedded within each application. While this may be an option in a limited number of environments, most mid- to large-scale domains cannot afford to deploy multiple point solutions—especially when a single security infrastructure can meet the needs of multiple applications, thereby leading to a much more cost-effective solution.

However, in small, closed-enterprise domains, point solutions may still turn out to be the most cost-effective way of meeting specific security requirements.

Standard Versus Proprietary Solutions

A solution is said to be based on *standards* when it is based on industry accepted standards, and there are no unique implementation details that would pose a threat to interoperability with another technology vendor that is also based on the same standards. A solution is said to be *proprietary* when it is based on unique implementation details that will, by definition, prevent interoperability with other technology vendors.

Given the current interest in and the level of activity with respect to standards and multivendor cooperation, it is difficult to see a business case for adopting proprietary solutions. However, there still may be a small number of environments where this may be the best choice. Again, this is all part of the cost/benefit trade-off analysis. However, if interdomain interoperability is even the slightest concern (and in most cases it will be), only standards-based solutions should be considered.

As the "Closed Versus Open Environment" section of this chapter pointed out, it is important to be careful when adopting proprietary solutions, even in an intra-domain context. This is because adopting standards-based solutions will decrease (or even eliminate) the danger of being locked in to a single vendor.

Interoperability Considerations

A number of interoperability issues go beyond the standards themselves. As discussed in Chapter 18, "Standards: Necessary but Not Sufficient," vendors can legitimately claim standards compliance, but multi-vendor interoperability still might not be possible for a variety of reasons. Understanding these reasons, and ensuring that the vendor community cooperates to provide acceptable and interoperable solutions, is essential.

Certificate and CRL Profiles

Even when standards-based techniques are adopted, it is still possible to dictate implementation specifics that can vary from one domain to another. This is the case with the X.509 certificates and CRLs. Specifically, different certificate and CRL profiles (which are discussed in Chapter 18) are being defined to meet a variety of needs. As a deployment consideration, it is important to select technology vendors that offer flexible certificate and CRL generation so that meeting the requirements associated with multiple certificate and CRL profiles is easy to do.

Multiple Industry Accepted Standards

It is not sufficient to simply adopt a technology that is "standards based," especially when multiple standards and protocols are available. For example, end-entity certificates can be initialized through different mechanisms, cross-certification can be facilitated in both on-line and off-line operations, and revocation information can be disseminated in a variety of ways. It is important to make sure that the technology meets the needs of the organization from a requirement perspective. The more flexible a vendor product is, the more likely it is that the vendor will be able to meet the needs of the organization (both now and in the future). Thus, vendors should offer multiple solutions based on standards and practices that are in widespread use throughout the industry.

PKI-Enabled Applications

For a given application to consume the services of a PKI, it must be *PKI enabled*. This enables the application to invoke the necessary security services and key/certificate life cycle management functions. Technology vendors should offer standard PKI-enabled applications (for example, secure e-mail via S/MIME) as well as generic toolkits to use to easily integrate other applications into the PKI as necessary.

Policy Issues

As Chapter 6 discussed, certificate policies must also be addressed to facilitate inter-domain interoperability. Specifically, formal agreements need to be established between enterprise domains that want to communicate under one or more inter-domain policies.

From a technology perspective, a PKI should be capable of supporting these policies both on certificate generation and on client-side processing. Chapter 6 provides descriptions of the certificate extensions that can be used to support certificate policy enforcement.

On-Line Versus Off-Line Operation

On-line operation is the situation in which the end-entities are directly connected to the network. Typically, the end-entities are capable of consuming all PKI-related services. *Off-line operation* enables end-entities to consume at least a subset of the PKI services even though they are not directly connected to the network.

Some techniques (for example, revocation information dissemination using the On-line Certificate Status Protocol) require end-entities to be on-line, in order to perform particular PKI-related operations. These techniques are clearly not suitable for off-line operation (for example, verifying signed e-mail on a laptop during circumstances in which access to the organization's PKI is not possible). In order to facilitate off-line operation, recent revocation information could have been cached that would enable the revocation status to be verified (within a certain window of time). Alternatively, the revocation information could have been supplied along with the e-mail in this example. Offline operation would also require that the necessary certificates and certification paths are available, which can be facilitated through caching or by including the necessary certificates with the e-mail.

Whether or not off-line operation should be permitted within a particular environment is a policy decision. After the policy is determined, a technology commensurate with the policy can be selected.

Peripheral Support

In addition to any hardware normally associated with the infrastructure components (for example, CA, RA, repository, and client systems), it should be determined if a cryptographic hardware module is required in association with the operation of the CA. This would enable the CA's keying material to be generated and stored on a hardware crypto-module rather than in software, which provides additional protection of the keying material.

Further, end-user hardware tokens or smart cards may also be required. For example, some environments may require multi-factor authentication (see Chapter 12, "PKI Operational Considerations"), and they may levy a requirement to store private keying material on a peripheral module rather than on the end-user's personal computer. Biometric devices also may be required—either in lieu of, or in addition to, the hardware tokens or smart cards.

Not all technology vendors support these peripheral devices to the same degree. However, standard *Application Programming Interfaces (APIs)* have been defined (for example, PKCS#11) that vendors should adhere to if they do offer support for peripheral devices. Once the policy decisions surrounding the requirement for these devices have been made, it will be easier to identify a technology vendor that meets the needs of the organization.

Facility Requirements

As discussed in Chapter 12, all sensitive PKI components must be adequately protected. As CAs are the most sensitive component within the PKI, appropriately-protected facilities must house them. Appropriate physical and procedural safeguards must also be established. Essentially, unauthorized access must be prevented and individual accountability should be maintained at all times.

Although the physical and procedural security associated with the RA components is typically not as stringent as that for a CA, it may be necessary to protect these components to some degree as well. Each organization should determine where these components will be placed and how they will be attended.

Personnel Requirements

As Chapter 21 "Benefits (and Costs) of a PKI," mentioned and as the "In-Source Versus Out-Source" section of this chapter alluded to, qualified personnel are required to maintain and operate the aspects of the PKI that fall under the direct control of the enterprise. The enterprise should determine the number and skill level of the appropriate personnel, which will depend on the scale of the PKI as well as how much of the PKI is in-sourced. The types of personnel that may be required include

- *Security officers* responsible for enforcing the security policies dictated by the enterprise

- *Operators* to perform system installs, backups, reboots, and so on

- *Administrators* to perform day-to-day operations such as end-user registration

Also, it may be necessary to enlist the services of skilled consultants and legal council to develop and/or analyze certificate policies and/or Certification Practice Statements (CPSs).

Certificate Revocation

As Chapter 8 discussed, it is possible to implement a number of possible certificate revocation mechanisms. Variables associated with the dissemination of revocation information include protocols, timeliness, size, performance, scalability, and so on.

It is up to each organization to determine its revocation requirements, and it is up to the technology vendor to meet those requirements. As Chapter 8 discussed, it is likely that PKI technology vendors will offer multiple solutions to maximize the chances that they will be capable of meeting the variety of needs in an extremely diverse market. In any case, ensuring that the technology vendor meets the organization's requirements (both now and in the future) is essential.

End-Entity Roaming

Many organizations have a requirement to support personnel while traveling on business or personnel who are always moving from one place to another as part of their everyday job (for example, in association with parcel delivery companies). This is sometimes referred to as *roaming*.

The requirements associated with roaming can vary substantially. On the one hand, the roaming user may carry a laptop at all times and, therefore, have the necessary credentials and client software to engage in PKI-related operations whenever required. In other cases, the roaming user may move from computer to computer, and the software may or may not be the same at each desktop or kiosk. The roaming user may also be unable to personally carry the necessary credentials (for example, a signing private key).

If it is determined that roaming is a requirement for a given organization, it is important to ensure that the technology vendor can support this capability in a secure and robust manner.

Key Recovery

As Chapter 7, "Key and Certificate Management," discussed, key recovery deals with the secure storage and distribution of encryption keys to recover corporate data that would otherwise be rendered unrecoverable. A given organization must assess the need for this functionality and determine the requirements associated with its implementation if required.

Note

Legal restrictions or legal mandates associated with key recovery may exist in some countries. Although not devoted solely to the topic of key recovery, *The Limits of Trust* [LOT] identifies existing legislation pertaining to confidentiality and digital signatures on a country-by-country basis.

It is possible to implement a key recovery facility as part of a CA or to implement a separate key recovery component. If an organization determines that key recovery is essential to respond to a legitimate business need, the implementation alternatives should be weighed carefully. Note that some vendors already support this capability, but they may offer only one option for achieving key recovery (for example, it may be supported only as a CA function, and a third-party key recovery center may not be available). Note that you can find a draft U.S. Federal Information Processing Standard (FIPS) on "requirements for key recovery products" at http://csrc.nist.gov/keyrecovery/.

Repository Issues

As Chapter 11, "PKI Information Dissemination: Repositories and Other Techniques," discussed, a number of options can be implemented to disseminate end-entity certificates, revocation information, and policy-related information. A number of technology vendors that support one or more of these services also exist. It is important for each organization to understand these requirements and to select a technology vendor that can best suit the needs as identified.

As in the case of PKI technology vendors, it is also important to ensure that the repository vendor offers flexible functionality and that the vendor is committed to multi-vendor interoperability. This is important because inter-repository communication and information exchange may be required in support of the certificate and revocation information dissemination requirement (as Chapter 11 discussed).

Disaster Planning and Recovery

While careful planning and the implementation of redundant components can minimize the risk associated with many sources of disaster, it is important to consider worst-case scenarios and to make sure that the best possible contingency plans are in place; this will expedite the recovery of the PKI in the event that a serious disaster does occur.

As Chapter 12 discussed, perhaps one of the most serious disasters that can occur with respect to the PKI is when a CA's key is compromised (or even suspected that it has been compromised). An organization should ensure that the appropriate safeguards are in place to minimize the risk of this event, and that the technology vendor understands the problem and is able to provide recommendations and tools to help expedite recovery if such an event were to occur.

Security Assurance

Security assurance has to do with how much confidence an organization can place in the proper and secure operation of the PKI components. There are a number of criteria that can be used to gauge the level of confidence that should be associated with a given product, and there are likely to be specific certification or accreditation programs that can help determine this confidence level in a formal manner. For example, the "Federal Information Processing Standards Publication 140-1" [FIPS140-1] establishes criteria for evaluating cryptographic modules, and there are independent laboratories approved to perform FIPS 140-1 evaluations. Other criteria and evaluation procedures are available, including government- and industry-sponsored endorsement programs that are based on evaluation criteria such as the "Common Criteria for Information Technology Security Evaluation" (see `http://www.csecst.gs.ca/cse/english/cc2dwnld.html` to download Version 2.0 of the Common Criteria). There are also industry sponsored testing laboratories that can be used to certify products against industry-specific criteria (for example, the BITS Financial Services Security Lab).

PKI products that have been demonstrated to meet specific criteria may be much more attractive to an enterprise than products that do not. In fact, it is not unreasonable for an enterprise to specify minimum criteria that must be demonstrably met by a PKI product before that product will be considered acceptable to that enterprise.

Mitigating Risk

In all cases, it is simply in the best interest of an organization to mitigate risk as much as possible. Understanding the organization's needs and requirements, both now and in the future, partially accomplishes this.

When it comes to selecting a specific technology vendor(s), a number of things should be considered to help ensure that the selection is as sound as possible, including

- Reputation—What do their existing customers have to say about the vendor?

- Market penetration—How pervasive is the vendor, and what is the estimated market share?

- Longevity—Is the vendor viable from a long-term perspective?

- Cooperation—Is the vendor willing and able to cooperate with the customer, especially if is the vendor knows in advance that some customization will be required to more fully meet the needs of the organization?

- Support—What is the level of support (for example, help desk and software upgrades) offered by the vendor?

- Standards compliance—Is the vendor standards compliant, and does the vendor offer multiple alternatives?

- Security—Does the vendor offer products that have been formally endorsed by industry established criteria (for example, FIPS 140-1)?

- Multi-vendor interoperability—Is the vendor committed to multi-vendor interoperability (as demonstrated, for example, through public, formally-organized interoperability trials)?

- Cost—Is the vendor cost effective, and will the organization realize cost savings?

Summary

This chapter has focused on many of the deployment issues to consider before an organization selects one or more technology vendors and launches its initial PKI deployment. The key is to understand the issues to the maximum extent possible and to make educated decisions based on facts and requirements rather than on marketing hype. If necessary, it is highly recommended that an experienced, vendor-independent consultant be hired to help the organization work through these issues.

See Chapters 21 and 23 for topics related to the deployment issues discussed in this chapter.

References

[FIPS140-1] FIPS 140-1. "Security Requirements for Cryptographic Modules." Federal Information Processing Standards Publication 140-1, U.S. Department of Commerce/NIST, National Technical Information Service. Springfield, Virginia. January 1994.

[LOT]   Baker, Stewart A. and Paul R. Hurst. *The Limits of Trust*. Kluwer Law International, 1998.

CHAPTER 23

Barriers to Deployment

The purpose of this chapter is to briefly discuss some of the issues that can impede the successful deployment of a PKI within a given organization. While solutions are being found to reduce or eliminate some of these potential obstacles, it is important to be aware of some of the difficulties that can be encountered in an early adopter market.

Repository Issues

As Chapter 8, "Certificate Revocation," and Chapter 11, "PKI Information Dissemination: Repositories and Other Techniques," discussed, many enterprise domains utilize a ubiquitous on-line repository to allow for the timely and robust dissemination of certificates, certificate revocation information (for example, *Certificate Revocation Lists*, or *CRLs*) and any other PKI-related information (for example, policy information). Early PKI deployment experience has demonstrated that this is not without its problems—although these issues are expected to be corrected as the products offered by the vendor community continue to evolve. The purpose of this section is to discuss some of these issues.

Lack of Industry-Accepted Standard

One of the concerns with a ubiquitous directory service is that there is no single accepted industry standard for offering these services. Some market segments have adopted the X.500 Directory standards [X.500], but there are also numerous (and usually competing) repository-related standards already developed or in the process of being developed. For example, the *Lightweight Directory Access Protocol (LDAP)*, which was developed under auspices of the *Internet Engineering Task Force (IETF)*, defines an access protocol between a client and a remote repository. LDAP is in direct competition to the X.500-based *Directory Access Protocol (DAP)*.

> **Note**
>
> It appears that, at least for now, LDAP has won the battle in terms of an access mechanism between a client and a remote repository. In fact, most X.500 vendors recognize this and now offer LDAP support in addition to DAP.

There are still a number of open issues when it comes to other functions associated with both client-to-server and server-to-server interaction and information exchange. For example, the IETF LDAPext Working Group is developing a number of additional proposed standards, such as access control mechanisms and access control models. Further, the IETF *LDAP Duplication/Replication/Update Protocol (LDUP)* is also under development, which may compete with the X.500 counterpart, the *Directory Information Shadowing Protocol (DISP)*. There are also proprietary solutions, as well as solutions based on standard remote database access. Certificates and CRLs can also be distributed as part of a *Domain Name Service (DNS)* function [RFC2538].

Although any one of these solutions may be well suited for a given organization's needs, the breadth of choices can lead to interoperability difficulties when it comes to inter-organizational communication. Selecting standards-based solutions may help to reduce some of these problems. Chapters 8 and 11 discuss certificate and certificate revocation information dissemination in more detail.

Multi-Vendor Interoperability

In addition to the standards issue, there is also the issue surrounding multi-vendor interoperability. Not all directory products are created equal, and early experience has demonstrated that all vendors do not implement some functions; or, if they are implemented, they are not necessarily implemented in a consistent manner from one vendor to another—even if these solutions are based on the same standards. (Chapter 18, "Standards: Necessary but Not Sufficient," discusses some of the reasons why standards themselves do not guarantee multi-vendor interoperability.) However, this is clearly an issue that will improve with experience, and the directory vendors appear eager to eliminate these types of issues by cooperating with their technology partners, customers, and even their competitors.

Scalability and Performance

Finally, potential scalability and performance issues are associated with the deployment of a ubiquitous repository service. Given the limited number of large-scale PKI deployments, there is little implementation experience with respect to how many repositories are required to effectively service a given organization. Clearly, this will be a function of the number of end-users, but the validity period of the CRLs (assuming caching is allowed) and other implementation variables (for example, whether or not Delta CRLs are supported, as discussed in Chapter 8) will have an impact as well. Also, the repository is unlikely to be devoted solely to the operation of the PKI; additional load is likely to be introduced by other uses (for example, a generic "white pages" service also may be supported).

Knowledgeable Personnel

Even though public-key cryptography was introduced over two decades ago [DH], the widespread availability of the technology itself has come to fruition only in recent years. Due to the fact that this technology is still fairly new from an implementation and deployment perspective, the number of knowledgeable personnel in this particular field is rather limited. There is evidence that the number of PKI-knowledgeable personnel is growing, but it is also clear that these resources may be difficult to hire and to retain.

From a resource perspective, it is important to recognize that personnel requirements are not simply limited to one or two administrative personnel. Not only are PKI-knowledgeable administrators needed, but also fairly senior-level personnel are required to help develop policy-related doctrines, such as Certificate Policies and Certification Practice Statements (CPSs) (as discussed in Chapter 13, "Legal Framework") in many enterprise environments. Further, the PKI deployment strategy itself needs to be well thought out and documented appropriately. This also requires fairly knowledgeable, senior-level personnel. Of course, it is possible to outsource some or all of these positions, depending on the specific needs of the organization.

Recent trends illustrate that the resource situation is improving dramatically, and as the technology continues to gain widespread acceptance and more information and formal training becomes available, this will become a less-significant issue. In the meantime, it may be beneficial to institute internal training programs (which can be outsourced from a variety of reputable training organizations) to help educate the appropriate personnel.

PKI-Enabled Applications

For a PKI to be useful, the software operating on behalf of end-users, processes, or devices must be able to consume the services that the PKI has enabled. Specifically, encryption/decryption and digital signature generation and verification (as discussed in Chapter 2, "Public-Key Cryptography") must be supported. In addition, the software must be able to access the key/certificate life cycle-management functions, as discussed in Chapter 7, "Key and Certificate Management."

When the software is able to "tap into the PKI," it is often said to be *PKI-enabled* or *PKI-aware*. The list of PKI-aware software is growing, and this trend is expected to continue. For example, many of the more popular e-mail and electronic forms packages are now PKI-aware. This trend is also evident in the *Virtual Private Network (VPN)* market, in which multiple vendors implement public key techniques (for example, those based on the *Internet Key Exchange (IKE)* proposed standard [RFC2409]).

In addition, Web browser and server technology may be viewed as "partially" PKI-enabled. However, even though the *Secure Sockets Layer (SSL)* or the *Transport Layer Security (TLS)* [RFC2246] protocols (which base authentication between a client and a server on public key techniques) are typically supported, it is clear that the browser/server technology that is currently available requires significant improvements before the Web environment will support full certificate-based services and key/certificate life cycle management.

Numerous applications (for example, legacy applications) will likely remain outside the PKI-enabled list, however. This is due to a variety of factors, including the inability to modify these applications so that they are capable of consuming the services offered by the PKI (because of a lack of available resources and/or the exorbitant cost associated with the necessary software modifications).

Corporate-Level Acceptance

We cannot overemphasize the need for corporate-level "buy-in." Without the appropriate champions in place to usher in the deployment of the new technology, it will be extremely difficult to overcome many of the hurdles likely to stand in the way of a successful deployment. It is, therefore, necessary to build a solid business case and to "sell" that business case to the critical decision-makers within a given organization.

As more and more business is conducted electronically, the need for a pervasive security infrastructure will become critical. Furthermore, as the number and visibility of PKI deployments continues to rise, achieving corporate-level buy-in will become much easier. This will become even more straightforward when the early-adopter market we see today matures to a market in which you are behind if you have not yet deployed.

Summary

This chapter briefly discussed some of the issues that might impede the deployment of a PKI within a given organization. However, the chapter also noted that, in many cases, significant improvements are being realized that help to reduce or even eliminate these issues. Eventually, it is expected that most, if not all, of these issues will be effectively reduced to only minor considerations within many organizations.

The remainder of Part III, "Deployment Considerations," (especially Chapter 21, "Benefits (and Costs) of a PKI," and Chapter 22, "Deployment Issues and Decisions") provides additional information related to PKI deployment issues.

References

[DH]   Diffie, W. and M. Hellman. "New Directions in Cryptography." *IEEE Transactions on Information Theory* IT-22, no. 6. (November 1976).

[RFC2246]   Dierks, T. and C. Allen. "The TLS Protocol Version 1.0." Internet Request for Comments 2246. (January 1999).

[RFC2409]   Harkins, D. and D. Carrel. "The Internet Key Exchange (IKE)." Internet Request for Comments 2409. (November 1998).

[RFC2538]   Eastlake, D. and O. Gudmundsson. "Storing Certificates in the Domain Name System." Internet Request for Comments 2538. (March 1999).

[X.500]   *The Directory*, Joint ITU-T X.500 Recommendations and ISO/IEC 9594 Standards. 1997.

CHAPTER 24

Typical Business Models

Part III, "Deployment Considerations," concentrates on PKI deployment considerations in an enterprise context. This chapter discusses several different business models that might drive the deployment of a PKI. Although this may not be an exhaustive list, we do concentrate on some of today's more prevalent business models, as evidenced by many of the PKI deployments around the globe.

There are also several initiatives designed to offer scalable inter-domain trust paths between organizations. Because these initiatives may have an influence on the external communications business model described here, this chapter also gives a brief discussion regarding these initiatives.

Internal Communications Business Model

From a corporate-security perspective, the overall goal in any organization is to provide cost-effective, useable security that is commensurate with the perceived level of risk. If the cost of providing the security is too great, or if the deployed security services are too difficult to use or administer, the business case for deploying that solution cannot be justified.

It is extremely difficult (if not impossible) to justify anything of this nature without considering the true benefits that will be realized through the judicious deployment of a comprehensive security infrastructure. For example, significant cost savings can be realized by reducing the amount of time individuals spend logging in to multiple applications each day. Further, the proper protection of corporate information can help reduce significant financial losses that can result from the theft of unprotected electronic information (either in storage or in transit). Of course, cost considerations are not the only benefits realized from providing comprehensive security services. Improvements in workflow efficiency, reduction in administrative overhead, and even revenue generation are all factors that may contribute to the business case. These considerations are discussed further in Chapter 21, "Benefits (and Costs) of a PKI."

Generally, it is the case that the business drivers for deploying a specific security solution center on several specific areas, such as the following:

- Enhanced authentication and accountability

- Secure e-mail

- Desktop security (for example, encryption of sensitive files stored on a disk drive)

- Secure remote access

- Secure internal communications (for example, secure intranet)

- Secure external communications (for example, secure extranet)

- Reduced sign-on (see Chapter 3, "The Concept of an Infrastructure")

- Paper reduction through adoption of secure electronic forms

- Secure (and robust) audit trails

In many cases, a single application is selected to help launch the initial PKI deployment, which is then used as a vehicle to prove the utility and necessity of the PKI itself. As discussed in Chapter 21, launching a small-scale pilot that focuses on a single application enables an ordered and controlled PKI deployment. Over time, additional applications are folded in, which eventually leads to a single infrastructure that is capable of supporting a variety of applications in a number of different contexts.

Thus, the prominent intra-organizational business model is to enhance overall security in a number of areas but in a cost-effective, structured, and user-friendly manner. Ultimately, the benefit of a PKI-based solution is to provide a single infrastructure that can support myriad security services in a complex, heterogeneous, multi-application, large-scale business environment.

Note

Benefits associated with the deployment of a PKI are discussed further in Chapter 21. Specific deployment considerations (for example, the number and location of CAs, insource versus outsource, and so on) are addressed in Chapter 22, "Deployment Issues and Decisions."

External Communications Business Model

The purpose of this section is to briefly discuss some of the business models presently being adopted for external corporate communications. These will be addressed from two perspectives:

- Business-to-business

- Business-to-consumer

Business-to-Business

The main business driver for business-to-business communications is to provide secure and cost-effective inter-organizational communications. Although this may seem to be a rather obvious statement, ubiquitous business-to-business interaction is not guaranteed. Solid business drivers must be in place to motivate corporations (or governments) to interconnect their PKI domains. To many, this falls under the general umbrella of secure electronic commerce.

A given business may want to communicate with a variety of external sources that have deployed or outsourced their own PKI, including the following:

- Partners

- Separately incorporated subsidiaries

- Suppliers

- Peers

Further, a given business may want to communicate with these external sources for a variety of reasons, including

- Purchase order exchange

- Collaborative research

- Pre-authorization of financial transactions

- Payment transfers

- Inter-organizational correspondence

- Supply chain management

- Secure document exchange

Not surprisingly, many of the applications listed in the "Internal Communications Business Model" section of this chapter can be used to accommodate the secure communications between two or more businesses. For example, secure e-mail might be suitable for collaborative research and inter-organizational correspondence. On the other hand, some sort of automated payment-transfer protocol would be more appropriate to facilitate payment transfers between financial institutions.

In any case, an agreed-upon set of common security capabilities is required to realize effective business-to-business communications. Many view PKI technology as the very foundation to achieve these capabilities.

> **Note**
>
> Each organization can run the PKI services independently. In this case, *cross-certification* can be used to establish the necessary trust relationship(s) between the two organizations. Alternatively, a parent organization may offer PKI services to one or more of its subsidiaries, especially if the subsidiary is a relatively small organization and it does not have the business need to run an internal PKI. Specific deployment considerations such as these are addressed further in Chapter 23, "Barriers to Deployment."

Business-to-Consumer

Much of today's business-to-consumer electronic commerce would not be possible without the Internet or the World Wide Web (WWW). However, it is important to distinguish between two prevalent business models when it comes to providing business-to-consumer electronic commerce.

The first model is *user-centric* (see Chapter 9, "Trust Models"). Individuals obtain their own certificates from a third-party service provider, or they generate their own certificates (as in the case of OpenPGP, as discussed in Chapter 6, "Certificates and Certification," and Chapter 16, "Major Standards Activities"). In many cases, the individuals use standard "Web technology" to conduct their business. This is largely an unstructured and uncontrolled model, in which even the most basic certificate/key life cycle management (see Chapter 7, "Key and Certificate Management") is simply unavailable. In this model, electronic commerce is typically based on the *Secure Sockets Layer (SSL)* protocol or *Transport Layer Security (TLS)* [RFC2246] protocol, which provides a confidentiality pipe between a browser and a server. Server-only or mutual client-server authentication can also be supported. However, the use of SSL/TLS has been criticized because client authentication is generally considered optional and is rarely used in today's Web environment.

In addition, there is generally no way to preserve a persistent digital signature in association with a given transaction, which is a serious limitation in many transaction-based applications. Nonetheless, many of the merchants on the Web rely on SSL/TLS for the protection of the transactions (for example, to protect credit card numbers while in transit between the client and the server).

The second model is more "*organization-centric.*" This second model, which has been adopted by a number of organizations, is arguably more controlled and more secure than the first. This model is where an organization (a bank, for example) operates as a

Certification Authority (CA), and certificates are issued to that organization's constituents for the specific purpose of conducting business between the individual and that organization. This model may also include the use of special purpose software, typically issued from the organization to the individual, to offer more comprehensive certificate/key life cycle management and more secure communications than would normally be available. It also enables the organization to more easily control the purpose and scope of the certificates it issues.

Internal/External Business Model Hybrids

Of course, it is natural for many organizations to offer both internal and external security services based on PKI technology. These two models must not be viewed as being mutually exclusive. In fact, many of today's PKI deployments begin with a modest-scale internal pilot (for example, deployment of a single PKI-enabled application with a community of users on the order of tens or hundreds). This is followed by larger-scale initiatives (for example, incorporating additional applications and increasing the number of users), including external business-to-business and business-to-consumer deployments.

Business Model Influences

In addition to internal business requirements, external events sometimes significantly influence the business model. For example, the U.S. health care industry is witnessing the introduction of legislation that is likely to cast an unprecedented focus on the protection of electronic health care information. Specifically, the Medical Records Confidentiality Act of 1995 levies severe penalties associated with the unauthorized disclosure of medical information. In addition, the Health Information Portability Accountability Act of 1996 (also known as the Kennedy/Kassebaum Bill) mandates that the U.S. Congress enacts federal laws for the protection of patient information no later than August 1999. Implementation of the technology necessary to meet the criteria identified by those laws is required within two years after the legislation is enacted. Clearly, this will have a profound impact on the business model of any health care organization.

As more and more of the paper-based medical records are replaced with *Electronic Medical Records (EMRs)*, care must be taken to ensure that those records are accessed and updated in accordance with sound business (and ethical) practices *and* all applicable legislation. For example, the technology used to access EMRs can vary significantly, and the individuals that access EMRs also vary. Specifically, access to the EMR can be local or remote (including remote access over the Internet). Personnel accessing the EMR can be a primary care physician, a consulting physician, a nurse, or even the patient himself/herself.

This brief example helps to illustrate how secure electronic forms, secure remote access, and individual access control and accountability are required in a business model that must address the proper protection of EMRs.

> **Note**
>
> A document titled "For the Record: Protecting Electronic Health Information" [NAS] summarizes many of the issues associated with the protection of health care information.

Government-Sponsored Initiatives

A number of government-sponsored initiatives exist (for example, the Government of Canada Public Key Infrastructure and the U.S. Federal PKI) that can be modeled in the same way as the internal, business-to-business, and business-to-consumer models described in the preceding sections. In this case, the internal business model is driven by a need to facilitate inter-departmental communications among civil servants. The business-to-business model is representative of the need for peer-to-peer communications between governments on a national, regional, or local basis. The business-to-consumer model reflects the need for a government to offer services to its citizens—although the specific applications may vary substantially due to the nature of services traditionally offered by a government (as compared to a private organization).

The deployment strategy of the known government deployments also reflects that of an internal/external business model hybrid discussed previously in the chapter. Specifically, the government-based PKIs tend to begin with modest internal deployments (on the order of tens or perhaps hundreds of users), with the plan to expand and extend the reach of the PKI to offer external services to the citizen and to provide for inter-governmental communications.

Inter-Domain Trust

Although it is possible for individual businesses to forge their own inter-organizational trust relationships on a bilateral basis, a number of initiatives are designed to establish business-to-business trust relationships on behalf of these organizations. The purpose of this section is to briefly discuss a few of these initiatives.

Entrust Worldwide

Entrust Worldwide is a global, policy-partitioned trust network. It is designed to facilitate inter-organizational trust through the concept of *hubs*. (The purpose of a hub is to "introduce" one organization to another.) This concept is similar to the bridge CA component discussed in Chapter 9, "Trust Models." The hub uses cross-certification (as opposed to a rooted hierarchy approach) as the basis for establishing the trust relationships between organizations. This enables an organization, which has established its own independent PKI, to establish an interoperability path with other autonomous PKI domains, as needs dictate. See Chapter 9 for more information regarding trust relationships.

Even though the name may suggest an Entrust-only infrastructure, this is not the intent of Entrust Worldwide. The infrastructure is designed to be vendor-neutral, as long as a given vendor product can support the minimum technical requirements necessary to seamlessly interoperate with the infrastructure as a whole. Interoperability is promoted through the use of industry-accepted standards.

Identrus

Identrus (once known as the *Global Trust Organization*, or *GTO*) is an organization that is designed to help establish business-to-business trust relationships for the purpose of conducting global electronic commerce. Identrus was founded by eight major financial institutions. It is expected that additional financial institutions will join the Identrus "network" over time. The infrastructure itself is based on a rooted hierarchy. Thus, each participating financial institution will "fall under" a common root. The basis of trust will rest with the participating financial institutions.

Like Entrust Worldwide, it is intended that the Identrus infrastructure will be open to multiple vendors, as long as the vendors are capable of offering products that conform to the Identrus infrastructure guidelines.

VeriSign Trust Network

The *VeriSign Trust Network (VTN)* exists because VeriSign has several root keys embedded in the Web browsers, and both individual and server certificates issued by VeriSign "fall under" one of those root keys. This model can be extended to encompass inter-organizational trust, as long as the certificates issued by each organization fall under a common VeriSign root. Thus, VTN is based on a rooted hierarchy trust model (see Chapter 9 for further discussion of trust models).

GTE CyberTrust OmniRoot

In May 1999, GTE CyberTrust announced a new service offering that is referred to as *OmniRoot*. From a "trust network" perspective, the GTE CyberTrust OmniRoot is analogous to the VeriSign Trust Network. Specifically, GTE CyberTrust has several root keys embedded within the popular Web browsers available from Microsoft and Netscape. If an organization chooses to operate CAs that are subordinate to the GTE CyberTrust root CA, browsers will recognize certificates issued by those CAs.

Other Trust Networks

It reasonable to suggest that any organization that issues certificates under the authority of a CA, whose root key is embedded in the browser and/or that issues organizational certificates under a common root, is in a position to claim that it, too, offers a "trust network." (As long as the individuals and the organizations are confident that the CA itself provides a solid foundation to enable those trust relationships.) However, it may be important to appropriately constrain these CAs in the future (see Chapter 9 for more information on trust relationships), perhaps through the use of the Name Constraints and/or Policy Constraints certificate extensions (Chapter 6 discusses certificate extensions).

Summary

This chapter addressed some of the more common business models that may drive PKI deployment. In particular, this chapter discussed the following business models:

- Business models related to internal communications requirements

- Business models related to external communications requirements

It was also noted that hybrids of these two models are possible (that is, an organization may implement both business models).

The goal of a PKI is to establish a single infrastructure that is capable of supporting multiple applications across multiple domains. This infrastructure must be cost-effective, capable of evolving over time, and based on industry-accepted standards to help ensure interoperability with other domains.

Although the initial PKI deployments may be modest internal efforts, the objective for many organizations (and governments) is to extend the "reach" of interoperability across multiple PKI boundaries. In other words, internal corporate communications is only the first step. Secure communications with external trading partners, subsidiaries, communities of interest (for example, collaborative research among many universities), or even peer organizations within a given industry (for example, the financial sector or the automotive industry) is also a highly desirable goal.

A number of national and regional government initiatives reflect the business models discussed here. For example, the Government of Canada Public Key Infrastructure is designed to facilitate secure inter-departmental communications for many of the applications that might be associated with the internal operations of a large corporation. This model can be extended to include the capability to offer governmental services to Canadian citizens and to facilitate secure communications with other governments. Other national and regional government initiatives also reflect this business model.

Finally, this chapter briefly discussed several global trust infrastructures.

In addition to the other chapters in Part III of this book, two related topics will help form the foundation for a more complete understanding of the business models and associated business drivers behind PKI deployment. Specifically, you should review the infrastructure concepts provided in Chapter 3 and the concepts associated with trust models provided in Chapter 9.

References

[NAS]   Committee on Maintaining Privacy and Security in Health Care Applications of the National Information Infrastructure, Computer Science and Telecommunications Board, Commission on Physical Sciences, Mathematics, and Applications, National Research Council. "For the Record: Protecting Electronic Health Information." U.S. National Academy of Sciences, 1997.

[RFC2246]   Dierks, T. and C. Allen. "The TLS Protocol Version 1.0." Internet Request for Comments 2246. (January 1999).

CHAPTER 25

Conclusions and Further Reading

This chapter provides a summary of the significant issues discussed in Part III, "Deployment Considerations." It also includes a few suggestions for further reading.

Summary

Part III of this book concentrated on the benefits of, and the issues associated with large-scale PKI deployments in the enterprise domain. It was noted that the key to achieving a successful deployment of a large-scale enterprise PKI rests in several areas:

- First and foremost, cost-justification and the development of a solid business case are essential. Attempting to deploy technology for technology's sake alone is doomed to failure.

- It is important to achieve the maximum amount of corporate-level buy-in. Lack of support within an organization will make deployment extremely difficult, if not impossible.

- It is important to be aware of the various deployment issues before deployment of the PKI actually begins. This can be tempered with the rollout of a small-scale PKI—which may help to expose any remaining issues that may not have been obvious initially.

- It is essential to understand the obstacles to deployment and to have a solid deployment strategy.

- Finally, ongoing operational support, including training and help desk support, must be provided.

Addressing each of these areas will aid in the smooth transition from a small-scale, single application rollout to a large-scale, multi-application deployment.

Part III also discussed some of the factors that should be taken into consideration before selecting a specific PKI vendor or service provider. As discussed in Chapter 22, "Deployment Issues and Decisions," some of the criteria to consider include the following:

- Reputation

- Market penetration

- Longevity

- Standards compliance

- Demonstrated security (for example, through formal endorsement programs such as FIPS 140-1)

- Commitment to multi-vendor interoperability

- Level of operations support

- Relative cost

Various business models were also discussed, and some of the global trust initiatives were introduced.

Suggestions for Further Reading

Given the current state of the market in terms of large-scale PKI deployments, few sources of vendor-neutral information are available on this topic. It is expected that this situation will improve with time. Nevertheless, the following articles may prove to be of some benefit to you:

- "Banking on Trust." *Data Communications Magazine* (21 May 1998).

- "In Focus: Public Key Infrastructure—the Key to Unlocking Data Access." *Internet Week* (15 February 1999).

- "Pioneers . . . or Guinea Pigs?" *Information Security Magazine* (June 1999): 34–40.

Index

The *Macmillan Network Architecture and Development Series* is a comprehensive set of guides that provides computing professionals with the unique insight of leading experts in today's networking technologies. Each volume explores a technology or set of technologies that is needed to build and maintain the optimal network environment for any particular organization or situation.

Currently available titles in the *Macmillan Network Architecture and Development Series* include

The DHCP Handbook, by Ralph Droms and Ted Lemon (ISBN: 1-57870-137-6)

The DHCP Handbook provides network architects and administrators with an authoritative overview of the Dynamic Host Configuration Protocol, as well as expert information on how to set up and manage a DHCP server. This book will give networking professionals already working with DHCP systems guidance on how to take full advantage of the technology to solve their management and address assignment problems. An essential resource, *The DHCP Handbook* provides the reader with critical information and expertise from author Ralph Droms, the chair of the IETF Dynamic Host Configuration (DHC) working group on automated network configuration, and author Ted Lemon, who wrote the ISC DHCP server code.

Designing Routing and Switching Architectures for Enterprise Networks, by Howard Berkowitz (ISBN: 1-57870-060-4)

A critical resource for network architects and engineers, *Designing Routing and Switching Architectures for Enterprise Networks* teaches the reader how to select the optimal switches and routers for their network environment, as well as guidance on their effective deployment. This book provides the unique insight and experience of real-world network design from Howard Berkowitz, an experienced network designer, developer, and contributor to the standards process.

Wide Area High Speed Networks, by Dr. Sidnie Feit (ISBN: 1-57870-114-7)

Today, conventional telephony, ISDN networks, ATM networks, packet-switched networks, and Internet data technologies coexist in a complex tapestry of networks. This book clearly explains each technology, describes how they interoperate, and puts their various uses and advantages into perspective. *Wide Area High Speed Networks* is an authoritative resource that will enable networking designers and implementers to determine which technologies to use in their networks, and for which roles.

Switched, Fast, and Gigabit Ethernet, Third Edition, by Robert A. Breyer and Sean Riley (ISBN: 1-57870-073-6)

Switched, Fast, and Gigabit Ethernet, Third Edition is the one and only solution needed to understand and fully implement this entire range of Ethernet innovations. Acting both as an overview of current technologies and hardware requirements as well as a hands-on, comprehensive tutorial for deploying and managing Switched, Fast, and Gigabit Ethernets, this guide covers the most prominent present and future challenges network administrators face.

Understanding and Deploying LDAP Directory Services, by Tim Howes Ph.D., Mark Smith, and Gordon Good (ISBN: 1-57870-070-1)

This comprehensive tutorial provides the reader with a thorough treatment of LDAP directory services. Designed to meet multiple needs, the first part of the book presents a general overview of the subject matter. The next three sections cover detailed instructions for design, deployment, and integration of directory services. The text is full of practical implementation advice and real-world deployment examples to help the reader choose the path that makes the most sense for the specific organization.

Designing Addressing Architectures for Routing and Switching, by Howard Berkowitz (ISBN: 1-57870-059-0)

Designing Addressing Architectures for Routing and Switching provides a systematic methodology for planning the wide area and local area network streets on which users and servers live. It guides the network designer in developing rational systems that are flexible and maintain a high level of service. Intended for people who are—or want to be—responsible for building large networks, this book offers a system and taxonomy for building networks that meet user requirements. It includes practical examples, configuration guides, case studies, tips, and warnings.

Wireless LANs: Implementing Interoperable Networks, **by Jim Geier (ISBN: 1-57870-081-7)**

This book provides both a context for understanding how an enterprise can benefit from the application of wireless technology, and the proven tools for efficiently implementing a wireless LAN. Based on the most recent developments in the field, *Wireless LANs: Implementing Interoperable Networks* gives network engineers vital information on planning, configuring, and supporting wireless networks.

Upcoming titles in the *Macmillan Network Architecture and Development Series* include

Local Area High Speed Networks, **by Dr. Sidnie Feit (ISBN: 1-57870-113-9)**